АГ 608154

POPULAR MEMORIES

POPULAR

Studies in Rhetoric/Communication *Thomas W. Benson, Series Editor*

Commemoration,
Participatory Culture, and
Democratic Citizenship

POPULAR MEMORIES

Ekaterina V. Haskins

The University of South Carolina Press

Published by the University of South Carolina Press
Columbia, South Carolina 29208

www.sc.edu/uscpress

Manufactured in the United States of America

24 23 22 21 20 19 18 17 16 15 10 9 8 7 6 5 4 3 2 1

Library of Congress Cataloging-in-Publication Data can
be found at http://catalog.loc.gov/.

For my family

Contents

Illustrations

Series Editor's Preface

In *Popular Memories: Commemoration, Participatory Culture, and Democratic Citizenship,* Professor Ekaterina V. Haskins offers a fresh look at the study of what she calls popular memories, examining how "participatory forms of communication" have "redefined the rhetoric of democratic citizenship." She explores in detail how four very different campaigns for participatory public memory—the Postal Service's "Celebrate the Century" commemorative stamp program, the September 11 Digital Archive, the first post-Katrina New Orleans carnival, and the *Eyes Wide Open* project of the American Friends Service Committee-suggest, guide, and sometimes limit genuine democratic participation.

Haskins explores the now familiar distinction made by memory scholars between popularization—the engagement of mass audiences through invocation of the idioms and practices of the popular arts—and democratization, which at a minimum would involve the participation of ordinary people in the production of memory practices, and suggests that the distinction may not fully explain what happens in actual cases. "Popular participation in memory work does not render it instantly more democratic, nor does the stamp of approval from government or mainstream media necessarily diminish the political charge of grassroots efforts."

Haskins asks how each of the cases she examines represents civic identity and how if at all it prompts democratic encounters among people of differing opinions about issues and about citizenship itself. The "Celebrate the Century" commemorative stamp program did invite citizens to participate in choosing the final designs from a menu of choices, and did depict an America of inclusiveness. On the other hand, the program equated consumerism with civic responsibility, promoting a neoliberal and self satisfied mythology in which each person has a place and an identity, but in which there is no space for strangers to mingle and debate. In a similar way, the online September 11 Digital Archive created an open web site for the uncensored contribution of diverse responses to the attacks of September 11, 2001, but while the structure of the archive encouraged a diversity of contributions, it did not enable the interactive potentials of the technology to encourage potentially transformative conversation, debate, or deliberation.

The first Mardi Gras festival after Katrina was highly complex and widely participatory for the citizens of New Orleans, though from the perspective of public memory it was ephemeral, especially for those who witnessed the carnival at a distance through the mass media. Haskins admires the complex treatment of the events by National Public Radio, and even more the fictional depiction of New Orleans in the television series *Treme.*

Eyes Wide Open was a traveling memory exhibit sponsored by the American Friends Service Committee, in which the war in Iraq was commemorated by the display in a large field of empty combat boots, each pair with the name of an American soldier killed in the war, and a display of civilian shoes representing dead Iraqi civilians. The exhibit was supplemented with a "memory wall." Haskins finds that *Eyes Wide Open* drew ongoing and productive contributions to the memorial itself in the sites to which it traveled, and that it was also recorded as having created a space for genuine citizen encounter with those of differing views and commitments.

Popular Memories is a fresh, vivid, theoretically sophisticated, and critically astute work of scholarship.

Thomas W. Benson

Acknowledgments

I became fascinated with the subject of this book over a decade ago, when I was completing my dissertation at the University of Iowa. At the time I was applying for academic jobs and making frequent trips to the post office in downtown Iowa City. This is where, in the fall of 1998, I first encountered the "Celebrate the Century" stamp program and its enticing slogan, "Put your stamp on history!" Although I was writing a thesis on ancient Greek rhetoric, the idea of a democratized memory culture struck me as so important that I could not get it out of my mind for years to come. As the tech bubble–induced euphoria of the 1990s gave way to the shocks of 9/11, the Iraq War, and Hurricane Katrina in the first decade of the twenty-first century, putting one's stamp on history became not just a way of looking back at distant past but a vehicle for citizens' response to recent events. My fascination grew into an abiding scholarly interest as I immersed myself in the multidisciplinary field of memory studies.

On this intellectual journey, many amazing scholars offered guidance, encouragement, and constructive criticism. I am particularly grateful to Kendall Phillips, Mitchell Reyes, Brad Vivian, and Anne Demo for including me in the many workshops, panels, and conferences on public memory they have organized in the last decade. Thanks are also due to Carole Blair for her sage advice on writing book proposals; to Steve Browne for his infectious enthusiasm and careful reading of my work; to Greg Clark, David Depew, and Tom Goodnight for being tireless champions of my career; to Michael Halloran for his gentle yet incisive criticisms of several drafts of this book and for being a pedagogical role model; to Joan Faber McAlister and Pete Simonson, my fellow University of Iowa alums, for their generous and thoughtful engagement with my writing; to Liz Wright for her insights into *lieux de memoire;* to Sara VanderHaagen for her astute remarks on the early version of the carnival chapter; to Studies in Rhetoric/Communication series editor Tom Benson and acquisitions editor Jim Denton at the University of South Carolina Press for steering the project through revisions; and to anonymous journal, conference, and manuscript reviewers whose high standards have goaded me to be a better scholar and writer. If this book doesn't quite live up to their expectations, the fault is entirely mine.

I am indebted to colleagues, students, friends, and family who have supported me in different yet equally valuable ways throughout the years. My colleagues and students at Boston College were first to see me wrestle with the topic of participatory memory culture. Elfriede Fursich and Greg Elmer commented on several drafts of what is now chapter 1 in addition to making my sojourn in Boston so much more fun. The late Justin DeRose, my most extraordinary undergraduate advisee and dear friend, coauthored with me a paper on commemoration of September 11 that in turn inspired the essay that became chapter 2.

At Rensselaer Polytechnic Institute, I was fortunate to be able to test many of this book's ideas in a graduate course, Media and Memory. My students have been the most receptive and inquisitive audience. Amy Scarfone, Jason Waite, Marcy Szablewicz, Michael Rancourt, and Hillary Brown Savoie deserve special recognition for their contributions to my thinking. My colleagues have been a wonderful group, as well. June Deery and Jim Zappen have shared their knowledge of participatory culture; Ellen Esrock expanded my understanding of photography; Jan Ferheimer read my chapter drafts and taught me salsa steps; Nancy Campbell helped me articulate the project's social relevance; and Abby Kinchy was the best writing buddy one could ask for. I am also grateful to the School of Humanities, Arts, and Social Sciences for the various forms of institutional support that enabled me to complete this project.

My friends near and far have shared my frustrations and cheered me on in moments of triumph. Mari Shopsis, Eliza Kent, Jennifer Burrell, Alex Dupuy, Pam Revak, Stephen Cartier, Dan Glaser, Erin Glasheen, Christine Tracy, Olga and Felix Ivanoff, Sat Kriya Kaur, Julia Arakelova, and the late Svetlana Kovalyova—your kindness and positive energy have buoyed me and kept me going when the going got tough.

I dedicate this book to my family for motivating me to finish what I started so long ago. My parents, Ludmila and Valeriy Chugaev, have never failed to remind me that I came from a line of headstrong and accomplished people. Dereck, my partner and best friend, has been steadfast in his support of everything I do. And my daughter, Alex, has been a source of joy, wonder, and hope. I pray that one day she will read this book and forgive me for all the weekends I spent at the office writing it.

Introduction

For the United States, the twentieth century closed on a high note—the soaring economy at home, the steady spread of democratization and free enterprise in the former Communist bloc, the end of oppressive regimes in South Africa and Central and South America. Domestic and international peace and prosperity seemed at hand. Despite the political rancor in Washington of the late Clinton era and incidents of domestic terrorism, Americans were encouraged to believe that they had reason to celebrate their country's triumphant march through history. Retrospection became something of a national pastime, with numerous anthologies, museum exhibits, and festivities marking the end of the millennium. The United States Postal Service even launched the "Celebrate the Century" commemorative program and invited the public to participate by selecting the most memorable events from the last five decades.

Just a few years later, after the shock of terrorist attacks on the World Trade Center and the Pentagon, the ill-justified and costly deployment of U.S. troops in Iraq, and the spectacle of devastation in New Orleans in the aftermath of Hurricane Katrina, the optimism of the late twentieth century seemed like a sentiment of a bygone era. In the face of fear and uncertainty, politicians and mainstream media repeatedly conjured images of national glory and resilience from a distant past in place of unsettling images of the present. Franklin D. Roosevelt's "Day of Infamy" speech after the Japanese bombing of Pearl Harbor was invoked to make sense of September 11. The photograph of three firefighters defiantly raising the U.S. flag atop the rubble of the destroyed World Trade Center echoed the iconic Iwo Jima photograph from World War II. At the same time, the government forbade the media from disseminating pictures of U.S. military caskets returning from Iraq and Afghanistan and largely ignored the plight of Katrina's victims.

Although traditional symbols of patriotic pride have been ubiquitous in national discourse since September 11, 2001—the flag-raising scene was even re-created as a tableau vivant during televised sporting events—other, less conventionally patriotic commemorative efforts have sprung up around the country to mourn the loss of civilian and military lives, to recollect the recent events from multiple perspectives, and, perhaps most important, to forge new bonds of community. Some of these efforts, such as the 9/11 History Archive, harnessed the power of new electronic media to collect and display diverse fragments of recorded experience provided by thousands of people. Others, such as the ephemeral memorials of the ongoing war in Iraq, relied instead on the power of repetitive display of simple symbols—military boots and civilian shoes—to engage their audiences in reflection about the cost of war. Still others, like Mardi Gras revelers in New Orleans after Katrina, used the liminal space and topsy-turvy symbolism of carnival to remember the recent disaster and reassert their agency. What unites these dissimilar commemorative endeavors is their dependence on the participation of diverse publics to produce and share stories and symbols. And although their tenor and purpose differ from the unequivocally positive "celebration of the century" organized by the U.S. Postal Service in the late 1990s, these popular commemorations, too, have emerged from an assumption that ordinary people must be able to "put their stamp on history."

Popular Memories examines this ideal of popular participation by asking how and with what consequences participatory forms of commemoration have redefined the rhetoric of democratic citizenship. Along with other scholars who subscribe to a discursive understanding of citizenship, I regard it as a relationship among strangers that is modeled by discourses of public culture and embodied through performance. Approaching commemorations as both representations of civic identity and sites of stranger interaction, I analyze four distinct examples of participatory memory practice: the U.S. Postal Service's "Celebrate the Century" stamp and education program, the September 11 Digital Archive, the first post-Katrina carnival in New Orleans, and a traveling memorial to the human cost of the Iraq War. Despite their differences in sponsorship, genre, historical scope, and commemorative purpose, all of these examples stressed their reliance on voluntary participation of ordinary people in selecting, producing, or performing interpretations of distant or recent historical events. These collectively produced interpretations—or popular memories—in turn became mnemonic prompts for interactions among people who were summoned by them to celebrate, to mourn, or to bear witness.

In this book I distinguish between "participation," understood as active contribution to the content and form of a text or performance, and "reception," which designates engagement and response by audiences. Some of my readers may object that all public memory is inherently participatory insofar as memory artifacts or performances are intended for a public audience and so must recruit members of this audience as attentive participants. On this view all acts of reception and interpretation by audiences constitute participation of a kind, even if audience members do not—or cannot—take part in the *production* of memory artifacts. Like most scholars of rhetoric, I see reception as an important aspect of meaning construction and therefore embrace the imperative to attend not only to the symbolism or generic features of memorial artifacts but also to the ways such symbolism gives rise to interpretation and response by various audiences. But to regard all kinds of participation as equal runs the risk of ignoring the influence of cultural and technological change on memory practices. For example the fact that the Lincoln Memorial was "reinterpreted" by Martin Luther King Jr. in August 1963 through his performance of the "I Have a Dream" speech in the "symbolic shadow" of Abraham Lincoln does not render the memorial's form, function, and historic significance similar to that of the NAMES Project AIDS Memorial Quilt, a multiple-authored, traveling memorial to the victims of the AIDS epidemic. To maintain that all memorials are open to interpretation and thus participatory at least to some extent would commit us to a view that there is no substantial difference between memorials with which audiences interact in idiosyncratic ways and those that, like the NAMES quilt, purposely integrate contributions "by the many, for the many."

Contemporary participatory memory practices certainly do not constitute an entirely new species—one could think of earlier forms of popular cultural politics in the United States, such as anniversary parades and historical pageants of the nineteenth and early twentieth century.[1] While driven by agendas of economic and cultural elites, these festivities still made room for spectatorship and even occasional performances by laboring classes, women, and people of color. By taking part in festivals and commemorative rituals of the early American Republic, ordinary Americans "affirmed that they were far more than simple subjects of power; . . . they continually demonstrated that power was not inherent in a single individual or a small group, but was instead exercised in the negotiations between rulers and ruled."[2] During the era of the "pageant craze" of the late nineteenth and early twentieth centuries, civic officials sought to "display the illusion of consensus through mass participation," which occasionally led them "to include dissenting voices in their public historical representations."[3] However, as Susan Davis points out in her study of festive street culture in nineteenth-century Philadelphia, "parade-making access was limited by wealth, opinion, custom, and everyday practice."[4] Today the belief that ordinary people should be able to "put their stamp on history" reflects the desire and ability of nonelite actors to coproduce narratives of public memory, not merely to experience them as spectators or interactive extras. What sets contemporary participatory commemorations apart from their historic predecessors is their self-conscious emphasis on inclusiveness, diversity, and access.

So far, public memory scholarship has made a strong case for considering memory practices as a key cultural technology of citizenship insofar as narratives and images of the past promote a consensual notion of collective identity or, on the contrary, contest conventional narratives of national or cultural belonging. Scholars across several disciplines have explored the construction of citizenship and nationhood through commemoration and have established the significance of public memory as a major cultural arena for defining and challenging what it means to be a citizen. Heeding Benedict Anderson's call to regard nations as "imagined communities," many studies have demonstrated how images, rituals, and sites of remembrance enshrine particular—often exclusionary—definitions of national character.[5] An equally impressive number of scholars have shown that, because of their partiality, these memory sites often become hotly contested.[6]

In addition to critiquing the power structure embedded in memorial artifacts and practices, a recovery of the voices and perspectives of ordinary people as agents of history has become one of the central preoccupations in contemporary memory studies. Implicit in many of these efforts is a presumption of authentic historical experience that underlies—or is subsumed by—publicly observable representations of the past. Because of the politicized nature of historic retrospection and the uneven distribution of power and resources, "ordinary" experiences remain marginalized or, worse, transformed into something that obscures their origins and deforms their meaning. As a result what may have begun as a radical and potentially destabilizing narrative ends as an inert element in the hegemonic construction of the past by the elites. Or so the argument goes. The interpreter's task then becomes that of salvaging the remembrances of the marginalized or, conversely, of exposing the machinations behind the facade of official memory.[7]

The participatory memory practices described in this book involve actors with unequal cultural capital, different levels of commitment, and dissimilar political allegiances in the production of nationally visible memorial artifacts and performances. The picture I paint here complicates the often polarized view of public memory as a struggle between elite narratives of civic virtue underwritten by political and economic powers that be and expressions of marginalized identities. In particular I question the reductive equation of certain modes of representation and forms of cultural expression with already existing identities. Taking a cue from rhetorical theories of identification and citizenship, I argue that mnemonic practices serve not only as tools of ideological domination or political self-assertion, but also as rhetorical invocations of identity that can expand or limit our civic horizon as well as induce or discourage identifications with various others. Participatory memory practices can model civic identity by collectively constructing images and narratives as well as by staging encounters among strangers. In the remaining pages of this chapter, I distinguish my approach to popular memories from other notable treatments of the subject, explore the connection between memory practices and citizenship, and outline the reading strategy at work in subsequent chapters.

Popular Memories at the Intersection of Popularization and Democratization

Participatory memory practices, including the ones discussed in chapters to come, tend to blur the distinction between production and reception. I use the term "popular memories" to highlight this ambiguity. On the one hand, "popular memory" evokes the mass appeal of a particular historic representation. On the other hand, the phrase suggests participation of the many in memorial practice. These trends seem to have converged in contemporary culture—the consumption and production of memories are no longer distinct activities. Academic historians, however, typically avoid this ambiguity and prefer to talk about "popularization" and "democratization" as rival, although at times overlapping, tendencies.

Popularization can be understood as a way to render history more relevant and engaging to mass audiences. Films, serialized television programs, historic working farms, reenactments, and amusement park rides have enjoyed great popularity and steady tourist traffic since the 1950s. In other words historic representations began to speak the language of popular culture to gain traction in popular imagination.[8] Professional historians and educators have observed this trend with a mix of ambivalence and suspicion, given the tendency of popular representations to promote a simplistic, decontextualized, and often self-congratulatory relationship with the past.[9]

Democratization, on the other hand, describes the broadening of participation of "ordinary" people in producing—and not just consuming—public memory. Frequently seen as acting in opposition to the official culture, or at least existing in tension with it, memories "of the people, by the people," harbor the potential to deepen the democratic self-understanding of citizens as agents of history.[10] In this sense public memory can no longer be viewed as a mere historical pageant staged for the entertainment and distraction of audiences and instead becomes a politically consequential arena of competing visions of "the people."

But how significant is the gulf between these two senses of popular memory? Many scholars have adopted the term *vernacular* to describe popular memory work as distinct from narratives and pageants sponsored by the government and corporate entertainment industry. Historian John Bodnar famously contrasted "official" and "vernacular" modes of cultural expression at the intersection of which public memory emerges. According to Bodnar official culture expresses "the concerns of cultural leaders or authorities" who "share a common interest in social unity, the continuity of existing institutions, and loyalty to the status quo" and "relies on 'dogmatic formalism' and the restatement of reality in ideal rather than complex or ambiguous terms."[11] Vernacular cultural expressions represent "an array of specialized interests" that are "diverse and changing" and "convey what social reality feels like rather than what it should be like."[12]

Bodnar presents "vernacular" expression, tied to particularities of historical experience and localized sense of belonging, as a challenge to the hollow "dogmatic formalism" of the official discourse of patriotism and citizenship championed by "cultural leaders." Yet he suggests that vernacular expression flows organically from, rather than constitutes, the identity he designates by the term "ordinary people." Vernacular expression, thus conceptualized, must originate from without, not engage from within, the rituals and discourses of official culture. The trouble with this conception of the vernacular is that it hypostatizes discourse, turning it into an ideologically and historically static category. Consequently it posits "ordinary people" as authentic bearers of such expression rather than as subjects whose identities are continuously formed and reformed through a complex process of enculturation and rhetorical negotiation.

Although Bodnar sees "official" and "vernacular" expressions occasionally working in tandem, he nevertheless asserts that vernacular expression's "very existence threatens the sacred and timeless nature of official expressions."[13] In this way his definition of vernacular memory is aligned with the sense of "popular memory" as "resistance" history advanced by Michel Foucault in a 1974 interview with the French film journal *Cahiers du cinéma.* Accusing recent French films of erasing the memory of popular resistance to the Nazis during the Occupation, Foucault stated: "It is an actual fact that people—I am talking about those who are barred from writing, from producing their books themselves, from drawing up their own historical accounts—that these people nevertheless do have a way of recording history, of remembering it, of keeping it fresh and using it. This popular history was, to a certain extent, even more alive, more clearly formulated during the nineteenth century where, for instance, there was a whole tradition of struggles which were transmitted orally, or in writing or songs, etc."[14]

In both cases "ordinary people" are presumed to possess authentic historical knowledge that is ignored or suppressed by the powers that be. Their method of representing and transmitting this knowledge—by recording "what social reality feels like" in oral media such as songs or stories—thus forms an aesthetic and political counterpoint to official representations put on display by museums, monuments, and history books. This notion of popular memory, with its related connotations of unvarnished authenticity, genuine connection to lived experience, and, perhaps more crucially, marginalized political status, animates much of the scholarship that valorizes memory's "subaltern" status and works to recover the voices of marginalized "others."[15]

Maintaining the line between "official" and "vernacular" expressions becomes difficult, however, if we take into account the success of some grassroots projects and the impact of their success on institutions of memory. Consider, for example, the case of the Foxfire project, which historian Michael Kammen pronounced "the triumph of vernacular culture at a truly grass-roots level."[16] Initiated in the late 1960s by Eliot Wigginton, a high school teacher in Rabun Gap, Georgia, Foxfire grew from a homework assignment to interview residents of rural Appalachia about their craft traditions into a major oral history project that went on to become a best-selling magazine and book series. As much as the Foxfire phenomenon highlighted the existence of formerly invisible folk histories, it also demonstrated that oral history is not, in itself, a marginalized activity that depends on premodern methods of recording and dissemination. For Foxfire participants and many others inspired by them, audio and video recording devices helped to project local traditions and memories onto the national scene.[17] Affordable tape recorders and, lately, a whole range of sound and visual recording technologies have altered the oral transmission that Foucault envisioned as a paradigm of popular memory work. In the last decade especially, as digital recording devices and online file-sharing became widespread, both grassroots movements and mainstream media organizations began to rely on "lay" contributors.

Foxfire's commercial viability also indicated the growing popularity of stories and traditions outside the American white middle-class mainstream. As Kammen describes this influence, "vernacular culture and traditions . . . unquestionably achieved their apogee thus far in terms of visibility and influence upon Americans' sense of who they are collectively and how they came to be that way. The weak and the meek may not yet have inherited the earth, but at least they found that they were on the map."[18] The "mainstreaming" of vernacular culture therefore complicates the distinction between official and vernacular expressions, even though it does not dissolve social, economic, and political differences.

Scholarly critics have often accused the popular culture industry of distorting and simplifying historical understanding in the service of commercial interests.[19] At first sight spectacle and entertainment typical of genres of popular culture may seem antithetical to the authentic expression of historical experience. But any presentation of historical content, commercial or not, relies on spectacle at least to some extent. Even the most "serious" museums, including those that address traumatic pasts such as the Holocaust, must employ display mechanisms to draw their visitors in.[20] Groups that wish to advance oppositional memories and identities, too, often resort to spectacle to attract wide audiences. For example, costumed reenactments, stock-in-trade of commercial heritage sites, can be appropriated to serve different political purposes. Thus a 1980 reenactment of a woolen-mill workers' strike in Lawrence, Massachusetts, reawakened suppressed memories of working-class struggles at the turn of the twentieth century and did so at a moment in history when the union movement was rapidly losing ground.[21]

Popular historic attractions are viewed with suspicion not only because of their potential distortions of the past but also because they arguably foster a tourist attitude toward history. According to Marita Sturken, this attitude implies "a detached and seemingly innocent pose": "tourists typically remain distant to the sites they visit, where they are often defined as innocent outsiders, mere observers, whose actions are believed to have no effect on what they see."[22] These mnemonic practices thus breed a depoliticized body of citizen-consumers. This does not have to be the case, however: as Kammen suggests, "heritage that heightens human interest may lead people to history for purposes of informed citizenship, or the meaningful deepening of identity, or enhanced appreciation of the dynamic process of change over time."[23] Furthermore as studies of "dark" and "toxic" tourism have shown, such activities can engender empathy, awareness, and political commitment in those who choose to travel to places with violent or ecologically disastrous legacies.[24] Therefore tourism comprises a variety of experiences that, while they form part of the leisure economy, can range from superficial sightseeing for purposes of recreation to more profound and politically transformative engagements with past and present.

However analytically attractive the distinction between popularization and democratization may seem, it is inadequate to capture the realities of public expression. Part of this book's purpose, therefore, is to question the strict dichotomies scholars invoke to evaluate practices of public memory: popularization versus democratization, vernacular versus official, authentic experience versus spectacle, and informed citizenship versus tourism. I suggest that it would be limiting and perhaps even misleading to align one set of memory practices and social actors on the side of official culture, spectacle, and tourism and the other on the side of vernacular culture, historical knowledge, and citizenship. Instead I envision a spectrum of engagements with the past that draw on available cultural resources and employ various forms of mediation in order to recruit participants and involve them in memory work.

Popular participation in memory work does not render it instantly more democratic, nor does the stamp of approval from government or mainstream media necessarily diminish the political charge of grassroots efforts. *Popular Memories* is not a celebration of the triumphant emergence of "memory of the people, by the people, for the people." Despite the democratizing aura of the term *participation,* this book's case studies illustrate that there is no univocal emancipatory narrative waiting to be told. It is by exploring how participation works in specific examples of public memorialization that we can discern its promise for democratic citizenship.

Memory and Citizenship

In its strictest sense, the term *citizenship* denotes a legal status of persons and a set of rights and responsibilities that come with this status. But the purview of citizenship expands dramatically if one considers it not as an abstract legal category but as a "relation among strangers who learn to feel it as a common identity based on shared historical, legal, or familial connection to a geopolitical space."[25] A host of institutional and social practices—beyond voting, serving on a jury, and paying taxes—are thus implicated in the reproduction of citizens and defining who counts as "the people." Memory practices constitute a major cultural technology of citizenship: memorials, commemorations, and other rituals of retrospection mediate citizenship both by envisioning models of civic identity and by staging experiences through which people come to embrace or reject these models.

Although scholars of rhetoric share many of the premises of public memory scholars from other disciplines—such as the assumption that representations of the past are dictated by the interests of the present and are tied to particular relations of power—they pay special attention to the discursive mechanism by which rituals and artifacts of memory participate in the construction of citizenship as an embodied identity.[26] Because commemorative practices tend to present or visualize, rather than argue, their subject matter, rhetoricians have traditionally aligned them with the rubric of display (or "epideictic") rhetoric, which since Athenian democracy has functioned as a primary site of civic discourse.[27] Jeffrey Walker's appraisal of the epideictic as "the central and indeed fundamental mode of rhetoric in human culture" is instructive: "Epideictic appears as that which shapes and cultivates the basic codes of value and belief by which a society or culture lives; it shapes the ideologies and imageries with which, and by which, the individual members of a community identify themselves; and perhaps more significantly, it shapes the fundamental grounds, the 'deep' commitments and presuppositions, that will underlie and ultimately determine decision and debate in particular pragmatic forums."[28]

Because of its appeal to "the 'deep' commitments and presuppositions," display rhetoric was frequently attacked as flattery or empty show by idealist philosophers. It is, in fact, Plato who left us one of the most dramatic portrayals of the rhetorical mechanism of patriotic indoctrination. In the dialogue *Menexenus*, under the pretense of reciting the Athenian funeral oration to a young student, Socrates unleashes a scathing condemnation of populist rhetoric: "For a man obtains a splendid and magnificent funeral even though at his death he be but a poor man; and though he but a worthless fellow, he wins praise" (234c). On Plato's view the listeners become vain and insolent when they identify with the constructed splendor of the polis. Socrates thus mocks the seductive appeal of funeral orations: "Every time I listen fascinated I am exalted and imagine myself to have become at once taller and nobler and more handsome. . . . And this majestic feeling remains with me for over three days: so persistently does the speech and voice of the orator ring in my ears that it is scarcely on the fourth or fifth day that I recover myself and remember that I really am here on earth, whereas till then I almost imagined myself to be living in the islands of the Blessed" (235c).

Socrates's critique of *epitaphios logos* charges it with deceptive selectivity (reshuffling and embellishing historical facts to make Athens look better than it was in reality) and corruption of the audience through political flattery. At the same time, Socrates depicts the nearly irresistible force with which such rhetoric affects its listeners on both ideological and somatic levels. Civic piety can be mocked, but as an affective investment, it cannot be rationalized away.[29]

What Socrates satirized as the intoxicating effect of funeral orations on Athenian audiences has been recognized by contemporary rhetorical theorists as a constitutive function of discourse, its ability to conjure into being collective identities. Before the publication of Benedict Anderson's "imagined communities" argument, Michael Calvin McGee's 1975 essay "In Search of the People" defined "the people" as a rhetorical process that organizes the dormant "seeds of collectivization" into "incipient political myths, visions of the collective life dangled before individuals in hope of creating a real 'people.'" "The people" ceases to be a mere symbolic construct when "masses of persons begin to respond to a myth, not only by exhibiting collective behavior, but also by publicly ratifying the transaction."[30] Citizenship may be a political fiction, but its existence depends on the involvement of those whom it nominates as citizens.

If for ancient Greeks ceremonial speech making and theater were primary venues of invoking and sustaining collective self-understanding, the scope of contemporary display rhetoric is much broader. Rhetoric scholars therefore investigate a variety of technologies of memory. For example Robert Hariman and John Louis Lucaites examine how U.S. iconic photographs—such as the flag raising on Iwo Jima and the Depression-era "migrant mother"—"equip the viewer to act as a citizen, or expand one's conception of citizenship, or otherwise redefine one's relationship to the political community."[31] They also suggest that iconic representations "might foreclose on some possibilities of action, restrict civic membership, or otherwise limit identification with others."[32]

The rhetorical power of images and narratives to model—and to mold—citizenship has been frequently exploited by political, cultural, and economic powers that be, especially during periods of crisis. A number of rhetorical analyses of commemorative discourse in the United States at the turn of the millennium have investigated how the state and the culture industry have sought to inspire civic consensus by narrowing the understanding of citizenship and political agency. Commemorative projects such as the World War II Memorial in Washington, D.C., and films such as *Saving Private Ryan* served as "civics lessons for a generation beset by fractious disagreements about the viability of U.S. culture and identity."[33] As Barbara Biesecker argues in her critique of these and other contemporary memory texts, the civics lessons they proffer embrace "a certain idea of what it means to be a 'good citizen'" and as such "promote social cohesion by rhetorically inducing differently positioned audiences—by class, race, ethnicity, sexuality, and gender—to disregard rather than actively seek to dismantle the inequitable power relations that continue to structure collective life in the U.S."[34] Cinematic and monumental expressions of praise of the "Greatest Generation" thus work rhetorically as a way to mute oppositional memories and identities. In a similar vein, V. William Balthrop, Carole Blair, and Neil Michel interpret the World War II Memorial in conjunction with its dedication ceremony as evidence of the "hijacking of the Good War" by the Bush administration to justify its imperial policies and to prescribe "a role for the US citizen and soldier—silent dependence and deference to national leadership."[35]

The solemn invocation of the nation's past in the face of present political exigencies is strikingly illustrated by the performance of "patriotic liturgies" in New York City on the first anniversary of the September 11, 2001, terrorist attacks. Opting not to compose new speeches to eulogize lives lost, public officials recited instead time-honored orations of past U.S presidents, including Lincoln's Gettysburg Address and Franklin Delano Roosevelt's "Four Freedoms" speech. According to Bradford Vivian, by offering "incantation rather than invention," the ceremony asked the audience to "ritually affirm a tacit yet indelible communal bond" and thereby to ignore potentially troublesome aspects of this collective identity.[36] Vivian terms this form of commemorative speech "neoliberal epideictic," the type of discourse that "sponsors a democratic yet apolitical speech . . . —*democratic* in its presumably universal dissemination and self-evident significance for all citizens but *apolitical* insofar as it transfigures documents historically cited as warrants for civic participation into allegorical paeans to the virtues of private life over public advocacy."[37] Despite its apolitical appearance, however, neoliberal epideictic gives prominence to a politically consequential ideal of citizenship marked by values of "privacy, consumption, and spectatorship" rather than those of "equality, justice, and mutual responsibility."[38]

Display rhetoric does more than perpetuate the status quo and assist in the reproduction of civic identities, however. "Epideictic is not limited to reinforcement of existing beliefs and ideologies," points out Walker; "it can also work to challenge or transform conventional beliefs."[39] What may seem like a prison house of collective memory is, indeed, a warehouse of rhetorical tools that can aid us in expanding or revising current definitions and models of citizenship. The abovementioned Socratic parody illustrates how dominant constructions of citizenship can be engaged—and subverted—*from within* the conventions of ceremonial rhetoric. In the *Menexenus* Socrates does not simply attack the formality, pomposity, and disregard for truth he finds in the funeral oration ritual; he draws attention to the genre's ideological function in the act of performing it. This critical performance asserts an alternative vision of Athenian citizenship—the role that Plato's *Apology* famously likened to that of a fly attached to a large thoroughbred horse. Yet Socrates's subversive engagement of commemorative rhetoric is antidemocratic, because it presents his fellow Athenians as ideological dupes and implies that only philosophers can resist the siren voice of ideology.

Consider, by contrast, how politically and socially marginalized rhetors have exploited conventions of dominant discourse to further a more inclusive vision of what it means to be a U.S. citizen. One such example is furnished by the woman suffrage pageant staged in Washington, D.C., in March 1913 on the eve of Woodrow Wilson's inauguration. Historical pageants were among the most popular public memory rituals in the United States in the early twentieth century. Featuring colorful tableaux of characters to dramatize historical development of communities and to bolster social cohesion, these displays typically "depicted class, ethnic, and race relations as a stable cohesive hierarchy."[40] In pageants' portrayal of gender relations, women were content with their domestic role and, "like labor and recent immigrants, were left out of scenes depicting crucial turning points in local economic or political history."[41] The five-thousand-member woman suffrage pageant, while echoing the use of women in allegorical roles then common in historical pageantry, nonetheless made a poignant statement about women's ambitions beyond the domestic sphere by prominently featuring a scene of women workers in the professions. The pageant's author, Hazel MacKaye, contended: "Through pageantry, we women can set forth our ideals and aspirations more graphically than in any other way."[42]

This instance of creative—and subversive—engagement with tradition illustrates the central premise of a rhetorical understanding of citizenship: that citizenship is a performance, not a possession.[43] In this way, those who through either law or custom are excluded from citizenship can still engage in meaningful symbolic action that has the potential to "reformulate collectively held understandings of who may be and what it means to be a citizen."[44] However, the cases discussed so far suggest that what matters in defining citizenship, whether it is definition by exclusion or by expansion, is the *representation of models* of citizenship. Monuments, films, photographs, speeches, and pageantry all have the rhetorical power to conjure compelling images of civic identity and invite audiences to inhabit them, or at least to consider them as legitimate claims on the collective imaginary. As representations, models of citizenship inscribed in memory texts become dominant or not depending on a variety of conditions, including the legibility of rhetorical conventions deployed by these texts, their timeliness in response to given historical exigencies, and the visibility and continuing circulation of similar representations in public media.

Yet memory texts make up only one part of the process by which individuals and groups come to identify with particular representations of the past and models of citizenship that these representations valorize. Even though the authorial intent may determine the text's genre, imagery, and form of mediation in anticipation of a desired audience response, it is the audience's attentive uptake that completes the rhetorical transaction.[45] In other words it is not only the values and beliefs that memory texts *inscribe* but also the *experience* of these texts by listeners and spectators that contribute to the performance of citizenship.

It is not surprising that the experience of audiences can be at variance with the desires of those who create or sponsor memory texts. Consider the 1927 pageant at the Saratoga battlefield in upstate New York (the site of the most important battle of the Revolutionary War). In his study of the event, S. Michael Halloran describes two kinds of commemoration, the scripted and the spontaneous, in competition with each other: "The scripted pageant at Saratoga attempted to set before its vast audience a nostalgic image of the social order rooted in post-World War I anxieties about some of the transformations American society was undergoing. But the effort was constrained by conditions at the pageant site and the consequent lived experience of all present. The scripted pageant was in effect upstaged by a larger spectacle enacted by the audience as well as the designated performers, and the image of social order that they enacted together was significantly different from that encoded in the pageant script."[46] At the Saratoga pageant, those present "enacted together . . . a carnivalesque order that may have had substantially more democracy and freedom than did the aristocratic world order" of the pageant text.[47] Here the script's failure to control the goings-on at the pageant highlighted the role of improvisation and copresence in transforming those assembled on the battlefield into a community of citizens.

Indeed places and rituals of memory produce civic lessons and conjure civic identities not only because of *what* they represent (for example, narratives of nationhood or class identity) but also because of *who happens to be there* at a particular time. "Memory places cultivate the being and participation together of strangers," write Carole Blair, Greg Dickinson, and Brian L. Ott, "but strangers who appear to have enough in common to be co-traversing the place. Memory places are virtually unique among memory apparatuses in offering their symbolic contents to groups of individuals who negotiate not just the place, but stranger relations as well. The presence of others may be experienced by a visitor as belonging to a constituted, if provisional, public sphere."[48] Spectatorship in common is regarded by many scholars as something that constitutes the shared ground for citizenship. To perform as citizens, we need to see and be seen; "political actors . . . are legitimated when they appear in social space."[49] Public spaces such as the agora in ancient Athens and its modern descendants have long been associated with the production of citizenship through public performance.[50] But less obviously "rhetorical" places such as public parks, too, have functioned as "socializing vehicles for the democratic experiment" by providing both scenic vistas away from the bustle of workaday life and a spectacle of strangers partaking in the same sort of recreation.[51]

A clear theme emerging from scholarship on democratic citizenship is the need for common experiences that would expose people to others unlike themselves and nurture the habits of trust, reciprocity, and collaboration. To quote political philosopher Danielle S. Allen, for our own sake as citizens and for the sake of democracy as a whole, we need to "talk to strangers."[52] And to be able to do so, we need shared spaces, whether virtual or physical, that would allow us both to express our beliefs and to interact with others whose attitudes may have been shaped by a profoundly different set of circumstances. The urgency of the theme stems in large part from the perception that in today's liberal democracies, the citizenry has become increasingly fragmented and polarized. Benjamin Barber makes this point emphatically when he states, "In our mostly privatized, suburbanized world, there are not enough physical spaces where citizenship can be easily exercised and civil society's free activities can be pursued."[53] We have an abundance of spaces of material consumption—"places for me"—and too few "places for us" where "we can govern ourselves in common without surrendering our plural natures to the singular addictions of commerce and consumerism."[54]

In evaluating the impact of participatory commemorations on citizenship, then, it is important to examine not only models of citizenship offered to audiences by memory texts but also the ways that experiencing together might invite audience members to affirm or reconsider their previously held notions of who counts as a citizen and what citizenship means. This insight is especially relevant to commemorative projects that actively seek to blur the line between invention and reception, between those who produce texts and performances for public display and those who experience them. While it is true that even traditional artifacts and sites of memory such as monuments, memorials, and museums largely depend on their audience's engagement for the meanings they generate, conspicuously participatory commemorations highlight the interdependence of invention and reception, of spectacle and spectatorship.

Let us pause to contemplate one such participatory memorial, the NAMES Project AIDS Memorial Quilt. A massive grassroots memorial to the lives lost in the AIDS epidemic, it enacts its complex rhetoric of mourning and advocacy through multiple handcrafted panels. Although the idea of the quilt belonged to a San Francisco gay rights activist Cleve Jones, who made the first panel, the quilt rapidly expanded thanks to thousands of contributions from lovers, family members, and even complete strangers who seized upon the quilting idiom to convey their grief and anger and to honor the dead. An important strand in the quilt's origin story, then, is its appropriation of the existing visual vocabulary and popular practice associated with the private sphere in order to make a public statement.

As the panels eulogizing individuals were joined together in public display, the memorial became a national site, where contributors were transformed into audience members "among a great many others, some Quilt panel makers, others not."[55] Each new showing of the quilt, besides testifying to the spread of the epidemic, also "became the impetus for new additions to it, again transforming audience members into rhetors."[56] At each display the NAMES Project added signature panels on which visitors could write their responses. These "patches of grief and rage," too, became "part of the Quilt's rhetoric of display."[57]

How did this multiply authored memorial text display (or advocate) citizenship? As Blair and Michel note, one of the quilt's signature legacies as a late twentieth-century commemorative artifact is its "foregrounding of difference as a legitimate marker of democracy."[58] In the words of Charles Morris III, the quilt thereby achieved "a queer transformation of . . . *e pluribus unum*."[59] Commemorated as individuals, the persons eulogized by the quilt's panels are presented as worthy of public regard not because they stand for some abstract ideal of citizenship (as, for example, the commemorated war dead typically do) but because their lives were unjustly cut short by a disease that the U.S. government long refused to acknowledge as a major public health threat. Challenging the government's negligence and the mainstream media's stigmatizing portrayal of the epidemic as a "gay disease," the quilt effectively argued that "America has AIDS."[60]

In addition to making visible collective loss and asserting the worth of multiple individuals who perished in the epidemic, the quilt's appearances in various public places around the country became transformative scenes of stranger relationality. Jeffrey Bennett describes the quilt as "a peripatetic site of public emotionality that engenders repertoires of public citizenship" and "embodies the emotive aspects of citizenship typically shunned in democratic practice."[61] The quilt "offered communal spaces for working through the syndrome's perplexities" and allowed strangers to come together "around reflection, loss, despair, anger and hope."[62] Moreover because experiencing the quilt is an emotional act, those who witness it often "become active participants in the creation of knowledge about the impact of AIDS and its circulation in the polity."[63] Whereas the quilt's critics have argued that the memorial's therapeutic qualities—its capacity to engender healing and allow mourners to move on—are a threat to its function as political advocacy, the situated performances that the quilt invites may mitigate against any kind of ideological closure. As Bennett points out, the quilt's arrangement defies any reassuring trajectory from the past to the present, its "panels featuring present day" reminding visitors "that everything has changed, but nothing has."[64] And because of its peripatetic character, the memorial localizes the quilt's rhetoric and fosters stranger relationality by "adapting to local communities and appealing to regional identifications."[65]

The legacy of the quilt as a landmark participatory memorial for the rhetoric of citizenship is profound. It demonstrated the inventive power of popular participation by inviting anyone, regardless of artistic skill or proximity to the epidemic's victims, to submit memorial panels to the NAMES Project. The project involved individuals with various and unequal cultural capital in the process of redefining their political community through the medium of commemorative public art and created the most diverse patchwork of commemorative expression in the late twentieth century. This diversity brought private emotion into the public and authorized this emotionality as a legitimate and civically consequential form of remembrance and political address. As Blair and Michel point out, the quilt's focus on the individual does not lessen "the spirit of collectivity marked by mutual obligation."[66] No less important, the quilt's multiple displays, in iconic locales such as Washington, D.C., as well as in smaller communities, created provisional spaces of civic spectatorship and promoted experiences of being together with strangers. Indeed it is through its function as a prompt to remembrance and political action—not only as a textually rich depository of expressions of loss and anger—that the quilt has done its work as a technology of citizenship.

The quilt is an apt illustration of a rhetorically informed understanding of citizenship and a vivid demonstration of how participatory commemorations can serve both as public displays of *e pluribus unum* and as sites of civic engagement. Therefore case studies in chapters to come will assess multiply authored "memory texts" in terms of their representation of civic identity as well as their ability to prompt transformative encounters between people subscribing to different notions of citizen rights and obligations.

Reading Popular Memories

What makes popular memories popular? This may seem like a simple question, but answering it requires us to reexamine some fundamental assumptions about the nature of commemorative activity, the relationship of memory with other symbolic and material cultural practices, and the role of reception in the commemorative process.

Despite its multidisciplinary nature, public memory scholarship often subscribes to an axiom that artifacts and practices of memory are "materialist modes of privileging particular histories and values."[67] In other words publicly visible manifestations of memory—such as memorials, museums, and rituals—are not politically neutral symbols but partisan expressions of identity. Contemporary memory practices seem to track the rise of identity politics in the late twentieth century. As Erica Doss observes, "contemporary American commemoration is increasingly disposed to individual memories and personal grievances, to representations of tragedy and trauma, and to the social and political agendas of a diffuse body of rights-bearing citizens."[68] From this perspective popular memories are popular because they represent an expanding range of histories and experiences and thereby establish political visibility and worth of their subjects. This is a plausible argument. But to focus on manifestations of memory solely as more or less faithful representations of already existing political identities stops short of explaining the persuasive power of representations to multiple audiences with different experiences and group allegiances.

Why do certain representations of the past appeal to audiences and others fail? Scholars of rhetoric have long considered the question of persuasive appeal central to their inquiry. They assume that all public expression is inherently selective; yet this selectivity—or "invention," in the rhetorical parlance—has to do not only with the author's political bias but with available cultural and symbolic resources that are deployed to inspire identification and adherence. Rather than see various material manifestations of memory as political ideologies and identities "written in stone,"[69] a rhetorically inflected approach regards them as modes of enacting "attitudes toward history."[70] While these attitudes may be inspired by the needs of the present, their power to influence others resides in part in their ability to use symbolic resources possessing cultural legibility and emotional power for particular audiences. These resources—such as iconic images or cultural narratives—are themselves products of historic and cultural developments.[71] Tracing the genealogy and current cultural resonance of symbolic forms pressed into service in any commemoration is therefore crucial to ascertain their particular appeal in the present.

All of this book's case studies, accordingly, attend to the evolution of formal and iconographic resources deployed in the service of public remembrance. To explain the prevalence of popular culture icons in the "Celebrate the Century" commemorative stamp program, chapter 1 examines historically the iconography of images reproduced on postal stamps. To evaluate the role of electronic media in collecting and displaying popular memories, chapter 2 addresses the changing curatorial and exhibition strategies of museums and archives. In chapter 3 New Orleans carnival traditions of the last century and a half form a background against which one can appreciate the multivocal pageantry of the first post-Katrina Mardi Gras. To understand the rhetorical strategy of the touring antiwar memorial *Eyes Wide Open,* chapter 4 explores the visual conventions of commemorating the war dead.

However, the issue of antecedent forms of commemoration, while necessary to understand how particular enactments of memory employ and sometimes transform available cultural resources, is not sufficient to account for their persuasiveness. Although it is often overlooked in studies of individual memorials, the relation of commemorations to other practices that form the cultural landscape of the present is also important for audience engagement. Contemporary audiences live in a multigeneric world in which discourses clamor for their attention wherever they go. Because of this oversaturation, perhaps, such old-fashioned memory artifacts as statues and permanent memorials languish as obscure landmarks. "There is nothing in this world as invisible as a monument," Robert Musil poignantly observed.[72] But this invisibility is not necessarily a sign of public disinterest in the national past—it is more likely than not a result of competing attractions.[73] Some would argue that distraction is a default state of mind among today's audiences and that attention, as Richard Lanham claims in his *Economics of Attention,* is a precious commodity.[74] Drawing in a distracted spectator may well be the first step toward the sort of experience that may, to quote Gregory Clark, "do the rhetorical work of prompting people to adopt for themselves a common—even a civic—identity."[75]

Therefore, to stimulate public participation, contemporary commemorative projects must rely on a variety of strategies, often leveraging their audience's familiarity with and involvement in cultural practices that on their face bear only slight resemblance to traditional commemorations. The "Celebrate the Century" program appealed to its prospective participants by conjuring a nostalgic trope of stamp collecting and stimulated their interest in telling the story of the twentieth century by appealing to their shared knowledge of mass culture's genres and artifacts. The September 11 Digital Archive emulated then-emerging social media by soliciting personal contributions from anyone who cared to share narratives or images related to the events of September 11, 2001. In making room for a variety of contributions, both pious and profane, the archive also mimicked the raucous diversity of ephemeral popular expression that temporarily invaded the landscape following the terrorist attacks. In post-Katrina New Orleans, residents used carnival as a venue for commemorating their experience because of the festivity's status as a central civic ritual *and* a tourist and media magnet. In order to engage passersby in a conversation about the cost of the Iraq War, the traveling memorial *Eyes Wide Open* visited multiple locales around the country, often timing its appearance to coincide with nationally significant dates such as Tax Day, Memorial Day, or Independence Day. In all of these cases, commemorations drew in various measures on their audiences' experiences as consumers, tourists, and spectators in order to invite them to celebrate, to mourn, or to bear witness.

Ultimately it is not so much the antecedent tradition or aesthetic innovation of a particular commemorative project but the investment of participants and audiences that establishes its popularity and vitality as a form of cultural politics. "The issue of reception," writes Alon Confino, is "that ogre that awaits every cultural historian"; "many studies of memory," he points out, "are content to describe the representation of the past without bothering to explore the transmission, diffusion, and ultimately, the meaning of this representation."[76] Some memory scholars have argued that reactions of multiple audiences are even more important than the symbolism of a particular monument and memorial. James Young made this point emphatically when he declared that memorials are "dependent on visitors for whatever memory they finally produce."[77] Young's insistence on the "fundamentally interactive, dialogical quality of every memorial space"[78] is a useful starting point for understanding those commemorative projects that actually rely on audience participation as an inventive strategy rather than simply anticipate it as an aftereffect.

Yet "reception" remains an elusive construct, since it can encompass a range of experiences, many of which leave few traces for the analyst to track down. Case studies under analysis here afford dissimilar opportunities to evaluate the extent and intensity of public involvement. In some, as in the case of the "Celebrate the Century" stamp program, I relied largely on media coverage to reconstruct controversies over stamp subject selection and audience reactions at stamp unveiling ceremonies and exhibits. In other cases, especially the September 11 Digital Archive, the role of contributors was evident in the contents of the archive, which made it a priority to solicit and preserve as many expressions of attitudes toward history as its technical capacity allowed. The controversy over the appropriateness of celebrating carnival in the wake of Katrina, still and moving images of costumes and parades, and the impressions of participants and spectators have been preserved in both mainstream media and a myriad of locations online.[79] Finally, when researching *Eyes Wide Open,* I had access to organizers and volunteers through interviews, observed exhibits in situ, and perused mainstream and alternative media to trace the life of the memorial beyond its temporary appearances in multiple locales. With few exceptions my access to audience experience depended on archival resources rather than firsthand observations and interactions.

My reliance on preserved traces of reception and contestation does not entail the tacit privileging of the "text" as the source of meaning, however. Following Young's suggestion that we interpret every memorial space dialogically, I inquire how textual, visual, and spatiotemporal arrangements, both deliberate and spontaneous, position participants as actors in scenarios of history enacted in the present.[80] In other words I hold that experience, while always individualized and embodied, is also a product of mediation.[81] Experience is prompted and framed by technologies of memory. Whether visiting physical memorials and museums or virtual destinations, we often "encounter experiences that have been composed for us to experience, that have been designed to influence and even direct the outcome of our own composition process."[82]

As part of the discussion of audience experience, the chapters to follow address diverse types of display and mediation. Chapter 1 examines strategies of display and promotion that invited the public to view the results of their participation in the selection of the most iconic images to represent the twentieth century, including the arrangement of stamps on collectible sheets, unveiling rituals, and the traveling train exhibit. In chapter 2 I assess how the September 11 Digital Archive positions its visitors as potential contributors to as well as users of its contents. In chapter 3 I distinguish between the ephemeral experience of New Orleans carnival in situ and the "prosthetic memories" of post-Katrina New Orleans made available by electronic media.[83] Chapter 4 explores how the physical setup, timing, and cultural particularities of different locations influence visitor interactions in the space of the *Eyes Wide Open* touring memorial as well as how different forms of mediation beyond physical locales affect its meaning.

By drawing a distinction between physical and virtual sites of memory in this study, I do not mean to construct a hierarchy of more or less authentic experiences. On the contrary physical spaces do impose a particular arrangement on encounters that may transpire there. Physical space can be therefore considered a "mnemonic technology."[84] But it is also important to recognize not only how different forms—modes—of mediation work to disseminate "products" of memory to distant audiences but also how a particular medium frames and enables subsequent audience experience.[85]

Examining participatory memory practices in relation to their cultural resources, other contemporary symbolic and material practices, and the mediation of audience experiences allows us to reconstruct commemoration as a multifaceted process that both displays representations of civic identity and occasions encounters among citizens. Looking at a range of recent nationally publicized commemorations from those most institutionally controlled to the least centralized, I inquire to what extent one's ability to "put one's stamp on history" contributes to the collective portrait of "the people" as well as to the likelihood of transformative conversation among strangers.

1

"Put Your Stamp on History"

Celebrating Consumer Democracy

In evaluating the impact of public participation on commemorations as a technology of citizenship, it is useful to begin with an example that seems to fit squarely into the category of "official" commemoration—a government-sponsored program intended to celebrate the nation's progress in the twentieth century.[1] Official commemorations, according to John Bodnar, tend to epitomize aspirations of political, cultural, and economic elites at the expense of ordinary citizens and take on forms that communicate "what social reality should be like" rather than what it "feels like."[2] As such they impose abstract ideals of citizenship onto the populace and in so doing disregard the lived experience of their audiences. This chapter's reading of the "Celebrate the Century" stamp program organized by the U.S. Postal Service (USPS) complicates the "official versus vernacular" polarity and provides a more nuanced account of an admittedly "top-down" commemoration. By exploring the sources of the program's appeal to its audiences and the manner in which participants were invited to experience the narrative of history that they helped to create, I show how popularity functions as a strategy to attract public participation and how participation, in turn, lends an appearance of democratic inclusiveness and authenticity to a project that benefits corporate interests and promotes individual consumption as a model of citizen engagement.

Joining the retrospection fever at the end of the millennium, the USPS unveiled its own commemorative stamp program, "Celebrate the Century." The program promised to become "one of the nation's largest and most inclusive commemorations of the 20th century."[3] Its scope—150 stamps were issued over a two-year period to honor the most significant people, events, and trends of each decade of the century—was matched by unprecedented public involvement and an array of promotional activities. The stamps representing the first five decades were chosen by members of the Citizens' Stamp Advisory Committee appointed by the postmaster general; the public selected the images representing the second half of the century. Ballots were available at post offices nationwide. In the balloting for "Celebrate the Century," all those interested, including schoolchildren, could vote an unlimited number of times if proper postage was affixed to each ballot.

Much financial and organizational effort was exerted to excite and sustain public interest in this commemoration. Post offices across the nation were transformed into minimuseums featuring electronic panels that counted the days, hours, and seconds remaining until the year 2000. On their way to the clerk's window, visitors were greeted by colorful panes of stamps issued under the aegis of "Celebrate the Century." In February 1998, as the ballots for the 1950s arrived, the USPS issued commemorative sheets for the decades of 1900 and 1910 and sponsored a series of unveiling ceremonies across the country, dubbed "thirty stamps in thirty days." Schoolchildren in some three hundred thousand classrooms were encouraged to "stamp history" as they learned about earlier decades from the "Celebrate the Century Kit." Before the series of ten panels was completed, stamps issued to date were integrated into a train exhibit, *Celebrate the Century Express*, a four-car museum that traversed the country from coast to coast, inviting visitors to "experience a century's worth of achievement and tragedy, entertainment and innovation, grit and greatness."[4]

"Celebrate the Century" manifested a significant shift in the aesthetics and politics of commemoration in several ways. The program's most conspicuous feature is a lack of discrimination between representations of historical events and persons and pop culture, between landmarks of social change and objects of mass consumption. One of the first mass-produced memorial artifacts, a commemorative stamp at the end of the millennium reproduces the imagery that has been rendered iconic by mass media. Thus the series is a mnemonic device in a cultural situation in which saturation by images or simulacra, to use Jean Baudrillard's term, threatens a stable sense of history and identity.[5]

By the same token, the program relies on the mass-produced quality of pop culture images—and their potential for intimate appeal—to distinguish itself as a novel way to commemorate. That half of these icons were chosen by popular vote emphasizes popularity as a mark of their historical significance and political legitimacy. "Celebrate the Century" valorizes the increasing role of ordinary people as coproducers of significant texts of public culture. In this respect the openness of commemoration to various publics promises to strengthen civic engagement.

Despite the success of "Celebrate the Century" as a popular program, however, its professed inclusiveness veiled the process through which the public's political agency as cocreators of history was manipulated to benefit private, corporate interests. Although it was promoted as the result of a popular and open selection process, "Celebrate the Century" used this process to authenticate a hegemonic narrative of consumer democracy, to convert the stamps and historical lessons they might teach into politically inert mementos, and to foreclose public dialogue across lines of difference.

To show how "Celebrate the Century" exemplifies a shift in the political aesthetics of commemoration, I first trace thematic and stylistic transformations in commemorative postal iconography and its relation to mass culture. Because contemporary icons serve an important emotional and political function in an ever-accelerating culture of obsolescence, they constitute a visual lexicon out of which both dominant and oppositional interpretations of history may emerge. Next I depict the politics of stamp selection as a struggle among competing interests to suggest that the public's participation in the process ultimately was appropriated by corporate interests. Finally I focus on several display mechanisms that helped to frame the collection as a commodity, the public as atomized consumers, and history as a progress toward consumer democracy.

From Civil Religion to Consumer Society

The evolution of commemorative aesthetics in general and postal iconography in particular forms the backdrop against which "Celebrate the Century" stands as an example of collective memory in the making. Some observers have frowned on the "pop" character of the series in which somber photographs of child laborers and Dorothea Lange's *Migrant Mother* share iconic status with neon-bright images of consumer products from crayons to Barbie dolls.[6] That a collective memory project should be so closely entwined with popular culture is not simply a matter of taste. Working from the assumption that icons "reflect social knowledge and dominant ideologies" and "shape and mediate understanding of specific events and periods,"[7] I begin my analysis of "Celebrate the Century" by surveying the changes postal iconography has undergone over some 150 years.

The current postal iconography can be seen as one of many manifestations of a transformation in individual and collective experiences of history in the West. Whether described as postmodernism, postnationalism, or post-Fordism, this change has affected the way citizens in liberal-democratic societies relate to past, present, and future.[8] In the United States, this shift was felt in part as a disenchantment with the legitimizing myth of "civil religion," itself a blend of religious faith in the nation as a chosen people and a civic republican ideal of the state as social covenant. Robert Bellah coined the term in 1967 in the midst of the social upheavals of the Vietnam War era, when the symbolic fabric signified by the term already had begun to unravel.[9] Bellah defined civil religion as "the myths that have developed to help us interpret who and what we are in America."[10]

Central to civil religion is the nation's myth of origin, which encompasses historical periods from the Declaration of Independence to the inauguration of Washington under the Constitution, and a host of religious and philosophical discourses that imagined America as a promised land.[11] The myth of the nation's beginning, as embodied by the founders, represents "the act of conscious meaning-creation, or conscious taking responsibility for oneself and one's society."[12] The theme of self-determination from the outset was complemented and complicated by the mythical teleology of the nation as a New Jerusalem, whose "natural" state connoted opposing visions of paradise and wilderness. These different strands of U.S. civil religion in all their dialectical complexity coalesced around the idea of common heritage.

For more than a century, U.S. postal iconography dramatized the dialectic of self-determination and destiny, stewardship and conquest.[13] Stamps promulgated the heroic imperative of leadership: presidents, statesmen, military leaders, and explorers remained the dominant themes of celebration well into the 1950s.[14] The style of depiction contributed to the sublime aura of the images. Statesmen were often shown in profile in the manner of Roman emperors. Heroes of the American Revolution were leading their troops to victory. Explorers were landing triumphantly on the shores of new territories or ascending mountain peaks. Thus, whether the subject is the landing of Christopher Columbus, Jacques Marquette's crossing of the Mississippi, or John C. Fremont's scaling of the Rocky Mountains, the composition of the images and the postures of those featured convey the momentousness of the event and the superhuman status of the central character, thereby establishing a kinship between the legendary conqueror of the New World and nineteenth-century pioneers.

In the meantime stamps bearing icons of the industrial age carried the story of progress. The locomotive, the steamship, the automobile, and the bridge—the images marking the Pan-American Exposition issue of 1901—assume a sublimity unrivaled by human beings. Representation of these technological wonders in the commemorative contexts acquires the aura of a national myth. A particularly vivid example is the stamp "Landing of Cadillac in Detroit 1701–1951," in which the image is formed by the juxtaposition of a familiar iconic scene of a hero's "landing" with Detroit's skyscrapers in the background. The center of the U.S. automobile industry and the birthplace of the assembly line is mythologized by its retroactive inclusion into the pantheon of the nation's civil religion.

From the mid-nineteenth century until the 1960s, the subjects and iconography of postal stamps replicate other commemorative practices of the era of nationalism. As John Gillis observes, "on both sides of the Atlantic, national commemorations were largely the preserve of elite males, the designated carriers of progress"; by contrast "the role of women was largely allegorical," and workers, minorities, and younger people "gained admission to national memories at an even slower pace than they were admitted to national representative and educational institutions."[15] The rhetorical legacy of the heroic imperative, the choice of individuals as subjects, and the grandiloquent manner of their depiction on postal stamps is evident even when ordinary Americans are the honorees. The Iwo Jima stamp of 1945 is a remarkable example. The stamp, reproducing Joe Rosenthal's photograph of marines raising Old Glory on the crest of Mount Suribachi, became an archetype of patriotic courage precisely because the group's posture so perfectly embodied the iconographic conventions that had been employed in national commemorations for more than a century.[16]

By most accounts the sixties were a watershed decade that transformed memory practices throughout the world. Although the heroic ideal had left its imprint in the form of imposing monuments, museums, cemeteries, and national holidays, there was a multiplication of subjects worthy of remembering and of contexts of commemoration. After the establishment of the Citizens' Stamp Advisory Committee in 1957, postal commemoration entered a new era, as cultural institutions became more open to influences from ordinary people. Although the final word still belonged to the postmaster general, all citizens could now propose postal themes and designs.[17] Official anniversaries continued to provide commemorative themes, but their representation no longer uniformly followed the heroic aesthetic of the nationalist era. For instance a laconic image of a broken chain—black links against a navy blue background—hailed the centennial of the Emancipation Proclamation. The abstract character of the image connotes a nonhierarchical value system without leaders or followers, wherein all are equally liberated by the freeing of an oppressed group. In the commemoration of the American Revolution's bicentennial, populist motifs mingle with the icons of the Founding Fathers. Issued over a six-year period, four stamp series—"Colonial Craftsmen," "Colonial Communications," "Contributors to the Cause," and "The Spirit of '76"—exemplify a turn toward reconsidering crucial events of U.S. history from the perspective of a common citizen.[18]

The popular turn also is signaled by the inclusion of mundane subjects expressing the seemingly apolitical interests of regular Americans. Alongside space exploration, achievements in electronics, the Civil War centennial, and the U.S. bicentennial, stamps of the sixties and seventies saluted amateur radio, professional baseball, and college football. In the post-bicentennial period, stamp subjects drew on popular culture more than on the traditional patriotic lore. In the eighties and nineties especially, commemoration ran the gamut from Will Rogers and Elvis to comic strip classics to classic movie monsters. Not only were women and minorities admitted to the national tableau, but a whole range of places, objects, holidays, and pastimes also acquired iconic status. This proliferation of icons is a symptom of the increasing speed of obsolescence and the increasingly sophisticated capacity to preserve the past. As Gillis remarks, "On the one hand, the past has become so distant and the future so uncertain that we can no longer be sure what to save, so we save everything. . . . On the other hand, never has the past been so accessible on film, on tape, and in mass-produced images."[19] Reproduction of mass-produced images on commemorative stamps captures the paradox of preservation and obsolescence that is the mark of contemporary historical sensibility.

According to Aaron Betsky, "part of our twentieth-century loss of faith has been a loss of the kinds of icons that are unapproachable, semidivine apparitions."[20] Nowadays, Betsky notes, "icons are all around us": "some of the most normal, run-of-the-mill objects we use in the United States have become iconic."[21] Ubiquity and ordinariness entail a corresponding aesthetic. In place of polychromatic and multilayered compositions reminiscent of nineteenth-century painting and neoclassical sculpture, today's postal iconography favors the bright, glossy look of a color photograph. Images are supposed to convey the feeling of three-dimensional similitude. This insistence on "hyperreality," as Umberto Eco argues, "suggests that there is a constant in the average American imagination and taste, for which the past must be preserved and celebrated in full-scale authentic copy."[22] If technology saves fragments of material culture from oblivion, their commemoration as fetishistic objects saves them from trivialization.

In "Celebrate the Century," for example, pop icons have the same ontological status as representations of significant past events. Showcasing the preceding decades from the perspective of the present, the series highlights the popular and the mundane along with major events and outstanding individuals. All ten panels contain the same five categories of subject matter: people and events, arts and entertainment, science and technology, sports, and lifestyle. Thus even the earlier decades include a gallery of artifacts and pastimes supposedly accessible to all Americans at the time. On the 1900 panel, a still from the 1903 movie *The Great Train Robbery* is sandwiched between President Teddy Roosevelt and a box of Crayola crayons, and W. E. B. Du Bois is next to the "Teddy Bear" stamp.

The principle of photographic verisimilitude is evident as well, although a number of stamps mimic the "authentic" look of original posters, sketches, and cartoons. Americans are introduced to the fashion world of the 1900s through an original sketch of a Gibson Girl, to U.S. involvement in World War I through the "I Want You" poster of Uncle Sam, to the Jazz Age of the 1920s through a cartoon, "Flappers do the Charleston," and to women's contribution to the war effort of the 1940s through the poster of Rosie the Riveter. Such stamps invoke the aura of the period "through stylistic connotation, conveying 'pastness' by the glossy qualities of the image."[23] Other stamps present a faithful copy of a person, artifact, event, or trend. Images of presidents Teddy Roosevelt, Woodrow Wilson, and Harry Truman depart from the iconography that once presented U.S. leaders as static profiles or larger-than-life heroes. Roosevelt resembles a businessman at a board meeting; Wilson is holding on to his top hat at an outdoor rally; a grinning Truman is lifting up the *Chicago Daily Tribune* with the headline "Dewey Defeats Truman." The image of Jackson Pollock, symbolizing the emergence of abstract expressionism in the 1940s, is based on a 1949 photograph of Pollock at work on one of his drip paintings.

The icons assembled under the aegis of the "American century" do not privilege a particular event as constitutive or a particular person as more important than others. There does not seem to be a grand narrative of origin but rather a host of random historical snapshots, in which all images appear to be of equal significance. A collage such as this, in which small-scale and large-scale history mingle and dissolve into one another, fits Fredric Jameson's description of the postmodern historical project as a "vast collection of images, a multitudinous photographic simulacrum."[24]

Yet the prospect of an engagement with the past via these images is not doomed simply because the manufactured "past" of mass culture substitutes a "simulacrum" for a real experience of history. Against the Platonic condemnation of images as false reality and Marxist critiques of the "society of the spectacle" as a negation of history and fabrication of "present frozen time,"[25] I maintain that popular icons represent a visual "vocabulary" equally available to all. As Alison Landsberg explains, "mass-mediated memories are not premised on any claim of authenticity or 'natural' ownership. One's engagement with them begins from a position of difference, with the recognition that these images and narratives concerning the past are not one's 'heritage' in any simple sense."[26]

As mass-produced quasi-fetishistic objects, stamps and the images they disseminate have acquired different meanings and valuations in the hands of stamp collectors and cultural institutions. Historically, as a hobby indulged in primarily by middle-class males, stamp collecting often functioned "as a metaphor for the free market: a leisure-time activity that trained boys in the techniques and values of commerce and confirmed the legitimacy of the market economy for adult males."[27] When women joined the ranks of philatelists, they presumably viewed stamps not as commodities with a market value but as "a medium through which they could express their creativity."[28] Women in fact pioneered topical collecting, arranging stamps according to pictorial subject matter rather than monetary value, chronology, or country of origin.[29] By the 1930s stamp collecting achieved the status of an educational hobby, having received "imprimaturs by educational and governmental authorities." Such endorsements stressed the role of stamps as lessons in geography and culture and affirmed philately as a wholesome leisure for both sexes insofar as it "occupied minds that would otherwise have been idle."[30] The framing of "Celebrate the Century" as a popular history lesson seems to echo the earlier institutional rhetoric about stamp collecting by assigning historic and educational value to potentially distracting representations of pop culture.

Instead of debating whether popular culture leads to a substitution of genuine experiences by mass-produced simulacra, then, it is more productive to think of pop icons as "magnets of meaning" that "change appearance depending on how you look at them, from what angle, in what context, or what you bring to your looking."[31] Accordingly the next section attends to politics of stamp selection for "Celebrate the Century" to show how the same image could serve different interests and how the process of appropriation and contestation alters the meaning of popular icons.

The Politics of Inclusion

Until the 1960s, the selection of persons and events to be honored on postal stamps had been the privilege of the political and cultural elites. Postal commemorations, like other state-sponsored memory practices, "were largely for, but not of, the people."[32] "Celebrate the Century" appears, by contrast, to be an expression of popular will. To quote then–Postmaster General Marvin Runyon, "through *Celebrate the Century,* Americans can save the past as they look toward the future. U.S. postage stamps have been integral to the fabric of American life since the founding of our great country, and they continue to be a source of learning and pride for all Americans. Capturing history on stamps is a part of the Postal Service's proud heritage. What makes *Celebrate the Century* such a unique continuation of this heritage is that for the first time, the public will play a major role in determining the stamp subjects that will become a permanent record of the passing millennium."[33]

This amalgamation of personal remembrance and collective history making confirms what social and art historians have been observing about commemorations in the late twentieth and early twenty-first centuries. John Gillis notes that memory work has become open to many and has shifted from national centers to local communities and living rooms: "Every attic is an archive, every living room a museum."[34] Although this "democratization of the past causes some anxiety among professionals" and "conservatives decry Americans' lack of factual knowledge about their national history," argues Gillis, "there is good evidence to show that ordinary people are more interested in and know more about their pasts than ever before, though their knowledge is no longer confined to compulsory time frames and spaces of the old national historiography."[35] Popular memory can also function as a form of political expression, as a way to create public visibility for individuals and interest groups. Calling this growing trend "memorial mania," Erica Doss comments: "Memorial mania is shaped by individual impulses and factional grievances, by special interest claims for esteem and recognition, and by efforts to symbolize and enshrine the particular issues and aspirations of diverse and often stratified publics."[36] If privatized remembrance deepens one's connection to a local or family past, "claims for esteem and recognition" publicly demand attention to issues of cultural identity and civic belonging.

The proliferation of sites of memory work and corresponding identities does not bring an end to officially sponsored commemorations. Rather, as analysis of the "Celebrate the Century" program reveals, official commemoration has found it vital to reinvent itself as part of the trend Gillis terms "democratization of the past," to craft an appearance of consensus, or at least of compromise, among historical and political interests of diverse publics. Public participation in stamp selection, coupled with popular iconography of the stamps, lent the project an aura of democratic inclusiveness and bottom-up civic engagement. Although "Celebrate the Century" was designed and promoted as a product of a pluralistic selection process, the program used this process as a strategy to authenticate a hegemonic narrative of the American century that disavowed sociopolitical differences and conflict.

From the beginning the selection process was marked by a division of labor between the Citizens' Stamp Advisory Committee (CSAC) and the "general public." The committee, composed of professional historians, business leaders, marketing specialists, and celebrities, selected subjects to represent the first five decades and suggested a list of designs out of which the public chose the icons capturing the 1950s through the 1990s. This division was justified by "extensive market research" that "showed the public was more familiar with events from the latter part of the century."[37] Presumably, through education and ease of access to archives, "the elites" could reconstruct the decades that the majority of the population did not experience firsthand; personal recollections would add an authentic touch to the mosaic of national icons from the remaining fifty years of the century.

As ballots for the last five decades began to appear in post offices, people realized that they could stuff the ballot box in support of their favorite icons, provided that they paid the postage to mail in their votes. Although the menu of images (thirty for each decade) consisted of nationally recognizable persons, events, and trends, some images became the focus of enthusiastic grassroots campaigns. Residents of Brockton, Massachusetts, fought to commemorate their local hero Rocky Marciano, an undefeated boxing champion.[38] Marciano was one of five sports figures and events listed in the stamp selection ballot for the 1950s; however, for the people of Brockton, he is an example of a successful tough guy who always remembered his blue-collar roots. At George's Café, a family restaurant owned by Marciano's boyhood friend, walls are covered with black-and-white photographs of his famous fights and of his frequent visits to the hometown. A framed first-day cancellation of the Rocky Marciano stamp from the "Celebrate the Century" series occupies a place of pride, yet it is one among many images of the boxing legend.[39] Marciano is now part of national history, but here he lives in local memory.

Postal customers could choose only from subjects recommended by the CSAC. Because records of the committee's deliberations were sealed from the public, the extent of outside lobbying to put particular subjects on the ballot is uncertain.[40] A notable exception is the National Council on Disability's effort to urge the Postal Service to issue a stamp commemorating the tenth anniversary of the Americans with Disabilities Act as part of the "Celebrate the Century" series. Posted on the NCD website, a letter to the CSAC chairperson, Dr. Virginia Noelke, outlined the reasons for turning the ADA into a national icon: "ADA is also distinctively American. It embraces several archetypal American themes such as self-determination, self-reliance, and individual achievement. ADA is about enabling people with disabilities to take charge of their lives and join the American mainstream."[41] Although such a stamp would have celebrated a crucial milestone in civil rights legislation for 54 million people, it was not considered for inclusion. Under the "people and events" rubric, the 1990s offered "Improving Education," "Cultural Diversity," "Sustained Economic Growth," "Gulf War," "Recovering Species," and "Active Older Americans."

What, then, was the official intent behind the series? Government officials, historians, and educators saw "Celebrate the Century" as an educational program to involve teachers, schoolchildren, and parents in a conversation about the nation's past and present. In its press releases, the USPS stressed its alliance with the Department of Education's "America Goes Back to School" program, "a coalition of more than four thousand businesses, community, religious and educational organizations nationwide," and promised to give teachers "the opportunity to take their students on a fun and interesting field trip through the twentieth century."[42] Not coincidentally, perhaps, "Improving Education" was one of the finalists for the 1990s, although it signified a collective commitment rather than an achievement. Then–Secretary of Education Richard W. Riley summed up the lofty aspiration of the program's government sponsors: "Exposure to the people and events of the twentieth century that will be honored on this series of stamps will give a dose of inspiration to the children who will some day perform great deeds of the twenty-first century."[43] The patriotic and pedagogical aspects of "Celebrate the Century" reflected an official concern about how to teach young Americans "not to forget something they had neither known nor remembered in the first place."[44]

The program's didactic goal of promoting a positive image of U.S. history to the younger audience can be gleaned from commentaries in the national press that followed "Celebrate the Century" for almost three years. Critical coverage highlighted two troublesome aspects of the collection: exclusion of some traumatic episodes of the century and positive modification of serious events that made the final cut. Commenting on the 1950s ballot, a *Boston Globe* writer noted with some sarcasm: "We can't choose stamps commemorating nuclear testing in Nevada, or the executions of Julius and Ethel Rosenberg, or the McCarthy hearings, or any of the more memorably awful events of the decade."[45] Reporters also were quick to point out that the Postal Service had put "a positive spin on some bad events: the Iran hostage crisis becomes 'American Hostages Freed,' the Depression becomes 'America Survives the Depression.'"[46]

What critics found most disturbing, however, was the manipulation of a Jackson Pollock photograph in order to match the atmosphere of the "smoke-free, drug-free, 98 percent fat free, child-friendly 1990s."[47] The image chosen to represent abstract expressionism in the 1940s collage, an original *Life* magazine photograph of Pollock working on his *Number 1, 1949,* was subjected to a series of alterations, including the removal of a cigarette from Pollock's mouth, before it became the picture on the stamp. CSAC chair Noelke, a history professor at Angelo State University in Texas, reasoned that the smokeless version was inoffensive historically and politically: "I think only a small percentage of the American public is going to be aware of that photograph—they're not going to realize there is even an issue here. If you leave the cigarette out, you're not giving a public message one way or another. If you leave it in, you are."[48] This compromise arguably sums up the institutional motivation behind the entire series: a desire to preserve the historical verisimilitude of images without losing control over their potentially unruly significations.

If the inclusion of a cigarette is an implicit endorsement of tobacco, what can be made of the many images of commercial Americana? Acknowledging that the program included a great many commercial products, Noelke suggested that public participation, rather than corporate lobbying, was responsible for this decision: "When you open things up for a public vote," she said in a telephone interview, "you end up with what is popular, not necessarily what is important."[49] To be sure, today popularity is often synonymous with commercial success. The Postal Service apparently agrees, because "Celebrate the Century" broke one of its rules for subject selection by commemorating a host of commercial subjects, ranging from Barbie dolls and automobiles to electronics and computer technology. Once the precedent was set, the rule was amended to permit commemoration of "commercial products or enterprises . . . to illustrate more general concepts linked to American culture."[50]

Private business interests benefited from the series through implicit image politics; however, the deployment of "Celebrate the Century" as an educational program depended on the active involvement of corporations and the use of advanced marketing techniques. In particular Microsoft and its search engine, MSN.com, were integral to developing the "Celebrate the Century Kit" for teachers of grades three to six. The purpose of the kit, besides motivating children to explore contemporary U.S. history by searching *Encarta* encyclopedia for background information on each stamp, was to encourage stamp collecting. The Postal Service's educational plan was a clever marketing strategy; because the program was to be implemented in some three hundred thousand classrooms nationwide, both Microsoft and the USPS stood to gain from the campaign.

The key to the marketing success of "Celebrate the Century" was a belief that stamp collectors, as nonprofessional history buffs, would cherish a chance to decide which stamps would become the permanent record of the passing era. Because schoolchildren could vote on stamp subjects along with the general public—student ballots were included in the educational kit—they were more likely to join the ranks of collectors. As *Promomagazine* remarked on the "pop-culture-tinged lunge after young collectors," the Postal Service had become a "competitor in the $4 billion collectibles market, doing battle not with Federal Express and Airborne but with Beanie Babies and baseball cards."[51]

Pop culture icons had been recognized on postal stamps even before millennial nostalgia set the stage for their commemoration en masse, yet soliciting the public's mandate for doing so is a recent marketing invention. The precedent was set by the popular vote for the Elvis Presley stamp in 1993; given the choice between a "young, studly King" and "the older, rhinestone-studded version," millions of Americans cast their ballots in favor of the young Elvis.[52] Nostalgia drew masses of noncollectors to post offices to buy stamps, and the USPS apparently drew its own conclusions about personal remembrance and commodification. Rather than calling on abstract patriotic values, "Celebrate the Century" elicited sentimental identification with material signs of popular culture. This identification, whose perceived authenticity marked the program as a genuinely collective commemoration, validated the process by which commodities are mythologized and history commodified. "Celebrate the Century," on its face, is a commemoration by the people for the people, but on closer inspection the professed inclusiveness turns out to have been a shrewd cashing-in on the public's desire to make history.

Yet some citizens refused identification, thereby proving that commemorative images are also politically charged representations of who we are as a people in the present. One case that attracted the attention of the national press was the protest against the proposed *Godfather* stamp, meant to honor one of the most popular film epics of the seventies. The Sons of Italy, a group representing the interests of Italian Americans, launched a "national-get-out-the-vote campaign" to oppose the stamp on the grounds that the portrayal of Italian Americans as Mafia killers would be unfair and inaccurate. Arlington lawyer Joseph Scafetta Jr., chairman of the Sons of Italy's stamp committee, told the *Washington Post* that he organized "a national campaign to get the fraternal organization's 450,000 members to vote for any proposed design other than 'The Godfather.'"[53] Notably this fraternal organization consistently has protested popular culture's depictions of Italian Americans while investing effort and money in support of positive national commemorations such as the World War II Memorial in Washington, D.C. The success of the Italian American protest against "defamatory" portrayals suggests that oppositional interpretations of mass culture's messages are more likely when message "receivers" are a relatively advantaged group with greater "access to oppositional codes."[54] To repoliticize a seemingly innocuous memento of pop culture requires effort and a measure of political visibility. By contrast no organized protests were mounted against the stamp representing the popular nineties sitcom *Seinfeld* despite its many jokes at the expense of less advantaged ethnic minorities.

Displaying the Century

The public could accept or reject individual images considered for "Celebrate the Century," thereby exercising a degree of control over the visual vocabulary of the series. But the rhetoric of the series was shaped through various strategies of display and promotion. Hence it would be a mistake to focus on the semantics of individual images in isolation. The critic's task, as Roland Barthes points out, is "rather of a syntactical order": one needs to go beyond the mythological lexicon to decipher "which articulations, which displacements constitute the mythic fabric of a mass-consumption society."[55] It is the "syntax" of the collection as a whole, not only the specific images of pop culture and commercial Americana that populate it, that also shapes the audience's relationship to these icons.

The different strategies of exhibition of the "Celebrate the Century" program fall between two approaches, known to critical ethnographers as "in context" and "in situ." The "in context" approach is traditionally used by museums: "Objects are set in context by means of long labels, charts, diagrams, commentary delivered by earphones. . . . Objects are often set in context by means of other objects, often in relation to a classification or schematic arrangement of some kind, based on typologies of form or proposed historical relationships."[56] Ten collectible panels of stamps of "Celebrate the Century" in which images are ordered thematically and chronologically through visual and verbal means are an instance of "in context" display. "In situ" installations, on the other hand, re-create an environment in which the object is only a part. They "privilege 'experience' and tend to thematize rather than set their subject forth."[57] Unveiling ceremonies for individual stamps were executed in this mode. The two modes are not mutually exclusive; the traveling exhibit *Celebrate the Century Express* incorporates both.

The narrative structure of the series is formed by the chronological progression of panels from the 1900s through the 1990s and by the interaction of visual and discursive components making up each of the ten commemorative panels. The stamps, each bearing an identifying title, are arranged diagonally in several rows against a background image. With the exception of the 1990s pane (where stamps are superimposed on a collage featuring U.S. currency and the steep graph symbolizing economic boom), all background images are decade-specific photographs. Each stamp sheet also features a title caption, a short description of the key events and trends of a given decade, and a list of new words that appeared during the period. According to Barthes in relation to images, verbal elements perform two functions, "anchoring" and "relaying." Anchoring occurs when the linguistic message (such as the title of each stamp) "fixes the floating chain of

1900s souvenir stamp sheet, "Celebrate the Century" stamp collection, United States Postal Service.

signifieds" by directing the reader "among the various signifieds of the image . . . ; through an often subtle dispatching, it teleguides him toward a meaning selected in advance."[58] Relaying refers to a complementary relation between language and image: "the words are then fragments of a more general syntagm, as are the images, and the message's unity occurs on a higher level: that of a story, the anecdote, the diegesis."[59]

The background images for each panel also can direct the reader by visualizing the "title" moment of each decade. Thus the first decade is summed up by the photograph of *Kitty Hawk*, one of the first of the Wright brothers' planes. Besides complementing the stamp image of the plane in flight, the photograph anchors the meaning of other stamps on the 1900s sheet, from the debut of the Model T Ford to the architecture of Frank Lloyd Wright. The first decade of the century is about progress in diverse areas of U.S. experience. Although one might perceive ideological tensions among the individual icons, say between the Ford and new immigrants (expensive commodity versus cheap labor), or between the Ford and John Muir's advocacy of preservationism (technological progress versus the environment), these contradictions are mitigated by the unifying aura of the background image.

The ambiguity of the collage is further reduced by the panel's discursive components, the caption and the short narrative. The 1900s are called "the Dawn of the Twentieth Century," and the story of the first ten years is dominated by achievements signaling the beginning of a more technologically developed, more just, and more prosperous society. Among the stated achievements are President Roosevelt's protection of national forests, the Pure Food and Drug Act, the exposure of corruption in industry by muckrakers Ida Tarbell and Upton Sinclair, and the beginning of the NAACP's struggle for equal rights for African Americans. Even the description of Ford's contribution to the decade—he "made automobiles more affordable with the Model T"—sounds unequivocally laudatory.

Importantly the first installment of the collection is set up as the beginning of a series of transformations leading to the technological and social state of grace at the century's end. This pattern is distinct from the old national mythology of civil religion that seeks to relate the present to a constitutive moment in the past, be it the landing of Columbus or the Revolutionary War. Instead of a historical and mythical beginning, the progression of the narrative is dictated by its end.

The final decade establishes the narrative teleology, thereby authorizing the mythical trajectory of the century. Images in the nineties collage connote the material and social success of the national experience at the end of the century. The stamps are set against the backdrop of a pile of cash and a soaring graph of the stock market, and the caption reads: "In the final decade, Cold War ends, economy booms." The stamp subjects resonate with the theme of post–Cold War U.S. lifestyle.

Curiously many of them are not uniquely American: the World Wide Web, cellular phones, and sport utility vehicles are tokens of modern lifestyle around the globe. Blockbusters *Titanic* and *Jurassic Park*, although bearing a distinct imprint of Hollywood, were distributed worldwide. Even baseball, an all-American pastime, is now a global phenomenon. The narrative role of these signifiers of prosperity and leisure become clearer in their articulation with images denoting social, environmental, and military concerns in the last decade. The domestic issues chosen for the collection—the threat of extinction of certain species of raptors and the decline in education—appear as positive strides thanks

1990s souvenir stamp sheet, "Celebrate the Century" stamp collection, United States Postal Service.

to upbeat captions "Recovering Species" and "Improving Education." Together with the stamp honoring the anniversary of the Special Olympics, these icons depict the nation's domestic concerns as a matter of protecting its nature and its future (children being the conventional symbol of the future). From the paucity of contemporary domestic issues, one might surmise that social and economic disparities at home have been resolved and that Americans have achieved a state of contentment and abundance. Not incidentally the cellular phones stamp depicts the user of the technology as an African American male in a business suit, thereby connoting the overcoming of racial inequality. The Gulf War stamp, on the other hand, suggests that the causes of our discontent lie elsewhere, which occasionally call for U.S. involvement in military conflicts overseas.

This inference is reinforced by the accompanying verbal description, which buttresses the link between national domestic progress and international leadership: "The Soviet Union collapsed, effectively ending the Cold War. Troops were deployed by the United States in the Persian Gulf, in Somalia and in the Balkans." At home, too, the nation was becoming seemingly more democratic: "In 1992—often called the Year of the Woman—a record number of women were elected to political office." Women also approached parity with men in athletics: "The U.S. women's softball, soccer and basketball teams proved themselves the best in the world." This narrative complements and augments the cumulative message of the stamps, that material prosperity and democracy go hand in hand. It also reassures Americans that they deserve their abundance and that their way of life is an example to other, less fortunate and less democratic countries.

If the nineties represent a historical and narrative climax, the preceding decades build toward it. I began my account of the syntax of "Celebrate the Century" with the 1900s, noting that most achievements presented therein foreshadow the resolution of social problems and the triumph of technology at the end of the millennium. The next decades follow the same narrative dynamic. In addition to icons of social progress (the regulation of child labor, the League of Nations, the ratification of women's right to vote, and so on), signifiers of enriched leisure, whether or not they were iconic at the time, provide a thematic leitmotif that becomes even more prominent in the post–World War II era. The collage anticipates the postmodern collapse of the line between "high culture" and "mass entertainment." The 1900s display Crayola crayons, motion pictures, ice-cream-eating children at the Saint Louis World's Fair, the teddy bear, and a Gibson Girl. The 1910s feature Charlie Chaplin's "Little Tramp," avant-garde art at the Armory Show, the first crossword puzzle, and construction toys. The "Jazz Age" is represented by the stamps depicting "Gatsby style," "Flappers do[ing] the Charleston," "Jazz Club" musicians, radio, American realism painting, and electric toy trains, while the verbal description mentions the first talkies and the first Academy Awards. During the Depression years, icons of entertainment abound: the Monopoly board game, the movies *Gone with the Wind* and *Snow White and the Seven Dwarfs,* comic book hero Superman, and the photojournalism of *Life* magazine. The World War II decade also accommodates abstract expressionism, Orson Welles's *Citizen Kane,* the Broadway production of Tennessee Williams's *Streetcar Named Desire,* jitterbug dancing, the big band sound, the "Slinky" craze, and the emergence of television as the nation's entertainer.

The serious and light subjects of the first five decades set in motion a progression toward a greater society and more democratized leisure, to be followed by a similarly optimistic trajectory from the fifties through the nineties. The fifties, the first decade for which the public selected the representative images, re-creates the atmosphere of the Pax Americana era of Eisenhower with its stereotypical ideals of suburban housing, nuclear families, and the living room TV set. Many of the fifties images—tail fins and chrome cars, teen fashions, drive-in movies, and rock 'n' roll—seem to have sprung directly from George Lucas's nostalgic film *American Graffiti.* The "rebellious sixties" is announced as the "decade of extremes," which signals that it was an aberration, a ripple in an otherwise steady flow of history. The panel elaborates the theme of "extremes" by juxtaposing the icons of rebellion and its chief source ("Woodstock" and "Peace Symbol" versus "The Vietnam War") with those connoting positive and unifying achievements ("Martin Luther King, Jr.," "Man on the Moon," and "The Peace Corps"). Considered from the vantage point of the nineties, however, even the rebellious counterculture of the sixties appears as one among many stylistic options, evidenced by the transformation of the peace symbol into jewelry and the staged spectacle of Woodstock's twenty-fifth and thirtieth anniversaries. Nostalgia-laden pop icons—the Beatles, *Star Trek,* the Ford Mustang, the Barbie doll—contribute to the toy-box aesthetic. On the seventies panel, the U.S. bicentennial (the Statue of Liberty), Earth Day, and the women's rights movement icon mingle with "Smiley Face," "70s Fashions," "*Monday Night Football,*" "Jumbo Jets," and VCRs. The eighties spotlight the space shuttle, the fall of the Berlin Wall, which "presaged the end of the Cold War," and the increasing closure of the gender gap in the workplace. Along with these momentous events, the stamps salute cable TV, videogames, personal computers, compact discs, Cabbage Patch Kids, and entertainment hits.

The collage of the century presents a chronological arrangement of images whose signification has been influenced by multiple repetition and commercial usage. Together they are an elaboration on the same theme that culminates in the nineties. This "in context" arrangement of the stamps illustrates Susan Sontag's argument about the malleability of photographic images: "Our unlimited use of photographic images not only reflects but gives shape to this society, one unified by the denial of conflict. Our very notion of the world—the capitalist twentieth century's 'one world'—is like a photographic overview. The world is 'one' not because it is united but because a tour of its diverse contents does not reveal conflict but only an even more astounding diversity. This spurious unity of the world is affected by translating its contents into images. Images are always compatible, or can be made compatible, even when the realities they depict are not."[60] The popular history lesson as presented by the ten "Celebrate the Century" panels, similarly, shapes the account of the passing century into a narrative in which social controversy and conflict are effaced in favor of a consensual consumer democracy. The narrative thus promotes what Lauren Berlant calls "infantile citizenship," or a sentimental attachment to the nation unburdened by a sense of "complexities of aggregate national memory."[61]

The chronological arrangement of "Celebrate the Century" narrows the signification of icons to a distinct teleology. In case of unveiling rituals and the traveling exhibit, one might argue that the narrative totality of the collection would dissolve into fragments, as the cognitive control of the narrative is replaced by more environmental and supposedly less constraining experiences. Even if these experiences seem more interactive and spontaneous, however, they are by no means neutral, because the environments in which they occur tend to convert visitors into "tourists of history," in Marita Sturken's sense of the term—those who remain "distant to the sites they visit."[62] In other words the "in context" and "in situ" displays of "Celebrate the Century" are complementary rhetorical strategies for positioning audiences as tourists and atomized consumers.[63]

Because a particular place confers depth and an aura of authenticity on what may appear as a mere succession of glossy surfaces, the collection's stamps were unveiled separately in a variety of symbolically significant locations. The unveiling rituals reenacted constitutive images of the century by making present a particular association or memory in a charismatic scene. In the words of Greg Dickinson, these sites "suggest the ways the spatial mnemonic triggers memories that come with a whole host of associations (this indeed is their rhetorical power), and the ways the mnemonics serve to cover over other absences."[64] Or, to paraphrase Kenneth Burke, each of these locations is a symbolic "container" that conditions, if not dictates, an appropriate response.[65]

The stamp "Immigrants Arriving" from the 1900s set, for instance, was uncovered at Ellis Island, New York, concurrently with a naturalization ceremony, thereby renewing the "land of opportunity" message in the present along with the message of inclusiveness extended to new immigrants. Rebuilt thanks to corporate philanthropy and now a museum, Ellis Island signifies a friendly passage point into the "new world," rather than a vigilant border post. The site's narrative, however, excludes immigrants who bypassed the island and those who are still barred from entering the United States by current immigration laws.[66] In this sense the location's "spatial mnemonic" both reveals and conceals. Although the hostility and suspicion toward new waves of immigrants was as serious at the turn of the twentieth century as it is today, Ellis Island's inclusion in the tableau of all-American icons is secure and uncontroversial, as opposed to locations along the U.S.-Mexico border.

Unveiling rituals were "containers" in yet another sense; not unlike niche marketing techniques that craft separate messages for separate segments of the population,[67] they simultaneously invoked and contained identities of the diverse publics commemorated by the stamps. Consider two occasions: the unveiling of the peace symbol stamp at a famous 1960s nightclub in West Hollywood and of the Gulf War stamp at MacDill Air Force Base. Admittedly these two events drew on incompatible political allegiances. The ceremony at the counterculture haunt

Whisky a Go Go conjured the oppositional identity of anti-Vietnam protesters, while the honoring of Gulf War veterans celebrated the sacrifices and patriotic commitment of military personnel who fought to protect what President George H. W. Bush called "our American way of life." Each occasion and place constituted a distinct rhetorical situation, a ceremonial moment of affirmation of a distinct group identity and political values. However, by separating the two ceremonies, postal officials betrayed unspoken apprehension at the possibility of a political disagreement erupting in the midst of celebration, again confirming the program's treatment of its participants/audiences as "infantile citizens" who must be shielded from the "inevitably rough edges" of their national memory.[68]

The ceremonial occasion of unveiling framed these stamps and assured each audience of its agency and political legitimacy within the larger historical context, but it also foreclosed questioning the temporal and mythical logic of commemoration. The peace symbol ceremony is particularly instructive in this regard: while acknowledging a representation of "the voice of a generation who spoke out for peace and humanity during a decade of social unrest," speeches by postal officials referred to the stamp as a "wonderful example of the diversity and richness of our *Celebrate the Century* stamp and education program" and described the purpose of the program as paying tribute "to the colorful events that have touched all of our lives in the history of this great nation."[69] By locating the peace movement and its political exigencies safely in the past, this framing neutralizes its political legacy. At the same time, in place of political radicalism as a model of civic identity, the commemoration substitutes a desire to possess the radical past in the present through "colorful" souvenirs—clothing, jewelry, and musical recordings. Similar to the commodification of other historical figures and social movements, the act of nostalgic consumption of counterculture insignia "plays its proper role as a legitimating citation for the commodity system as a whole."[70]

Not all unveilings succeeded in fixing the political in the past, however. At the uncovering of a stamp featuring Martin Luther King Jr., Atlanta mayor Bill Campbell stressed the continuity between King's civil rights crusade in the sixties and the current struggles of African Americans and other minorities. At the moment when Atlanta's affirmative action program was threatened by a civil suit from the Southeastern Legal Foundation, the mayor chose the ceremony to call attention to unresolved social and economic injustices: "Let us not let anyone, any organization or any movement stop our struggle for justice. We will continue to fight like Dr. King. Affirmative action is our Selma. It's our Edmund Pettus Bridge."[71] Mayor Campbell's framing of King's legacy as an enduring symbol of patriotic insubordination violated the decorum of the event, however. The *Atlanta Journal and Constitution* labeled Campbell's intervention "Mayor Gets Political at MLK Stamp Event," as if to emphasize its incongruity with the pathos appropriate to such an occasion: "The imagery Campbell used in his brief comments contrasted sharply with the scene in the hall at Atlanta's Martin Luther King, Jr. Historic Site. King's widow, Coretta Scott King, and a member of the Postal Service's Board of Governors released a royal blue banner to uncover the first-class stamp as a recording echoed the final words of King's 'I Have a Dream' speech: 'Free at last. Free at last. Thank God Almighty, I'm free at last.'"[72]

Whereas rituals of unveiling helped to authenticate the icons by their association with particular locales and people, *Celebrate the Century Express* combined "in context" and "in situ" modes of display. The traveling museum capitalized on its symbolic association with whistle-stop tours of political leaders of the past, reinforced by the inclusion of President Harry S. Truman's 1948 car in the four-car Amtrak train. With its restored vintage railway post office car and an exhibition car housing the interactive displays of stamps, the museum exuded historical authenticity. The *St. Louis Post-Dispatch* described visitors' reaction to the exhibit: "Fran and Bob Watson . . . liked the one of a laughing Truman holding aloft the *Chicago Tribune* front page announcing 'Dewey Defeats Truman,' and were thrilled to learn the original scene actually took place in the St. Louis station just two cars down."[73] If Truman's first-class car conjured the atmosphere of the late forties the way southern plantations reenact the antebellum era, the railway post office car offered a tour of the "postal time." Because railway post offices were discontinued in 1977, visitors were welcomed to experience what was no more: the working conditions of postal clerks as they sorted, processed, and delivered the mail. The exhibit did not offer technological and economic reasons for their discontinuance; the car was fashioned into an attraction to be marveled at, not a lesson in the politics of obsolescence.

A museum excursion typically culminates in a trip to a museum shop. Through various forms of display and promotion, "Celebrate the Century" created an appetite, in a Burkean sense, to complete the "museum" pattern by purchasing a souvenir.[74] Even before the last commemorative pane was issued, the public was urged to take advantage of this "once-in-a-century" opportunity. Collectors and noncollectors could purchase the entire series as a deluxe coffee-table display—"the special heirloom book," as the *Postal Service Guide to U.S. Stamps* called it. "Celebrate the Century" thus would make its way into a family archive as a collection with instant heritage and into the family room as a ready-made conversation piece. The direct-mail offering pictured an older man contemplating stamp sheets with his grandson, an image linking stamp collecting with memory passed from generation to generation, a nostalgic trope conjuring good "old times" when collectors hunted for rare stamps and when children received history lessons from their grandparents rather than from commercial television and the Internet. The agency of the popular vote was to be consummated and immortalized by acquiring a handsomely packaged visual relic.

Conclusion

An institutionally sponsored popular commemoration, "Celebrate the Century" demonstrates, to some extent, the vitality of participatory cultural politics. Although it was organized "from the top" by a government agency and supported by corporate and nonprofit organizations, the project's success depended in large measure on voluntary and enthusiastic involvement of citizens. In its rhetoric of democratic inclusiveness and a stimulating outreach campaign, "Celebrate the Century" acknowledged the importance of ordinary people as history makers.

The democratization of the program was arguably a consequence of popularization, or the choice of historical representations that were easily recognizable and possessed mass appeal. As citizens in a republic of signs, Americans could draw on a stock of images that not only appealed to them but also represented some aspect of their identity. In this way the thematic scope and eclecticism of "Celebrate the Century" responded to the need to remember serious historical events and civic achievements as well as consumer products and lifestyles. This inclusiveness allowed diverse participants in the commemoration to enter the discourse of national memory on their own terms and to interpret particular icons in their own way.

At the same time, the project also shows how popular memory practices can be subjected to the funneling process of selection through elimination as well as modification through a host of display mechanisms. In consequence what begins as an open museum of a postmodern life world in which "everyone is a curator of sorts"[75] ends as a historical amusement park where everyone is a sightseer. As distinct from individual icons—whose signification is open to different interpretations—the series weaves a unifying narrative. This unification was not to be sought in the past, as was the case with the old national mythology of civil religion. In the present Americans could see themselves as world leaders, free from social and political controversies that had divided them in the past, free to enjoy the material rewards of their membership in the consumer culture. "Celebrate the Century" thus promoted what may be called a neoliberal model of citizen rights and obligations, wherein individual consumption is equated with civic responsibility and ability to consume is equated with political self-expression. As a "neoliberal epideictic," the program hailed economic prosperity as a unifying democratic virtue and implicitly declared the end of "debilitating sociopolitical differences . . . —such as the political polarization, class and racial disparities, and vociferous debates over social mores that divided the public at the dawn of the twenty-first century."[76]

Popularization of memory culture is not a sign of the decline of civic consciousness. Popular images and narratives can stimulate interest in the past by eliciting sentimental identification and expanding one's "archive of experience." Yet the affective potential of popular forms is ambivalent insofar as it can encourage social solidarity across difference in opposition to the status quo but also permit solipsistic consumption and civic disengagement. The rhetoric of display of "Celebrate the Century" is troubling not because it elevates commodities to the status of cultural icons. A more problematic aspect of the program is the normative ideal of civic interaction it presents, particularly evident in the form of unveiling ceremonies for individual stamps. Each of these ceremonies assured each group whose heritage was being celebrated of its importance in the larger narrative of U.S. history. Yet by the same token, these ceremonies fragmented the audience of the program into nichelike segments and thus discouraged the mingling of strangers with different sets of political and cultural values. Unveiling rituals thus were crucial not only in framing the stamps but also as a mechanism to keep apart those with potentially antagonistic political ideals and interests. Along with the larger narrative of consumer democracy constructed by the souvenir stamp panels, these rituals projected a depoliticized view of civic life, in which "a place for me," to quote Benjamin Barber, triumphs over a more genuinely democratic "place for us."[77]

The broadening of participation by ordinary people in commemorative activity is therefore not in itself a recipe for democratic renewal. Although terms such as *inclusiveness* and *diversity* were successfully used to promote "Celebrate the Century" to the public, the kind of participation the program offered was both superficial and largely apolitical. While opening the program to participation by diverse publics and thus offering an ostensibly inclusive portrait of "the people," "Celebrate the Century" effectively silenced any profound reflection on the past and present. Given a menu of choices for which to cast a vote, participants were invited to contemplate them as taken-for-granted representations of the American century rather than as concrete, contestable values with deliberative implications.

2

The September 11 Digital Archive

Archival Memory and Popular Participation

The spread of participatory culture is credited in no small measure to the ubiquity and accessibility of new media technologies. Like other kinds of cultural production, memory work is becoming increasingly decentralized and democratized thanks in part to the ease of electronic archiving.[1] No longer a privilege of state and cultural institutions, the recording of events and experiences for posterity—and sharing them with intimates and strangers—has become a pastime of regular people. The emergence of the Internet as a medium of both private remembrance and public commemoration calls for a reconsideration of traditional distinctions between official memory, embodied by "compensatory organs of remembrance" such as memorials, monuments, and museums, and popular forms of memory that are often ephemeral and localized. Online memorializing, thanks to the technology's capacity for virtually unlimited storage and potential to engage many diverse audiences in content production, appears to mitigate against the ideological ossification associated with official memory practices and the fragility of ephemeral memorial gestures.

At the same time, in exploring the Internet's promise as a democratizing medium of public memory, it is important to realize that the contemporary Western obsession with recording traces of the past is an ambivalent cultural trend—it signals not only the "democratization" of memory work but also the acceleration of amnesia. Moreover the very features of electronic communication that make the technology friendly to popular participation in memory work can also abet political fragmentation.

This chapter examines memorial functions of the Internet in light of recent scholarly debates about virtues and drawbacks of modern "archival memory" as well as the paradoxical link between the contemporary public obsession with memory and the acceleration of amnesia. I suggest that "digital memory," more than any other form of mediation, complicates the assumed polarity between modern "archival" memory and traditional "lived" memory by combining the function of storage and ordering on the one hand and of presence and interactivity on the other. Although on its face such synthesis seems to posit the Internet as a panacea for both ideological reification associated with state-sponsored memory practices and the fragility of popular memory, the medium's potential cannot be discussed in the abstract, separate from its cultural and political milieu and institutions that have deployed it in the service of memory work. To illustrate the merits and limitations of new electronic media as vehicles of collecting, preserving, and displaying traces of the past, I will examine the September 11 Digital Archive, a comprehensive online effort to document public involvement in commemorating the tragedy of September 11, 2001. The archive participates in the contemporary cultural obsession over forgetting and amnesia by privileging capacity for storage and representational diversity as marks of civic significance. It does not, however, concern itself with how and to what effect the memories deposited by the contributors might be taken up and thus disowns its role as a scene of civic engagement in the present.

Between the Archive and the Repertoire

The notion of the archive looms large in public and academic discussions of history and memory. Associated with collection and preservation of traces of the past, the archive can be thought of as a location, container, or symbol of our desire to save the remnants of what is no longer present. As French historian Pierre Nora famously asserted, "Modern memory is, above all, archival. It relies entirely on the materiality of the trace, the immediacy of the recording, the visibility of the image."[2] For Nora archival "sites of memory" (*lieux de mémoire*) historically replaced organic "environments of memory" (*milieux de mémoire*) "by virtue of the de-ritualization of our world."[3] Instead of continuous transmission of shared cultural knowledge through participatory performance and ritual, memory work in modern societies is now carried out by museums, archives, and memorials.[4]

Despite the archive's status in modernity as a capacious repository of cultural knowledge and as a signifier for memory itself, archival institutions have been no neutral—or inclusive—receptacles.[5] In choosing what to preserve as traces of the past, museums and archives traditionally have valued objects and texts, selected for their enduring cultural value, over ephemeral manifestations of cultural heritage. Not incidentally artifacts and texts selected for preservation and veneration were often products of intellectual and artistic elites rather than illiterate artisans and performers. This preference, furthermore, contributed to the loss of contexts in which artifacts and texts were produced; as "fragments wrested from their pasts and elsewheres to be exhibited and categorized,"[6] they were subordinated to legitimizing narratives of historical progress and national identity.[7]

The archive's didactic function as an instrument of political power has not escaped criticism, either. Connected to the rise of capitalism and the modern nation-state, the archive played a major role in shaping nationalist sentiments and inculcating a civic identity in place of regional, ethnic, and class affiliations. Institutions of memory have tended to promulgate official ideologies of the ruling elites while claiming to speak on behalf of the people. As cultural theorist Tony Bennett tells the story, "museums were regarded by the end of the [nineteenth] century as major vehicles for the fulfillment of the state's new educative and moral role in relation to population as a whole. While late nineteenth-century museums were thus intended *for* the people, they were certainly not *of* the people in the sense of displaying any interest in the lives, habits, and customs of either the contemporary working classes or the labouring classes of pre-industrial societies."[8]

A similar narrative seems to apply to memorial architecture erected throughout the nineteenth and first half of the twentieth centuries. As a rule monuments and memorials of that era employed representational symbolism to convey narratives of victory and valor and diminished the historical role of nonelite social classes.[9] Museums of history and public art were fashioned after Greek and Roman architectural forms to emphasize the affinities between modern nation-state and classical forms of government.[10] The scale of memorials and museums, too, played its role in instilling a sense of awe and distance in their audience: dwarfed by their size, the visitor was cast in the role of observer and spectator rather than participant.

Although the archive has certainly enjoyed epistemological and ideological dominance in modernity, it has not erased embodied memory practices represented by "performances, gestures, orality, movement, dance, singing—all those acts usually thought of as ephemeral, non-reproducible knowledge."[11] The continuing vitality of cultural knowledge transmission, what performance studies scholar Diana Taylor refers to as "the repertoire," contradicts the displacement of living memory by the archive postulated by Nora.[12] Contesting the tendency "to banish the repertoire to the past," Taylor maintains that "the archive and the repertoire exist in a constant state of interaction."[13]

Taylor's argument is worth heeding not only because it questions the hegemony of the archive in modernity, but also because it cautions against romanticizing the repertoire as the realm of unmediated authenticity. The archive is distinguished by its separation of "the source of 'knowledge' from the knower," achieved by the process "whereby an object . . . is selected, classified, and presented for analysis."[14] The repertoire, on the other hand, "requires presence:

people participate in the production and reproduction of knowledge by 'being there,' being part of the transmission."[15] Still we should be careful not to polarize the repertoire and the archive as "true versus false, unmediated versus mediated, primordial versus modern," warns Taylor. Practices that fall under the rubric of the repertoire are also subject to mediation, as "performances . . . replicate themselves through their own structures and codes."[16] Moreover we should be wary of creating an ideological binary, "with the written and archival constituting hegemonic power and the repertoire providing the anti-hegemonic challenge," because "performance belongs to the strong as well as the weak."[17]

Therefore we might profit more from inquiring into the extent and nature of interaction between the archive and the repertoire than from maintaining a sharp distinction between them. From this perspective even a traditional museum (an archival institution par excellence) is not only a collection of objects and representations but also a "ritual" space that engages visitors in a kind of performance and guides them through some sort of programmed narrative.[18] To describe the museum's contents and exhibits as inscriptions of a particular didactic narrative would be insufficient in accounting for its ideological function, since this leaves out the fact that the museum "also makes visible the public it claims to serve."[19] Historian Carol Duncan proposes that the public museum "produces the public as a visible entity by literally providing it a defining frame and giving it something to do. Meanwhile, the political passivity of citizenship is idealized as active art appreciation and spiritual enrichment. Thus the art museum gives citizenship and civic virtue a content without having to redistribute real power."[20] The typical museum experience is a melding of the functions of the archive—particularly those of selection and display of objects taken out of their original contexts—with the functions of the repertoire, in this case of a bourgeois decorum of spectatorship and stranger relationality befitting a "proper" museumgoer.

Attending to the interaction between the archive and the repertoire can thus clarify how sites of memory enable certain citizenship roles both through the narratives they present and through the repertoire of performances visitors are invited to enact in these spaces in the presence of others. This is not an idle academic concern, since designers, museum professionals, and art critics have begun to ponder how "permanent" memorials and brick-and-mortar museums can engage their popular audiences in "experiences" instead of asking them to contemplate archival objects. The term *experience,* notes Barbara Kirshenblatt-Gimblett, "indexes an engagement of the senses, emotions, and imagination"[21]—in short the values associated with the repertoire. As a consequence of their effort to accommodate experience, institutions of memory, "once defined by their relationship to objects, . . . today are defined more than ever by their relationship to visitors."[22] There has been a similar shift toward a visitor-friendly mode in public memorials. Projection artist Krzystof Wodiczko, a champion of ephemeral public gestures, comments on this trend: "The previously respectful distance ('historical perspective') of the memorial from everyday life is now being broken. Cold, tombstone benches, regimenting, mountainous stairways, brainwashing fountains, architortured bushes, and windswept floors were intended to banish unofficial life from the memorial's territory. Today, the authorities want to add life and 'social function' to the memorial site, to turn it into a 'humanized' space for cultural relaxation, a zone of free festivity, tourism, permanent recreation, and so-called art in public spaces."[23] In other words contemporary institutions of memory are showing signs of opening up to "unofficial life" in allowing visitors greater latitude to define their roles with respect to sites they traverse.

In the United States, the precedent for an open-ended, experiential memorial appears to have been set by Maya Lin's design for the Vietnam Veterans Memorial in Washington, D.C.[24] Instead of glorifying the Vietnam conflict, the black granite chevron laconically conveys the cost of war by listing all American casualties in chronological order. In addition to its strategy of naming names, the memorial's physical form invites interaction: its polished black surface reflects the visitor's image, and its modest scale allows one to reach out and touch the names inscribed on the wall. Although its nonheroic stance initially angered some officials and veterans who wished to see an unambiguous affirmation of military valor, the memorial has become an iconic site of popular remembrance. To mark their pilgrimage to the wall, many visitors leave behind mementos that temporarily become part of the memorial composition. At first the National Park Service classified these traces of participation as "lost and found" but later on began collecting and archiving them for posterity, thus moving them "from the cultural status of being 'lost' (without category) to historical artifacts."[25] In the case of the Vietnam Veterans Memorial, then, "written in stone" official memory and ephemeral participation are interdependent as the archival function of the memorial supports a heterogeneous, unscripted multiplicity of performances of memory.

If the archive used to occupy a privileged cultural position, it is increasingly seen as a supplement to temporary, grassroots modes of memorialization. Ephemeral, multiply authored memorials, such as those spontaneously created at sites of tragedy, "have assumed honorific status in contemporary America," explains Doss, because of the perception that "they embody important public emotions, and that these emotions are eminently worthy of attention and preservation."[26] But felt experiences require presence and stranger interaction and therefore cannot be preserved as artifacts. Even as museums and archives take on the role of "compensatory organs of remembrance"[27] to save materially fragile traces of popular expression, they have to grapple not only with the technicalities of preservation but also with the question of how—and to what end—to furnish these traces for public consumption. In evaluating the success of these efforts, it is therefore important to examine their aspects that relate both to the archive and the repertoire—to see them as repositories of representations of *e pluribus unum* and as sites where strangers can see and engage each other's contributions to the patchwork of public memory.

Promises and Problems of Digital Memory

Although even "permanent" memorials and museums are now being built with an eye to stimulating public engagement, their capacity to share memory work with ordinary people arguably pales in comparison with "digital" memorials and archives. The Internet is a relatively new medium of public memory, however, and its promise of representational diversity, collective authorship, and interactivity is in need of exploration and critique.

At least in theory, online memorializing harbors a greater democratizing potential than any conventional archive insofar as it can accommodate an infinite variety of artifacts and performances. Because all new media objects are composed of digital code, it becomes possible to collect, preserve, sort, and display a vast amount of texts, drawings, photography, and video and audio recordings.[28] In addition to this capacity to "translate" other media into digital code, the function of hyperlinking facilitates interconnection among different sources, producing a cacophonous heteroglossia of public expression.[29] Alongside official accounts disseminated by mainstream media and the government, all kinds of stories can now become part of an evolving tableau of public memory. Formerly limited in time and space, ephemeral gestures can be preserved in still and moving images, ready to be viewed and replayed on demand.[30] Previously banished to dark storage rooms, mementos left at memorial sites can be displayed for all to see. The boundaries between the public and the private, the permanent and the evanescent will cease to matter, for all stories and images will be equally fit to represent and comment on the past.

Perhaps like no other medium before, the Internet has made the idea of collective authorship a practical reality, fulfilling many literary critics' desire to free texts from authorial constraints. Most new media texts are products of collaboration among multiple designers and users. Barbara Warnick states, "A hyperlinked, multimedia site including user contributions as part of its text is best described in Barthes' words as a de-centered 'tissue of quotations drawn from innumerable centers of culture.' It functions as 'Text' and not as 'work,' in that it appropriates and reproduces content from the networked system of which it is a part and may not lend itself well to critical approaches that assume authorial intent and linear structure."[31] George Landlow elaborates this point when he compares the process of generating digital hypertext with the tradition of appropriating or paraphrasing other discourses in print: "The text of the Other may butt up against that by someone else; it may even crash against it. But it does seem to retain more of its own voice. In print, on the other hand, one feels constrained to summarize large portions of another's text, if only to demonstrate one's command (understanding) of it and to avoid giving the appearance that one has infringed copyright."[32] The Internet levels the traditional hierarchy of author-text-audience, thereby distributing authorial agency among various institutions and individuals involved in the production of content and preventing any one agent from imposing narrative and ideological closure upon the data.[33] As web memorials depend on "the joint production of Web-accessible materials by disparate actors," they represent an evolving, multidimensional narrative of historical events and responses to them.[34]

Similar to multiple authorship, "interactivity" was hailed as a democratizing attribute of new media at the turn of the twenty-first century. As Laura Gurak puts it, interactivity embodies "one of the biggest potentials of cyberspace"—to act as "a two-way street in a world where the dominant medium (television) has been unidirectional."[35] While some consider the term itself too broad and even misleading,[36] the users' ability to supply content, provide feedback, and choose their own paths through the system of hyperlinks marks the experience of navigating the Internet as more active than that of flipping through television channels, scanning a newspaper, or following an audio tour through a museum. The audience no longer acts as a consumer of a linear story—it takes part in the experience by making choices to connect particular messages and images as well as to register responses to them. According to Yochai Benkler, participatory cultural content production enabled by Internet tools such as "cutting, pasting, rendering, annotating and commenting" can engender "a self-conscious conversation among users of the culture about its limits, its meanings, and its subversions."[37] As such this conversation fosters new forms of collaboration and sociality that are beneficial to democratic citizenship. Like John Dewey's vision of democracy as a way of life animated by "the faith that the process of experience is more important than any special result attained,"[38] online sociality facilitates potentially transformative encounters among strangers.

While diversity of content, collective authorship, and interactivity can stimulate broad public engagement in memory work, these features work in tandem with a larger cultural context and are subject to medium-specific constraints. One cannot ignore that today's memorializing occurs in a climate of rapid obsolescence and the disappearance of historical consciousness, that much of computer-mediated communication serves commercial and entertainment purposes, and that interactivity can nurture narcissistic amnesia no less than communal exchange.

Contemporary "democratization of the past"[39] is paradoxically entwined with the disappearance of historical consciousness. Andreas Huyssen attributes changes in both personal and social memory to "an emerging new structure of temporality generated by the quickening pace of material life on the one hand and by the acceleration of media images and information on the other. Speed destroys space, and it erases temporal distance. In both cases, the mechanism of physiological perception is altered. The more memory we store on data banks, the more past is sucked into the orbit of the present, ready to be called up on the screen."[40]

The glut of archival memory is a by-product of rapid obsolescence. In the words of Gillis, "The scale of collecting increases in inverse proportion to our depth perception. Now that old is equated with yesterday we allow nothing to disappear."[41] The will to remember is an internalized desire for documenting one's relationship to the present that is felt to be rapidly slipping away. The common worry about this expanding dossier is that active memory work—not just compulsive collection of traces—would be thwarted by the sheer volume of stuff that is being preserved as well as by the perceived (if not actual) ease of retrieving the past at will. When technology offers the ability of instant recall, the inclination to remember withers away. If archival preservation and retrieval are not balanced by rhetorical and political mechanisms that support citizens' engagement with the preserved traces of the past, electronic memory may lead to self-congratulatory amnesia.[42] In this case amnesia refers not to the individual inability to recollect the past but to collective failure to sustain communal practices in which "pluralist speech and action" can thrive.[43]

Another, related concern is that the typical user's participation in online interaction has been to a large extent shaped by commercial patterns of experience. As Manovich reminds us, "the logic of new media fits the logic of the postindustrial society, which values individuality over conformity."[44] The rhetoric of individual choice permeates contemporary commercial culture, reassuring consumers of their uniqueness and stimulating compulsive shopping as a form of identity-shaping performance. Perhaps it is not coincidental that a good portion of user-supplied web content consists of self-expression, most vividly represented by the genre of the weblog.[45] Although some bloggers engage in a sort of editorial activity by providing links and annotating other sources, the majority of blog authors relate their own experiences (whether real or imaginary) to a potentially limitless number of people.[46]

Blogging can be seen as a form of self-memorialization, and an impulse to save the most trivial details of one's past, however recent it might be, is one of manifestations of contemporary remembrance culture in the West: "Both Americans and Europeans have become compulsive consumers of the past, shopping for that which best suits their particular sense of self at the moment, constructing out of a bewildering variety of materials, times, and places the multiple identities that are demanded of them in the post-national era."[47]

However, this "customized" approach to one's past and sense of belonging, enabled by electronic media, may breed cultural and political insularity and lead to a fragmented body politic. Scholars of political communication and Internet activists warn that some of the Internet's assets as a political medium could also be its greatest weaknesses. The ability to narrow down one's web search thematically, for example, while allowing one to magnify one's exposure to information on a particular topic, simultaneously endorses a narrow focus on certain issues at the expense of a broad awareness of political matters.[48] Within the last few years, Internet search engines and social media have begun using algorithms that customize information even without the user's knowledge, creating the "filter bubble" that invisibly isolates media consumers within their own ideological and social worlds.[49] This tendency produces the fragmentation of social and political debate and the entrenchment of established niche groups. The tools of connectivity and interactivity can thus both support a Dewey-like vision of an open debate between people with different points of view and aid an insular process of group identification among like-minded participants.

The intersection of contemporary remembrance culture and new media technologies presents a mixed bag of promises and problems. The storage and sorting capacities of the Internet are certainly helpful in preserving, organizing, and linking vast amounts of data. Any motivated person can now engage in a free search for his or her past and identity, becoming his or her own historian. Thanks to interactivity, virtually everyone can also leave an imprint on the fabric of public memory by sharing images and stories with millions of other users. As a result of these technologically abetted cultural changes, professional historians, archivists, and museum curators find themselves compelled both to acknowledge the role of ordinary people in history making and to include diverse forms of popular expression into the "official" record of history. In so doing, however, they are facing a challenge to their traditional role as stewards of public memory. To remain relevant, they must strike a delicate balance, as it were, between a desire to accommodate as many different voices as possible, on the one hand, and a responsibility to provide a common ground for this diversity on the other. It is one thing to collect, digitize, and preserve large quantities of memorial artifacts; it is quite another to display them in ways that stimulate meaningful participation and interaction. Although online interactivity has been extolled for its potential to foster communitarian intimacy, it is necessary to ask what kind of exchange actually occurs—whether it indeed creates bridges between demographically and politically diverse audiences or furthers balkanization.

Between Archive and Public Participation: The September 11 Digital Archive

September 11, 2001, became deeply etched in collective imagination not only because of the brutality of the terrorist attacks and the magnitude of human loss, but also because it was one of the most mediated disasters in history. Broadcast live on television, the sudden collapse of the World Trade Center towers was witnessed by a global audience. Yet mainstream media were not the only narrators of the unfolding drama of those tragic events and their aftermath. Thousands of people, armed with digital cameras and personal computers, were recording history and reporting it on the Internet. In Dan Gillmor's description, "Another kind of reporting emerged during those appalling hours and days. Via e-mails, mailing lists, chat groups, personal web journals—all nonstandard news sources—we received valuable context that the major American media couldn't, or wouldn't, provide."[50] The tragedy mobilized the desire to record and interpret the events that had not yet been filtered by the U.S. government and media corporations.

Like grassroots journalism, the proliferation of memorial and discussion websites created in response to September 11 and its aftermath pointed to the diversity and robustness of popular expression. Memorializing online was often an extension of the spontaneous process begun in the streets, squares, and train stations of New York City and Washington, D.C. Thousands of ephemeral artifacts from posters and graffiti to makeshift memorials filled public spaces, interrupting the quotidian time and space of city life and creating a vivid counterpoint to mainstream media coverage. For several weeks after the attacks, Union Square in New York City and a number of other places became sites of lively debates about the meaning of the events and the nation's response to them. Political philosopher Marshall Berman recalls this hunger of "everyday people" for meaning as "a striking feature of New York life after 9/11 attacks": "These people stayed out and filled up the downtown streets and squares; they hung around the many clusters of 'missing person' signs, and brought candles and stones; they refused to go home and stayed up talking and arguing with total strangers through the nights even when they had to get up for work in the morning."[51]

The unregulated displays of mourning, sympathy, pride, and protest represented more than a range of reactions to the event that the media quickly dubbed "9/11." In Diana Taylor's words, "the new spatial inscriptions asked us to interact with the city in a different way, as actors in the public space and not merely passive recipients or consumers."[52] City residents, commuters, and tourists alike were made into witnesses of history as it was unfolding not on television or front pages of newspapers but directly in front of them. This liminal experience momentarily transformed a collection of passersby into a community of people who were, to paraphrase S. Michael Halloran, self-consciously present to each other as well as to the spontaneous street spectacle that brought them together.[53] Before the commemorative process migrated to cyberspace, it was actively experienced by thousands of people as they witnessed and contributed to the ephemeral tableau of memorial gestures.

When temporary memorials and posters of the missing began to be removed,[54] many museums and organizations stepped in to preserve these and other ephemera of 9/11 for posterity in order to add them as historical evidence to an already ample set of individual and corporate efforts to memorialize the victims of the attacks. The September 11 Digital Archive, organized by the American Social History Project at the City University of New York and the Center for History and New Media at George Mason University and now supported by the Library of

Congress, represents a comprehensive attempt to "collect, preserve and present the history of September 11, 2001 attacks."[55] The archive's stated purpose summarizes its desire to act as a mediator of a historical event as it was witnessed by regular people, to provide a well-sorted repository of materials for future historians, and to furnish a space where the disparate experiences and reactions could be relived and reflected upon. Accordingly the following discussion of the archive will focus on these three aspects of its mission—to collect, to organize, and to display—in light of this chapter's concern with the promises of "digital memory" as a technology of democratic citizenship.

"The utterly objective exhibition, like the completely unmediated photograph, is a phantasm."[56] Archivists and museum curators always mediate between the artifacts they choose for display and their audiences, but rarely do they explicitly acknowledge their own motives or recognize the role that visitors play in parsing an exhibit's narrative. As Bruce Ferguson argues, "Exhibitions are publicly sanctioned representations of identity, principally, but not exclusively, of the institutions which present them. They are narratives which use art objects as elements in institutionalized stories that are promoted to an audience."[57] For example the Museum of the City of New York, one of the institutions that participated in salvaging ephemeral artifacts of 9/11 for posterity, organized an exhibit of these objects on the first anniversary of the attacks to "underscore the role of museums as stewards of the nation's stories and as special places where communities can examine and reaffirm our basic freedoms."[58]

It is therefore noteworthy that the organizers of the September 11 Digital Archive not only "exhibit [their] intention" but also show their awareness of being "only one of three agents" in the field of exhibition (the other two being the maker of the objects on display and the viewer).[59] In so doing they do not promote a univocal, self-aggrandizing narrative. Their goal, instead, is to "foster some positive legacies of those terrible events by allowing people to tell their stories, making those stories available to a wide audience, providing historical context for understanding those events and their consequences, and helping historians and archivists improve their practices based on the lessons we learn from this project."[60]

Unlike traditional exhibitions, where the curator often exercises full control over the selection of materials, the September 11 Digital Archive epitomizes inclusiveness, which is made possible in no small degree by the interactive capacities of electronic media. The archive's "Contributor Information" link welcomes submissions in multiple forms and media (stories, e-mails, and images) and allows for participation by anyone who had been touched by the events of September 11. In particular the wording of answers to frequently asked questions emphasizes collaboration, positioning audience members as active participants in the unfolding of history regardless of their age, nationality, or location on the day of the attacks. For example those who may have doubted their story's importance because they were not at Ground Zero, at the Pentagon, or in Pennsylvania were reassured as follows: "Please! We want to hear from you. Your experiences need not have been at or near the directly affected locations, not [*sic*] do they need to be particularly heroic or harrowing tales. They can be short or much longer personal reminiscences about how you or the people you knew were affected by 9/11."[61]

Foreigners, too, were encouraged to contribute to the archive: "September 11 was an event that evoked many kinds of responses in many parts of the world. The Internet is similarly a global phenomenon. As such, we are eager to receive contributions of all kinds from all parts of the world."[62] Unlike many U.S. media organizations (including such trusted newspapers as the *New York Times*), the archive refused to frame September 11 as an "American" tragedy that split the world into "us" and "them" but instead invoked a global community.[63]

Launched in March 2002 on the six-month anniversary of the September 11 attacks, in the first three years of its existence the archive collected more than thirty-five thousand personal narratives and twenty thousand digital images.[64] In addition to these, the archive amassed and organized quantities of already existing individual, corporate, and government websites, documents, and online collections related to September 11 and its aftermath. Finally in the section "Frequently Asked Questions about the September 11 attacks," it provided links to a step-by-step account of the event by the *New York Times*. The estimated traffic to the site in its first two years—nearly 120 million hits and more than 2 million unique visitors—testified to the archive's success as a popular history project.[65]

In its sprawling totality, this collection of stories, images, and points of view reflects the unsettled and still-evolving quality of public memory of the 9/11 trauma. While mainstream media accounts assembled by the archive provide an overview of the events themselves, personal stories, photo essays, and artwork present a motley tapestry of sentiments and attitudes in response to the events. They echo the spontaneous popular commemoration begun in public spaces in the days after the attacks as well as reveal the connection between privately shaped memories and those furnished for public consumption by mainstream media.

Individual stories, arranged in reverse chronological order by the date of submission (similar to the way entries are displayed on electronic discussion lists), show a mix of the extraordinary and the banal. On the one hand, family members tell of their loved ones who perished, survivors recount the circumstances of their escape from the Twin Towers or the Pentagon, and volunteers relate their experiences of helping rescue and cleaning crews at Ground Zero or working at hospitals and blood banks. On the other hand, entry after entry describes its author's memory of television coverage of the terrorist attacks. Many of these register their shock at realizing that what they were watching was not an action movie but a live broadcast.

While scores of stories simply recall their authors' first emotional reactions—disbelief, terror, and sympathy for victims and their families are the most common sentiments—some also go on to reflect on the meaning of the tragedy and its aftermath. A sense of vulnerability and loss pervades many entries, especially those by schoolchildren, for whom September 11 was the first exposure to organized violence on a large scale. As one high school student puts it, "Sometimes we take things for granted and my generation really didn't know what it felt like to be under attack but now we do."[66] A ski patroller from Colorado recalls the confusion and misplaced jingoism that characterized the months after the attacks: "The desire to take revenge was very strong, although there seemed to be nobody to take revenge against. In this atmosphere calling French fries 'freedom fries,' or singing 'God Bless America,' were seen as dynamic actions rather than being auxiliary to the matter at hand, simply because it was unclear as to what, exactly, the matter at hand was."[67]

There are, of course, more emphatic statements that express politically polarized attitudes in support of or in opposition to the U.S. government's domestic and foreign policy in the wake of 9/11. For example a Chicago businessman who stockpiled firearms in case U.S. residents of Middle Eastern descent became "sleeper warriors" and took to the streets intones: "In short order—our Commander in Chief, George W. Bush, did what needed to be done in a very pragmatic and reasonable way. He went about the job he had to do and now the evil people that brought terror to us—are either dead, terrified or on the run and in hiding. They may well attack again. But for every one of us they kill, we will bring the wrath of God down on them thousand fold."[68]

On the other end of the spectrum, a college student who became an antiwar activist after September 11 voices her anger at the Bush administration: "September 11th made clear to me the importance of challenging and criticizing our governments [*sic*] blind move to bomb and murder thousands of innocent Afghanistani, and soon, Iraqi citizens. When the towers first fell I was in a state of shock, but as I listened to President Bush's rhetoric (laced heavily with calls for American Manifest Destiny), I found myself enraged and energized for action."[69] These two statements illustrate contrasting conceptions of patriotism and civic duty—one urging unification in support of the administration's military retaliation against "the Other" and the other advocating against American exceptionalism.

Similar to verbal accounts, images submitted to the archive represent a collage of perspectives. Among still photographs, which dominate the category, many document the devastation of Ground Zero and the neighborhoods around it, the recovery and cleanup work of the police and firefighters, and the proliferation of missing posters and impromptu remembrance shrines around New York City and the country. Some pictures capture the sights by then familiar to many through mainstream media coverage, such as the smoldering pile of wreckage that used to be the World Trade Center, while others focus on smaller details of the changed landscape, such as a poison dust warning posted days after 9/11 in a Tribeca park near where the North Tower stood[70] or a Burger King that became a makeshift triage center.[71]

"Notice concerning sandbox." September 11 Digital Archive. Photo by David Vogler.

Photographic entries often "voice" their authors' rhetorical intent, clarified by captions or short narratives. These commentaries tend to situate their subjects within some narrative frame, casting the events in a different light depending on the author's attitude. For instance an image depicting a unit of National Guardsmen arriving at the World Trade Center site on September 12 is titled "Redeemers."[72]

This entry contributes to a narrative of heroic sacrifice, which came to dominate the memory of 9/11 as it has been constructed in mainstream U.S. culture in the following years. A different narrative—of a community coming together to grieve and remember—is reflected in captions accompanying photographs of makeshift memorials. Such is the one describing the temporary shrine in Union Square Park, which in those fateful days became a site of mourning and debate: "Every day, all day hundreds of people would gather."[73]

Some authors attempt to explain the presence of revenge symbolism that dotted the landscape in the weeks following the tragedy. Commenting on the picture of a life-size doll of Osama Bin Laden that was hanging by its neck out of a

"Redeemers." September 11 Digital Archive. Photo by G. N. Miller.

window of a house in Massachusetts, the photographer explains: "For the last eight years I have driven by Wallaston Beach in Quincy, Massachusetts on my way to work. A couple of days after 9/11 this appeared on one of houses along the beach. It was an erie [*sic*] image considering that you can watch planes take off and land from Logan airport at the beach. They fly right over-head."[74]

A dissenting antiwar narrative is represented by a submission called "Liberty Street Protest," whose author interprets the significance of a Liberty Street building whose windows displayed "No War" signs and peace symbols: "Overlooking the memorial plaques and area where most tourists and onlookers from around the world visit when they want to see the emptiness that is now Ground Zero and the WTC site as well as pay their respects. Conceived by local artist Glen E. Friedman, . . . to let people of the world know that New Yorkers, who live so close to the actual destruction of 9/11/01, do not agree with the 'War on Terror' being waged in their name."[75]

The most prevalent narrative by far, however, is that of nostalgia for the World Trade Center and the postindustrial utopia it symbolized. Dozens of people sent in pictures of themselves and their family members photographed against the panoramic backdrop of the Manhattan skyline anchored by the Twin Towers.

Criticized as the epitome of bad urban planning and architectural hubris during their lifetime, in their haunting absence the towers became beloved martyrs whose resurrection was viewed by many as essential to the restoration of New York City and the old world order.

In gathering together these disparate fragments of post-9/11 discourse, the archive offers a panoramic view of the fractious cacophony of public expression that cannot be accommodated by a permanent, professionally designed memorial. Cultural geographer Kenneth Foote stressed the difficulty of constructing such a memorial to 9/11 because of "the magnitude of the losses, the diversity of the victims, and the fact that the entire nation feels it has a stake in the commemorative process."[76] Anticipating the debates over the Ground Zero memorial, the archive's virtual space played a crucial role in "forcing emotion and competing interpretations into the open."[77] By granting the authority to determine what is important (or appropriate) to individual contributors, the September 11 Digital Archive refrains from taking sides and imposing closure upon the audience's

"Union Square Park." September 11 Digital Archive. Photo by Paul G. Selders.

Effigy of Osama bin Laden. September 11 Digital Archive. Photo by Brian Merrikin.

interpretation of the different narratives.[78] And by allowing readers to continue submitting their stories and images, the archive acknowledges that public memory is, in fact, an evolving process.

Beyond providing a forum for public expression, the archive aims to offer a usable set of materials for professional historians who will revisit September 11 in the future. Toward this end the collection is sorted and organized by medium and subject matter, allowing one to search through the cornucopia of submissions and links. Brief annotations describe many items' content and occasionally indicate whether certain entries might offend some visitors, as in the case of several digital animation submissions that revel in the fantasy of violent retaliation against bin Laden and Al-Qaeda. In other instances the archive's wording more explicitly distances its professional agenda from those of its many sources: "The September 11 Digital Archive collects reports, studies, and white-papers written by a variety of organizations and institutions in response to the September 11, 2001 attacks and the public reaction to them. The Archive gathers and presents these items to preserve the historical record. These materials do not necessarily reflect the opinions and views of the Archive or its staff."[79]

Perhaps the clearest sign of the archive's desire to assert its status as a steward of history while allowing unrestricted public participation can be seen in the effort to distinguish between fact and fabrication. At the bottom of each individual submission, whether it is e-mail, story, or image, one finds a highlighted question: "How do I know that this item is factual?" Clicking on the question leads one to a manifesto of sorts that signals a tension between the archive's populist commitment to grassroots history making and its professional obligation to maintain impartial factuality:

> Every submission to the September 11 Digital Archive—even those that are erroneous, misleading, or dubious—contributes in some way to the historical record. A misleading individual account, for example, could reveal certain personal and emotional aspects of the event that would otherwise be lost in a strict authentication and appraisal process. That said, most people who take the time to submit something to the September 11 Digital Archive share the goal of its organizers—that is, to create a reliable and permanent record of responses to the 9/11 attacks—and therefore most contributions are authentic.

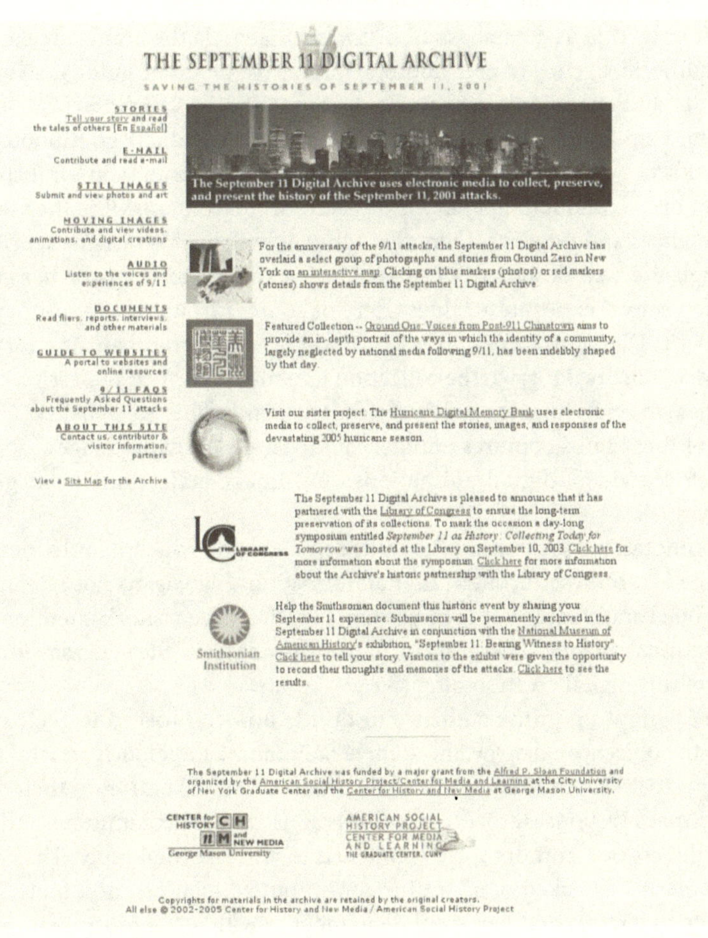

The September 11 Digital Archive original home page.

> Nevertheless, as with any historical sources (including, for example, newspaper accounts), there are always questions about reliability, and all researchers need to evaluate their sources critically. It is for this reason that the Archive harvests metadata from every contributor—including name, email address, location, zip code, gender, age, occupation, date received—and suggests that these metadata be examined in relation to one another, in relation to the content of the submission, and in relation to other authenticated records. Sound research technique is the basis of sound scholarship.[80]

The archive thus fashions itself as a space of interplay between attitudes toward history and historical facts, between the lay public and trained historians. It is a balancing act, however, and reservations in the passage above ("That said," "nevertheless") indicate how delicately one must tread to employ popular memory as a source of professional history writing.

If in its role as a database of historical materials the archive seeks to respect the authorial agency of contributors, in the role of a tour guide it strives to educate its audience while respecting its autonomy. As distinct from brick-and-mortar exhibitions, digital displays do not offer a spatially continuous sequence of artifacts but instead work by inviting one to choose an item for display from a menu or by conducting a keyword search of the contents. It is the viewer's own preferences and interests, then, that ultimately shape his or her experience, even though the web designer is responsible for the range of his or her choices. To guide visitors' exposure to the variety of sources in its vast repository, the September 11 Digital Archive makes use of several display mechanisms. First an interactive menu breaks down the collection into main categories—stories, e-mail, still images, moving images, audio, documents, and guide to websites. Clicking on any of these links conjures another subdivision; "moving images," for example, comprises video, digital animations, and image collections from groups and individuals.

Annotations further aid the visitor in choosing which item to view. If one is inclined to browse through "digital animations," labels do not so much dictate how one should interpret their content but direct the visitor's attention by noting the satirical quality of certain entries or warning that "viewers may find the content of this digital creation offensive."[81]

Leaving it up to the audience to decide how to proceed in their interaction with the objects on display, the archive maintains a judiciously neutral stance and assigns the responsibility for the content of individual entries to their authors. In some cases responses to certain submissions were so voluminous and polarized that the entries' authors were compelled to add a formal reply. Thus the author of "America Attacked 9/11," a nineteen-minute digital creation that combined a tribute to victims and heroes of September 11 with a call for military retaliation, posted a form letter to answer his critics' objections: "Please don't e-mail me about trying to understand the folks that did this. I have no interest in understanding them. I want them dead. Don't e-mail me about innocent people being accidently [*sic*] killed in a war zone. I am uninterested in their plight and if that sounds cold, go review my website again. None of THOSE people were at war on 11 September and they are not casualties of war. They were murdered. I don't want their murderers treated as war criminals; I want them treated as they are—subhuman criminals who committed crimes against humanity. I don't want to hug them, analyze them or anything other than annihilate them. Wipe them off the face of the earth."[82]

The letter not only reveals the author's frame of mind but also points to a deep political division that marked public response to the U.S. government's foreign and domestic policies in the aftermath of the attacks. After all, "depending on your political inclinations, the events of September 11, 2001 were either unique or inevitable, richly deserved or entirely unprovoked, a predictable product of generations of conflict or the dawn of an entirely new age."[83] The clash of perspectives ignited by the contributor's inflammatory rhetoric, however, did not arise as a consequence of the archive's display strategy. Indeed the creator's letter, a link to which appears next to the title of the submission, indicates that responses came to previous versions of the tribute posted on other Internet sites.[84]

Still, occasionally the archive conspicuously exercises its control over the arrangement of items on display to draw attention to entries that may otherwise go unnoticed. Similar to temporary special exhibits mounted by regular museums, the September 11 Digital Archive presents "featured items" that underscore its public mission to give voice to underrepresented views. The main page, for example, highlights experiences of Chinatown residents, "largely neglected by national media following 9/11," by providing a link to a collection, "Ground One: Voices from Post-911 Chinatown." Under the "Documents" rubric, the featured item is "American Backlash," a "report documenting press coverage of bias incidents and violent hate crimes that occurred in the first week after the September 11 attacks." Until the fifth anniversary of the attacks, the video collection gave center stage to a film featuring interviews with Arab American residents of Bay Ridge, Brooklyn ("Arab American Responses"), after which a commemorative montage, "September 11 Hero Tribute," took the spotlight. The "featured item" strategy, then, can be a mechanism for leveling the playing field by allowing politically marginalized groups to have their say.[85]

Ironically, in so doing the archive is trying to balance its open submission policy that generated plenty of politically incorrect and even offensive material in the name of popular participation. Assessing the archive's contents, historians Stephen Brien and Joshua Brown admit that "much of the material . . . was riddled with jingoistic, racist, xenophobic, and messianic attitudes and opinions." Yet they argue for the unique value of these materials to future scholars: "If we might hazard to find one word that succinctly captures what the quarter of a million digital items comprising the archive offer future scholars, it is a sense of the *zeitgeist:* an intricately detailed panoramic view revealing the myriad ways Americans and others throughout the world experienced, understood, deciphered, distorted, and rationalized—*located meaning in*—an epochal traumatic event."[86]

But how is the general public—the audience so solicitously cultivated by the archive—supposed to approach this panorama of meaning-making gestures? What conclusions about public values and citizen roles can contemporaries of the events draw from their exposure to the collection? Perhaps because of the tension between its commitment to unbridled populism, on the one hand, and political fairness on the other, the archive seems reluctant to lend its curatorial credibility to a particular way of commemorating September 11.

An example of this seeming objectivity is an "interactive map" of Manhattan unveiled on the fourth anniversary of the 9/11 attacks.[87] The archive selected from its collection those photographs and stories that captured the attacks against the World Trade Center and overlaid them on the map of Manhattan. Each photograph is represented by a blue marker and each story by a red marker. Visitors can click on them to relive, in painfully vivid detail, the events of that fateful day from the perspective of people who witnessed them firsthand. The virtue of this display is that it presents, in a visually compelling and dynamic way, images and accounts that until then had been separate fragments of a larger story. Seeing the burning towers of the World Trade Center photographed from various vantage points and reading accounts of commuters, train operators, and policemen gives one a sense of the event as it unfolded. However the display offers little beyond the now familiar spectacle of impending devastation, freezing in memory the moment before the towers' collapse. Reproduced repeatedly in various news media, the image of the World Trade Center still standing became iconic in the weeks and months following the attacks. As Barbie Zelizer explains its rhetorical power, "Not only did the images [of the towers] offer the appropriate degree of contingency for a message too harsh to be seen with the brute force of reality's depiction. . . . But the image also cut—and depicted—the story at precisely its most powerful moment, pushing spectators to recognize what came later while allowing them to prolong the experience of what had been before. The images hence created a space of (im)possibility, whereby spectators were able to linger in a moment when the full scope of the tragedy was not yet upon them."[88] Focusing on this moment in an anniversary display, then, the archive assimilated its audience's contributions into the mainstream media's strategy, which can be described as a symbolic refusal to come to terms with the events of September 11. It thereby cast its audience in the role of spectators stunned into inaction and unable to interpret the events in front of them.

Conclusion

As the most comprehensive effort to collect, organize, and display discursive traces of the momentous historical event commonly referred to as 9/11, the September 11 Digital Archive illustrates both the virtues and limitations of digital archives. Launched by professional historians, it is presented as an inclusive collection of contributions from both individuals and institutions. The archive's then director, Tom Scheinfeldt, argued for a connection between the size of digital storage and its democratic potential: "Unlike traditional 'brick and mortar' archives, there are no physical limits to the size of the September 11 Digital Archive's collection. If it needs to expand, it just adds more disk space. This means that no digital object is too trivial for the Archive to accept."[89] Indeed the strategy of defining any submission related to 9/11 as "historical record" allowed the archive to solicit and preserve a vast and diverse set of stories, images, and points of view that otherwise would have been lost or dispersed in cyberspace and private archives. In so doing the archive accented "the role of history's ordinary actors in creating the historical record even as they are living it."[90]

At first glance there is no downside to inclusiveness: the archive encourages ordinary people to participate in the production of public memory, furnishes future historians with a wealth of data, and generates a multiplicity of perspectives on the same event. Preservation of large quantities of digitized and "born digital" materials does not necessarily engender a robust civic dialogue, however. The task of interpreting this "burgeoning dossier," to use Nora's phrase, is deferred and entrusted to the archive's users, be they future professional historians or lay visitors. The archive gives minimal guidance to either group: historians are admonished to distinguish between fact and fabrication when sifting through the submissions; visitors are reminded to pay attention to underrepresented voices and to be wary of voices that may offend them. There is no other mechanism, however, for encouraging the audience to explore views different from their own, in the manner that pedestrians in the streets of New York City were in the weeks following September 11.

Although the archive admittedly could not replicate the experience of the post-9/11 civic spectacle in the streets, not taking full advantage of interactive possibilities of electronic media discussed earlier prevented it from exploring a vital connection between the production of memory and its consumption. This oversight is partially due to time pressures and the scarcity of resources that are needed to design and maintain a well-functioning user interface. As Scheinfeldt admitted in a recent interview, at the time the archive was launched, he and his colleagues "were focused on collecting," and "when it came to organizing the contents, we were just reacting." But there were other reasons as well. Although the organizers "did realize that there were limitations to the front-end user interface" and considered "adding a comments section," the idea was turned down because of the possibility that responses from users might act as a barrier to participation by requiring "more commitment on the part of potential contributors."[91] Minimizing interaction between contributors and audiences was thought to boost participation and bring in a greater number of submissions.

The archive's collection and display strategies may be seen as a self-conscious reaction against the traditional dictatorial role of official institutions of memory. By allowing users to participate in the shaping of the historical record on their own terms and by enabling them to take charge of their journey through its collection, the archive undoubtedly preempts possible accusations of professional elitism and political bias. Yet while making multiple fragments of the 9/11 discourse publicly visible and accessible, it stops short of allowing contributors to engage one another in discussion and debate. This approach relegates the burden of meaning making to private individuals and thus effectively disables the interactive potential of the virtual site of memory the archive assisted in forging.

The archive's open-ended submission policy and curatorial neutrality may have spurred on contributions from people who otherwise would have kept their experiences private. But its apolitical stance also suggests that one's responses to others' acts of memory should be kept out of public sight. Like the "Celebrate the Century" program, then, the archive embraces diversity only to render it politically neutral. It thus abets a trend toward displacement of civic spaces in which people from different parts of the ideological spectrum can come together to contest their shared history.

3

Carnival after Katrina

Popular Festivity in a Time of Crisis

For weeks after Hurricane Katrina inundated most of New Orleans and adjacent areas of the Gulf Coast in late August 2005, all major television networks and print media carried images of flooded neighborhoods, thousands of displaced residents, and scores of those who failed to evacuate and were stranded on rooftops awaiting rescue. The sights of the disaster itself and the astonishingly slow and inadequate response of the U.S. federal government led journalists, politicians, and intellectuals to denounce the Bush administration and particularly the Federal Emergency Management Agency (FEMA) for their incompetence and apparent lack of concern.[1] These images will no doubt form a prominent part of the public archive of Hurricane Katrina, for they offer a large-scale, panoramic view of what many now consider a human-made catastrophe. Yet the first collective commemoration of Katrina occurred a mere six months after the hurricane and took on a form of a giddy popular ritual—the carnival.

Although at first blush it may seem an unlikely site of public commemoration or civic engagement, the first post-Katrina carnival of 2006 merits consideration as an example of popular memory because it acted as a collective forum for remembering the recent disaster and debating the city's civic and cultural identity. If the previous chapter focused on the archival dimension of popular memories, this chapter accents the role of the repertoire in the display and experience of civic values. The many New Orleans carnival traditions exemplify "the political, affective, and mnemonic power of the repertoire," as Diana Taylor defines it, insofar as they transmit culturally significant knowledge through embodied performance and help to restage contests over political and cultural rights.

This particular carnival gave New Orleanians an opportunity to comment on their ongoing ordeal and to defend their civic and cultural identity in the face of "a cultural Chernobyl" wrought by forces of nature and political failures.[2] By performing their carnival traditions amid the ruins, the residents celebrated their collective resilience but also drew attention to the fragility of local culture as an embodied tradition, dependent on repetitive reenactment by people living in real neighborhoods. This interpretation of the 2006 carnival demonstrates that ritualized popular festivities, even the ones that seem to suspend political and economic concerns in favor of revelry and spectacle, can also become sites of citizenship—robust arenas for the display of communal identity and contestation of political and cultural values.

In what follows I first look to the history of the modern New Orleans carnival for insights into the role of carnival traditions in the struggle over political and cultural legitimacy and civic identity. I then consider the controversy over the desirability of celebrating the carnival after Katrina as an indication of the conflicted status of the festivity as both a lucrative tourist destination and an embodiment of cultural memory. The third major section examines the multifarious spectacle of the first post-Katrina Mardi Gras as a forum for coming to terms with the tragedy and for reclaiming New Orleans by its residents. The carnivalesque idiom provided participants with what Kenneth Burke calls "a comic frame of acceptance"—a symbolic mechanism for responding to their historical situation and displaying to themselves and the rest of the nation why New Orleans matters. I conclude by analyzing the archival role of news and entertainment media in "translating" the 2006 Mardi Gras and the New Orleans experience to television and radio audiences and their varying capacity to simulate "prosthetic memories" of New Orleans for the larger public.

Carnival Tradition: a Cacophonous Pageant of Ambient Citizenship

A variation of the European carnival, the season of celebration that usually begins on the Feast of Epiphany (January 6) and culminates with Mardi Gras (Fat Tuesday), New Orleans carnival was brought to the city by its French settlers. As the city grew into a major port and center of trade in the eighteenth and nineteenth centuries, the distinctive character of Mardi Gras formed as a synthesis of European, Caribbean, and African cultural traditions.[3] Carnival was the occasion that offered anyone—rich and poor, white and colored, free and enslaved, male and female—a license to assume a different identity. Carnival license temporarily turned the world upside down and allowed one to be someone else, to indulge one's senses, and to mock and invert social conventions.

The history of New Orleans carnival shows how such freedoms have been variously appropriated to assert or contest one's place in a social hierarchy as well as generate new forms of cultural expression. However it is important not to romanticize carnival traditions as a source of antihegemonic challenge to the status quo. As Taylor cautions in regard to the political function of the repertoire, "performance belongs to the strong as well as the weak."[4] New Orleans carnival has functioned as an informal arena for performances by the powerful and powerless alike. Carnival can thus be seen as a form of "ambient citizenship," as Lauren Berlant theorizes it: "a mode of belonging . . . that circulates through and around the political in formal and informal ways."[5] Defined through ambiance, citizenship "registers the normative distinctions in terms of who has the formal and informal right to take up soundspace."[6] This section's retrospective look at the carnival tradition confirms that the question of who can legitimately lay claim to the common space of the celebration has been tied directly to struggles for political and cultural legitimacy and even survival.

In the antebellum era, the permissiveness of carnival provided a space for self-expression and self-assertion to the city's racially and culturally diverse populations. Enslaved peoples from Africa and the Caribbean appropriated this Christian holiday to perform their festive and religious rituals, such as the Congo dance, so named after a square in New Orleans where people of color congregated on Sundays. New Orleans also had a substantial population of the free people of color, many of whom were educated and owned property. They used masking to gain access to venues—such as fashionable streets and masked balls—that would be closed to them during the rest of the year: "During Carnival, a black New Orleanian could mingle with white New Orleanians, drink with them, dance with them, deceive them about his race."[7] The fact that masking often obscured skin color and gender produced anxiety among the city's white elites, who eschewed street revelry and confined their celebrations to exclusive costumed balls.

After the Civil War, white elites took to the streets in an effort to redefine carnival as a civilized and orderly affair and to assert their cultural superiority at a time when people of color and former slaves were granted political rights. Comus and Rex, two oldest carnival organizations, or "krewes," led the way by introducing carefully planned, lavish parades in which masked participants rode on floats and wore costumes unified around a mythological or literary theme. Deriving its name from John Milton, the Mistick Krewe of Comus made its inaugural appearance before the war, in 1857. That year the city council adopted an ordinance that outlawed the usual masking by individuals; therefore the Comus parade, whose membership included Mayor Charles Waterman, was allowed to roll without impediment—or competition.[8]

Like Comus, Rex boasted themed costumes and elaborate theatrics meant to dazzle both the high society and the common folk when it entered the scene on Mardi Gras Day in 1872. True to its name, the parade crowned a mock king, chosen from the krewe's exclusive list of members, to rule over carnival festivities. To make the illusion complete, Rex issued an edict, disseminated by newspapers and delivered to local authorities, commanding the city and state government to relinquish their control for the day and allow citizens to obey their sovereign joyfully.

Both Comus and Rex attempted to redefine carnival as a performance by a few chosen actors for the benefit of the spectators. Parade floats elevated performers above the crowd both literally and metaphorically and pushed unaffiliated maskers to the periphery of carnival space. By the time of Rex's inaugural parade, individual maskers had returned to the streets, so Rex organized them to follow the "royal procession" as the king's subjects. Disciplining a motley and "promiscuous" crowd of revelers proved a difficult task, however, and several years later, "in order to march with Rex, maskers had to organize themselves and apply in advance for permission—and keep their assigned places."[9]

The innovations of Comus and Rex as well as several other krewes that sprang up after the Civil War were not merely aesthetic. In addition to making carnival processions more decorous and widening the distance between performers and audiences, Comus and Rex projected a particular vision of social order—one in which mock aristocracy protested the legitimacy of the state's lawful government. It was the time of Reconstruction and of the defeated Confederacy's violent reaction to the recent enfranchisement of people of color. Membership of several early carnival krewes overlapped with that of the Knights of the White Camellia, Louisiana's version of the Ku Klux Klan. In this context their extravagant Mardi Gras pageantry functioned as political theater, a display of culture that veiled—or perhaps complemented—the white supremacist terror against blacks and members of the Republican government.[10] In this way, to quote Taylor, these performances contributed "to the maintenance of a repressive social order."[11]

Faced with economic realities of a quickly industrializing nation, elite parade organizations transformed their pageantry into a vastly successful tourist enterprise, thereby adding economic legitimacy to their display of cultural prestige. By the end of the nineteenth century, with the turmoil of the Reconstruction period behind and their place in the social hierarchy restored, elite carnival organizations endeavored to promote their spectacle to tourists from the North. Railroad companies began to advertise reduced rates during the carnival season, and local hotels erected viewing stands along the main parade route.[12]

Building upon elite krewes' innovations, subsequent generations of New Orleans business leaders sought to expand the tourist season and encourage visitors' participation in carnival. The introduction of "throws" such as beads "turned once passive observers into active participants."[13] Moreover several new krewes actively recruited nonlocals by selling memberships and hosting tourist-oriented balls.[14] In the second half of the twentieth century, the number of parading organizations increased dramatically, serving to extend the carnival season and thereby keep visitors around for a longer period of time. Several "superkrewes," so named for their size and number of parade floats, democratized the celebration by opening their membership to nonwhites and out-of-towners; they also featured popular culture themes and national celebrities to make their parades even more spectacular and entertaining.[15] However, while racially and socially inclusive, these krewes were open mostly to the well-to-do; their democratization "was really about reinforcing the class insularity and exclusivity of Carnival while creating a new mechanism for the cultural reproduction of class inequality."[16]

At the same time, the proliferation of organized parades rejuvenated the once marginalized tradition of "promiscuous masking" and thus allowed the "weak" to reclaim their "ambient citizenship" in the space-time of carnival. Ironically the growing orientation of Mardi Gras toward tourism encouraged costumed revelry by pedestrians, because they both filled the gaps between grander processions in the carnival schedule and enhanced the effect of grassroots authenticity. Beginning in the late nineteenth century, New Orleanians have formed several so-called walking societies, many of which have made themselves open to all those willing to join the masked group of revelers and roam the streets.[17] They have no spectators, only participants, and the only requirement for membership "is that you know about it" and show up in costume.

The institutionalization of carnival forms also influenced those revelers who purposely lampooned "respectable" krewes, partially because of the practical need to secure permits for marching during the Mardi Gras season. Perhaps more important, the affiliation with a krewe also lent one social legitimacy and visibility. In the second part of the twentieth century, female, gay, and African American krewes joined the list of carnival organizations, thereby declaring their right officially to occupy the most prominent public spaces of New Orleans and to leave their imprint on the city's collective image.

The krewe of Zulu's evolution from a marginalized group of African American revelers to a pillar of the New Orleans Mardi Gras illustrates the sometimes problematic interdependence of grassroots cultural expression, the politics of race and class, and the logic of capitalist commodification. The Zulu parade originated in the activities of a social aid and pleasure club known as Tramps. Even before Jim Crow, African Americans across the South had established organizations that provided their members with burial insurance and other forms of social support. In New Orleans social aid and pleasure clubs have also sponsored jazz funerals and "second-line" parades in which whole neighborhoods participate by following the parade band and the club's members. Mardi Gras is but one of the many festivities celebrated by the African American community during the year, but it is the one that is seen by all New Orleanians and visitors to the city.[18]

In 1909 the Tramps appropriated the imagery from a comedy skit about the Zulus, a South African tribe most famous for their victory over the British colonial forces. That year club members emerged as the Zulus, dressed in raggedy pants and led by a king who wore a lard can instead of a crown and held a banana stalk as a scepter. Over the years the Zulu iconography came to include blackface makeup and grass skirts, probably in implicit parody of the mainstream culture's convention of representing African Americans.[19] Moreover the krewe made a point of mocking the pretensions of Rex: "If Rex traveled by water, coming up the Mississippi with an escort from the U.S. Navy, Zulu came down the New Basin Canal on a tugboat. If Rex held a scepter, Zulu held a ham bone. If Rex had the city police marching before him, Zulu had the Zulu police—wearing police uniforms until the municipal authorities objected."[20]

In a segregated society, the Zulu spectacle was a rare public opportunity for African Americans to lampoon white supremacy without fear of violent retribution. It was also a chance to display their creativity and political wit at a time when mainstream culture portrayed them as dimwitted simpletons.While black people were employed by white parades as brass band musicians or as torch carriers, their participation, however skillful, was ornamental to the main show. The Zulus, by contrast, lay claim to the city's performance space on their own terms, even though until the end of World War II their parade was confined to traditionally black neighborhoods. In 1946, for the first time, the club marched along Saint Charles Avenue and Canal Street, the main Mardi Gras route. When in 1949 jazz legend Louis Armstrong was crowned the Zulu king—his dream since childhood—the parade was witnessed not only by all of New Orleans but, thanks to media coverage, by the entire nation.

The Zulu parade became "blacks' most public means of critiquing New Orleans white order"; yet, as historian Anthony Stanonis points out, "white opinion considered the Zulu parade . . . to be nothing more than a natural outgrowth of the childlike foolery expected from blacks. Joyful black float riders suggested to white tourists and locals contentment with the social order."[21] The fact that the Zulus refused to take *themselves* seriously became controversial in the 1960s, when civil rights activists derided the convention of blackface as demeaning to African Americans and demanded that the club change its aesthetic to something more dignified and socially uplifting. However, after a period of reforms, the old Zulu look returned. After the civil rights victories of the 1960s, the parade has lost some of its political poignancy as a parody of white society and has been embraced by the black bourgeoisie as well as by many whites.[22] The krewe's website now invites nonmembers to ride on one of the Zulu parade floats and attend its ball for a handsome fee of $1,500.[23] The Zulus' hand-painted coconuts—the "throw" originally intended as a parodic counterpart to Rex's beads and doubloons—became parade goers' most treasured trophy. And—the ultimate sign of respectability—the parade now rolls on a Mardi Gras Day ahead of Rex along the main parade route. Now a central attraction among Fat Tuesday parades, Zulu has been pruned "from its black working-class roots and grafted . . . onto the branches of the tourism industry as an essential sight one must see to have truly 'done' Mardi Gras."[24]

Other notable traditions of African American Mardi Gras, however, have remained tied to their communities and, as a result, have been more difficult to appropriate for the tourist mainstream. The Mardi Gras Indian is one of the most spectacular forms of costuming that was developed by New Orleans working-class blacks in the late nineteenth century. It involves a number of "tribes" of men (occasionally women and children) who every year design and sew new costumes extravagantly decorated with feathers and beads and engage in ritual competition with other tribe members on Mardi Gras and Saint Joseph's Day.[25]

Like the Zulus, Mardi Gras Indians invented their tradition out of popular culture stock elements—their costumes resemble those of Plains Indians and were likely influenced by the touring "Wild West" shows of the likes of Buffalo Bill Cody. Their decision to identify as Indians was rooted in historical realities of Jim Crow and acted as an expression of solidarity with another oppressed ethnic group.Wearing headdresses and face paint allowed African Americans to outsmart the local law that forbade them from wearing masks during carnival, but it also gave them a chance to celebrate a native warrior culture all but destroyed by the white settlers. To dress as Indian on Mardi Gras is therefore not simply to escape one's everyday identity: "Other revelers may use carnival masking to escape the repressions of their everyday existence, but the Indian tribes' disguise brings out into the open dimensions of repression that the dominant culture generally tries to render invisible."[26]

If the Zulu club affirmed the right of African Americans to present themselves publicly on equal footing with the whites by venturing into traditionally "white" areas of the city, the Mardi Gras Indian tradition is firmly rooted in black working-class neighborhoods. The ritual anchors the community and would be devoid of its meaning if it were taken out of context—for example if the Indians were to follow one of the big parades on Canal Street.[27] While their frequently photographed extravagant costumes and skilled performances make a colorful contribution to the cultural image of New Orleans, their aesthetically dazzling display is even more important as a form of what scholars call "constitutive rhetoric," a symbolic invocation of community itself.[28]

Because their parade routes are not disclosed in advance, Mardi Gras Indians have resisted commercialization but also have faced frequent police harassment. Indeed the manner of the legendary big chief Tooti Montana's death—he collapsed at a city council hearing on June 27, 2005, where he was protesting the most recent police interference with the Indians' processions on Saint Joseph's Night—was symbolic of the link between festive performance of cultural difference and struggle for civil rights.[29]

Although the Zulus, second-lines parades, jazz funerals, and Mardi Gras Indians have been exploited by the tourist industry as marketable symbols of "multiculturalism" and "diversity," their role as living traditions embedded in the daily lives of residents cannot be discounted. The Zulu Social Aid and Pleasure Club and Mardi Gras Indians have acted as social safety nets for their neighborhoods and as "alternative academies"[30] for budding musicians. As social organizations they bolstered their communities against the crippling effects of segregation, discrimination, and institutional racism by providing financial support to the least fortunate and promoting cohesion through participatory events such as second lines. Music is the lifeblood of all African American cultural events in New Orleans, and many children grow up following jazz bands in second-line parades and listening to Mardi Gras Indians' call-and-response singing. Some of them, like Louis Armstrong, have developed into world-class musicians.[31] Because they are so deeply involved in "the living transmission of cultural knowledge and values," the Zulus and Mardi Gras Indians illustrate Raymond Williams's claim that "a culture can never be reduced to its artifacts while it is being lived."[32]

The New Orleans carnival is a 150-year-old tradition that has defined the city as a tourist destination for almost as long. Yet it is also one of the most crucial popular rituals of citizenship the city has produced. The story of modern New Orleans carnival can be seen as a struggle over who can legitimately occupy and traverse the city's public spaces, or as Berlant puts it in her description of ambient citizenship, "whose noise matters."[33] Carnival has served as a prominent public forum where a tension over who can be a citizen can be enacted in a spectacular—and relatively peaceful—way. Consequently it has also been a story of cross-pollination of cultural forms of expression that owes much to the influence from the margins, even though, as many critics have argued, these forms have been often spatially separated from their producers. Despite the legacy of hierarchical divisions and struggles over the meaning of carnival, the city's unique mixture of cultural and ethnic styles represented in the raucous pageantry and costuming during Mardi Gras marks New Orleans as a place of tolerance for diversity and difference—an image summed up by the local gastronomic metaphor of "gumbo." What would New Orleans—and the United States—be without this "gumbo"? It was this alarming prospect that compelled New Orleanians to reexamine their central ritual after Katrina.

"Now More than Ever": Contesting the Meaning of Mardi Gras

Similar to New York City after the September 11 attacks on the World Trade Center, post-Katrina New Orleans initially drew tremendous public sympathy (if not prompt federal relief). However, for outsiders as well as many displaced residents, it seemed unconscionable that the city should celebrate its Mardi Gras as if nothing terrible had happened. After all much of the area's infrastructure was laid waste, and many neighborhoods, especially in the Lower Ninth Ward, were left uninhabitable. Only the historic districts that had been built on high ground—including the traditional tourist precincts—suffered relatively little damage.[34] The storm's comparatively merciful treatment of these areas prompted some officials to praise this as a divine intervention into the city's vexed racial politics and to dream publicly of a "new New Orleans" unencumbered by "a teeming underclass."[35]

The 2006 carnival, then, was bound to stir controversy not only about the appropriateness of partying in disaster's wake but also about the significance of this event for the city's image and its future. In the wake of Katrina, New Orleanians asked themselves: What is carnival? Who is it for? And what purpose would Mardi Gras serve at this moment in history? In the weeks leading to the festivities, local press, business leaders, scholars, and residents debated the value of their popular tradition. These debates reveal that New Orleanians were conscious of the tensions—between tourism and cultural expression, commercial interests and local priorities, levity and seriousness—that permeate the modern carnival form.

The most obvious answer to the question "What is carnival?" has long been "a tourist attraction," and so it was in 2006. In a locale heavily dependent on tourist dollars, carnival is both a cash cow and a form of cultural expression, and the two are ambiguously entwined. By the end of the nineteenth century, New Orleans Mardi Gras had become a popular destination thanks to the expansion of railroad travel and the tantalizing accounts of the holiday in the national press.[36] In the second half of the twentieth century, as tourism supplanted the chemical and petroleum industry, Mardi Gras was transformed into the area's "single largest special event," with many tourism and marketing strategies built around it. By the beginning of the twenty-first century, carnival infused nearly a billion dollars into the city's economy and provided employment for many thousands of people in the food, music, and hospitality industries.[37]

Still for New Orleans' African American mayor, Ray Nagin, endorsing carnival was a delicate political decision, as unabashed celebration would imply that the city government was in favor of revelry and excess while many residents still had no electricity. Moreover many thousands of black residents were still living as evacuees in other states with no apparent prospect of return, so festivities might send a message that New Orleans was indeed better off without its citizens of color. After initially voicing his reservations about the carnival, the mayor declared that the city was committed to holding the festivity on a reduced schedule. Using a commercial justification, Nagin ultimately sided with New Orleans economic elites' wish to signal that the city was open for business.[38]

After Katrina, however, only half as many hotel rooms were available to tourists, and the city's diminished housing stock meant fewer guests rooming with friends and relatives.[39] While commercial justification may have been the authorities' default argument for Mardi Gras, the event's emotional value for locals was bound to be even greater. New Orleans residents needed their Mardi Gras to remind themselves and those who had fled from the storm why they would still want to live in the city. In the winter of 2006, for people who had already returned home, the collective mantra was "now more than ever,"[40] for carnival offered a respite from their ongoing physical and psychological hardships. Many residents—even those lucky enough to find their homes virtually intact upon return—suffered from symptoms of depression. The city's suicide rate nearly tripled in the months after the storm.[41] Temporarily forgetting the woes of Katrina by participating in the carnival was thus part of collective therapy.

Yet the seeming frivolity and therapeutic value of carnival disguised a more serious purpose—many saw it as a platform for airing grievances about the recent past and sharing hopes for the future. Local correspondent for National Public Radio Michael Depp observed: "In New Orleans, we have always used Mardi Gras' irreverence and absurdity to cope with the harsher sides of the city's reality: chronic poverty, economic stagnation, flagrant political corruption. . . . We can't fully make sense of what has happened to us until we bring it into the public sphere of our parades."[42] Mainstream media have treated Katrina mostly as a natural disaster rather than a political and social catastrophe and largely cast New Orleanians as victims of the storm, so Mardi Gras presented a unique opportunity for residents to tell the world about their situation from their perspective. As New Orleans author and Mardi Gras historian Reid Mitchell put it, "Observing Carnival hardly meant forgetting Katrina. . . . Mardi Gras does not ignore reality; it comments on it. Mardi Gras is one of the ways we New Orleanians talk about the world. Carnival, if only in its folk form, inevitably returned after Katrina. When could it have been more necessary? Mardi Gras was how we talked about Katrina."[43] These assertions testified to a strong local desire to use carnival as a forum for public expression rather than merely a magnet for tourist dollars.

Post-Katrina devastation and the loss of population have made the question "Who owns carnival?" more poignant than ever before. For decades the tourist industry has exploited the noncommercial image of New Orleans carnival as a "rollicking family party given by the people of New Orleans for themselves"[44] to distinguish the locale as a culturally unique destination in an increasingly homogenized travel and leisure economy.[45] To guard this image, political and business leaders have avoided conspicuous corporate sponsorship and advertising within parades while engaging in more subtle forms of commodification to draw tourism and business investment to the city.

On the eve of the 2006 carnival, New Orleans business leaders once again extolled the authentic quality of Mardi Gras even as Mayor Nagin accepted corporate donations to underwrite the city's costs of cleanup and police protection. By holding carnival the city's leadership was eager to send an uplifting message about New Orleans' recovery without appearing irresponsible. So the rhetoric of authenticity served to counter the stereotype of the celebration as a promiscuous street party perpetuated by inebriated tourists and scores of "girls gone wild" videos circulating in cyberspace. To uphold the image of the celebration as a family party, the local chapter of the American Marketing Association printed ten thousand fliers that outlined ten "rules of carnival attendance" and stressed that "Mardi Gras isn't paid by the city—it's a gift to the world from the people of New Orleans."[46] In an unintentionally ironic reversal of the carnivalesque "anything goes" license, the fliers admonished visitors to "remember the kids" and "keep it clean": "Just because we live in FEMA trailers doesn't mean we want to be trashed."[47] This plea echoed a similar appeal by the business leaders back in the early 1970s, when the festivity's popularity with counterculture youth was perceived as a major threat to the enjoyment of middle-class tourists.[48]

Whether or not all New Orleanians agreed on the definition of Mardi Gras as a time of wild abandon or as a wholesome family holiday, they emphasized collective ownership of the ritual. In the weeks when local authorities were debating the feasibility of holding carnival among the ruins, residents recalled the impromptu Mardi Gras revelry of 1979, when the city's police force was on strike and few "official" parades rolled. To illustrate the ritual's importance to residents from various walks of life, the *Times-Picayune* ran a series of interviews with New Orleanians under the rubric "My Mardi Gras." One resident summarized this collective attitude: "Mardi Gras is not held or hosted by the city of New Orleans. . . . Mardi Gras issues forth from the homes and clubs and bars and streets of New Orleans, a product of the city's collective imagination and shared history. It is the central and defining cultural event of the city, and if it were made illegal by government decree, New Orleans would still make it happen, like some bootleg, speakeasy Mardi Gras of revolutionary revelry."[49] Pronouncements about collective ownership of Mardi Gras underscored the nature of the festivity as a living tradition and confirmed that "New Orleans existed not only in the dreams of tourists but in the daily lives of its own people."[50]

Despite the apparently strong collective will to display the resilience of local traditions and culture, scholars, public intellectuals, and community activists warned against the official rhetoric of recovery on the grounds that such rhetoric dissociates "traditions" and "culture" from those who sustain them. Arguing that the "instant expectation of renewal" that came on the heels of the devastation "serves the rich" and "screws the poor," New Orleans poet and essayist Andrei Codrescu contrasted culture without quotation marks and "culture" in quotes: "The culture-sans-quotes of neighborhoods, bars, clubs, carnival societies, funeral societies, second-lines, burial customs, different types of music—all segregated by race and divided by neighborhoods—comes together in the Carnival season when the city of New Orleans becomes a single entity visible to locals and outsiders alike as the city of New Orleans. New Orleans 'culture' in quotes is the kitschified version of Carnival, an autonomous and marketable product that is the packaged, faked, and de-sacralised Carnival marketed to tourists. Its marketing and profits are not in the hands of people who have produced it, and there is very little incentive in this market to help create or maintain culture without quotes."[51]

Although Codrescu may have overstated the gulf between the "authentic" New Orleans and its commodified simulacrum—after all the two have been entwined for almost a century—he rightly highlighted the politics of place, race, and class that is displayed on Mardi Gras.[52] To leave this consideration out of the equation in the process of "bringing back New Orleans," Codrescu argued, was tantamount to pretending that New Orleans "culture" can be restored quickly and easily, without bringing back its people.

The massive exodus and continuing exile of thousands of African American residents, in particular, made the tourist industry's "diversity talk" in reference to Mardi Gras traditions sound hollow. In a book published on the eve of the first post-Katrina Mardi Gras, folklorist Roger Abrahams and his colleagues pointed out that "Carnival . . . has its home base in many of the neighborhoods that have been drowned by the recent natural disasters and political failings."[53] What might "a new cityscape . . . look like," they asked, "without the very neighborhoods that are the soul and source of much New Orleans music, food, fashion, religion, and building arts"?[54] Post-Katrina realities have called into question tourism promoters' practice of dissociating "the products of black culture spatially from their black producers in an effort to appeal to mostly middle-class white visitors."[55]

The annual festivity of Mardi Gras gave New Orleans residents a reason to set aside their cares as well as to contest the definition of their popular tradition. If some saw the celebration as a much-needed respite from the woes of post-Katrina existence, others viewed it as a forum for talking about Katrina. Arguments over authenticity and diversity of Mardi Gras raised the issue of ownership of the tradition—whereas the city's business elites planned to use carnival to advertise that New Orleans was open for business, many communities and carnival organizations reasserted their ownership of the tradition as a constitutive ritual of civic self-definition.

By mounting Mardi Gras in 2006, New Orleanians were not only proclaiming their tenacity and camaraderie—they were also doing their part in conjuring the city they wished to bring back. In this way they were both paying homage to the carnival tradition and issuing a collective plea to appreciate this tradition as a distillation of a rich, complex—and now endangered—culture.

Mardi Gras 2006: Talking about Katrina, Remembering New Orleans

The mix of traditions and performance styles that constitutes contemporary Mardi Gras is not an inert mass of symbols and forms—it is a living ritual that evolves in response to new historical, economic, and political realities while retaining its distinguishable features. A display of the city's cultural heritage, Mardi Gras can also shine a light on persistent sociopolitical tensions and inequalities. The first post-Katrina carnival, too, offered a communal spectacle of unification in the aftermath of a disaster *and* a poignant, if indirect, defense of the city's cultural diversity in the face of potential economic and cultural homogenization.

Remembering Katrina, New Orleanians thus also presented a collective argument for why people should still live in the city and why the rest of the country should care about the fate of New Orleans.

One way in which New Orleans residents talked about Katrina was through what rhetorical theorist Kenneth Burke calls a "comic frame of acceptance": "The comic frame, in making a man the student of himself, makes it possible for him to 'transcend' occasions when he has been tricked or cheated, since he can readily put such discouragements in his 'assets' column, under the head of 'experience.' . . . In sum, the comic frame should enable people *to be observers of themselves, while acting.* Its ultimate would not be *passiveness,* but *maximum consciousness.*"[56] Carnivalesque expression, by presenting situations in a comic light, allows one to gain agency by the fact of being able to name these conditions and thereby to exert control over them.

Festive New Orleanians—organized krewes and individual maskers alike—seized upon the rich heritage of carnivalesque expression to describe their experiences, to satirize all levels of officialdom responsible for the mishandling of the emergency, and to assert their civic identity. These gestures ranged from laconic tongue-in-cheek statements about survival, defiance, and government incompetence to elaborate satirical commentary.

New Orleanians felt victimized by the storm, "FEMAtized" by the government's slow and inadequate response, and insulted by the media portrayal of Katrina as a natural disaster affecting a city built on a swamp. Yet their comic take on the disaster—a man-made calamity, according to a widely spread conviction among locals—gave them a degree of symbolic power over their circumstances. Many of them literally transformed their physical tools of survival, the blue tarp being the most common, into symbolic "equipment for living." During Mardi Gras the "blue tarp couture," as the locals quickly dubbed it, was the most universal statement of defiance: "It was fashioned into gowns and tuxedos, body wraps, elaborate headgear, and utilitarian, hardware store lingerie, all of it folded, taped, bent, and tied like the origami of dark humor."[57]

Besides celebrating their collective resistance to forces of nature, revelers piled scorn on government agencies and public officials implicated in the mismanagement of the emergency and its aftermath. The Army Corps of Engineers, the federal agency responsible for the design, construction, and maintenance of the nation's flood protection system, received its share of blame for the levee failure in the greater New Orleans area. Months before official investigations into the matter identified flaws in levee design, Mardi Gras floats and maskers criticized the shoddy construction and poor upkeep that led to the catastrophic flooding of the city.

For his slow and inept response to the catastrophe, President George W. Bush was pictured as a demonic figure steering his "ship of state." The former director of FEMA, Michael Brown, nicknamed "Brownie" by Bush, was a particularly

The "Levee" float of the Knights of Chaos krewe at a Mardi Gras parade on Saint Charles Avenue. New Orleans, February 23, 2006. Photo by Alexey Sergeev.

"Ship of State" float of the Knights of Chaos at a Mardi Gras parade on Saint Charles Avenue. New Orleans, February 23, 2006. Photo by Alexey Sergeev.

"Department of Homeland Insecurity" float of the Knights of Chaos at a Mardi Gras parade on Saint Charles Avenue. New Orleans, February 23, 2006. Photo by Alexey Sergeev.

popular target. Alongside elaborate floats sponsored by carnival clubs, many unaffiliated maskers joined in the lampooning of Brown. True to the folk carnival tradition of cross-dressing, a group of men clad as "brownies"—sporting brown skirts and brown-smudged noses—furnished an eloquent metaphor for the pervasive cronyism of the Bush administration and the incompetence of its appointed officials. The brownies were accompanied by a woman impersonating "a stiff Margarita," another familiar trope of carnival season, when people often dress as alcoholic beverages. This time the reference was to Brown's e-mail during the time of Katrina in which he expressed his desire for the drink.[58]

Several parades directed their derision at local law enforcement authorities and citizens who acted inhumanely and sometimes criminally toward their fellow citizens stranded in the flooded city. The Krewe of Muses, for example, featured a float that satirized the infamous police blockade of the Crescent City Connection, during which the sheriff of Gretna, an unflooded town across the river from New Orleans, and his armed associates prevented desperate people from walking to safety.[59] Thanks to the presence of television networks on the scene, the incident received national attention, but the reporting of this instance of white vigilantism was overshadowed by many unconfirmed and later retracted news stories about black vandalism and looting.[60] Mardi Gras revelers' insistence on

"Red Rover" Mardi Gras float design, Krewe of Muses, 2006. Image courtesy of Goddesses, Inc.

commemorating this episode of post-Katrina chaos used shame as a symbolic tool and implicitly affirmed the need for cooperation and tolerance in the face of social panic and distrust.

Krewe du Vieux, an organization that opened the parade season, presented the most extensive comic-satirical commentary on Katrina. In contrast to the old-line krewes' genteel celebration of their European heritage or the businessmen krewes' reliance on commercial pop culture, Krewe du Vieux members distinguished themselves by their classically carnivalesque use of "material bodily lower stratum" symbolism, as literary theorist Mikhail Bakhtin called the European tradition of festive folk humor. This tradition, according to Bakhtin, "for thousands of years . . . strove at every stage of its development to overcome by laughter, render sober, and express in the language of material bodily lower stratum (in an ambivalent sense) all the central ideas, images, and symbols of official cultures."[61] Such expression brings down all ideas and images to the common level of bodily functions, but this debasement is also a kind of renewal: "The material bodily lower stratum is productive. It gives birth, thus assuring mankind's immortality. All obsolete and vain illusions die in it, and the real future comes to life."[62] Above all, it is a "symbol of the defeat of fear by laughter."[63]

During the 2006 season, Krewe du Vieux organized its parade around the theme "C'est Levee" and announced, in its publication aptly named *Le Monde de Merde,* that its seventeen "subkrewes" will "each present their own free-flowing, tree-floating, muckraking, trash-talking, trash-burning, Bush-burning,

FEMA-gated interpretation of the theme."[64] In keeping with the theme, the krewes offered a bawdy, occasionally lewd, but above all richly ambivalent perspective on Katrina.

Members of the krewe of K.A.O.S. parodied bureaucratic inefficiency of FEMA by electing Michael Brown their grand Marshal and appointing themselves "official FEMA carnival adjusters." In this role they invited parade goers to fill out a FEMA-like "Application for Carnival Throw," which asked them to select "only one" type of throw per application (from the menu of "beads, doubloon, spear, plastic rose, panties or cup") and to describe in detail their "entitlement to throw" (yelling "hey mister, throw me something," having connections to someone on a parade float, or displaying "body part in exchange for carnival throw"). At the bottom of the form, a mock-serious disclaimer assured one of the futility of the application: "FEMA recognizes the importance of throws to your Carnival enjoyment. Every effort will be made to ensure delivery of the throw selected by you in time for this year's Fourth of July celebration. However, delivery by that date is not guaranteed."[65] Rendering the bureaucratic idiom through the promiscuous imagery of the body (as in the request to describe the exposed body part "in complete detail"), the parody transformed the red-tape nightmare of many New Orleanians into a ridiculous, and therefore more manageable, kind of hell.

The Totally Orgasmic Krewe of Intergalactic Ne'er-do-wells mined the lexicon of sexual hedonism for their vision of good life. Describing returning citizens' hopes for a saner existence, they mused: "Amid the debris and devastation, meetings were being held on smoke-filled street corners all over town. Agendas were shared and new visions arose (and were aroused) from out of the muck. Back in their beloved but battered bacchanalian city, the Ne'er-do-wells were dreaming of good government, good schools, electricity and gas, FEMA checks, mail delivery, flood protection, elections, erections and being serviced."[66] The imagery of sexual abandon here evokes a rather sober and civilized social order. Whereas the lewdness of Mardi Gras customarily signals a suspension and inversion of social order, in this case it is employed to express a wished-for return to normalcy. This merging of two seemingly incongruous concerns—those of the lustful, festive body and of the weary body politic—can be seen as an effort to reenergize the latter, to spur it into productive civic action.

The comic-satirical antics of New Orleanians during Mardi Gras were not just a mechanism to release their collective frustration with life in a storm-ravaged city—they were a way to counter the pessimism and apathy with the liberating power of laughter. Carnival laughter, especially the kind linked to the body and its desires, is affirmative. Bodily imagery, in particular, asserts the continuity and regeneration of the collective body of the people.[67] Even in satirical form, its critical bite is almost always ameliorative, summoning a vision of a social order that is more humane and egalitarian than the actual social order. Illustrating Lauren Berlant's description of "the desire for the political," these performances acted as "alternative filters that produce the sense—if not the scene—of a more livable and intimate sociality."[68]

In contrast with many satirical parades and maskers, some of the big krewes—such as Rex and Bacchus—refrained from making any statements about Katrina. As lavish as ever, Rex floats presented the theme "Beaux Arts and Letters" and Bacchus rolled under the aegis of "The Wizard of Oz." As usual riders on these floats had their costumes made and fitted for them, and their function was to dispense beads and doubloons to onlookers in exchange for the customary "Throw me something, mister!" One local journalist who was invited to ride with Bacchus related his unease at the behind-the-scenes display of white privilege in which he reluctantly participated: "My float-mates and I have been designated to be apples, and the float itself is a Disney-looking apple tree. The theme of this year's Bacchus is The Wizard of Oz, but nobody I ask seems to know or care why. I feel absolutely ridiculous pulling on my shiny gold top, a huge apple emblazoned on the chest, then something akin to brown parachute pants. Around me, old and young alike, all white, all clearly well-to-do, do the same. Black men in black suits and white gloves busy themselves with tailoring the costumes for those who need it. I look at the people, nearly every one the rich, white Uptown type, drinking beer, eating huge po' boy sandwiches, drinking more beer, and wonder what I've gotten myself into."[69] If carnival is a forum for public expression and competitive self-assertion, these parades' display of opulence and apparent absence of concern for the city's suffering majority spoke volumes about the politics of place in New Orleans. It was no accident that they hailed from "The Isle of Denial"—the affluent uptown neighborhoods that largely escaped the ravages of the storm and whose residents were thus assured of their future in the "New New Orleans."

While the flooding of "white" suburbs such as Lakeview forced many relatively well-to-do residents into a prolonged exile, the dislocation was most keenly felt by African American neighborhoods and parading organizations. The Zulu krewe was hit particularly hard: at the time of the carnival, more than half of its five hundred members were still living outside New Orleans. The krewe was faced with a difficult decision: choosing not to parade would be an acknowledgment that many African American New Orleanians could not participate in that year's, and possibly any future, carnival festivities. Attorney David Belfield, a club member and one-time Zulu king, pleaded with Mayor Nagin to suspend carnival until African American residents could return. But other members argued that to cancel the parade would be tantamount to letting go of their place in the city, both symbolically and literally.[70]

In the end the Zulu membership voted in favor of Mardi Gras and chose the slogan "Leading the Way Back Home" as their parade theme. The slogan addressed multiple audiences: other Zulu members who wished to return but could not, displaced New Orleanians who found shelter elsewhere and considered not coming back, and all those who questioned whether African Americans would return to

A float of the krewe of Zulu at a Mardi Gras parade on Jackson Avenue, with an abandoned shotgun house in the background. New Orleans, February 28, 2006. Photo by Alexey Sergeev.

the city. In proclaiming their leadership and intent to return, the Zulus acted as stewards of their ravaged and demoralized communities and as ambassadors of the cultural traditions they had preserved for more than a century. Using their reputation as one of the most anticipated Mardi Gras attractions, the Zulus reenergized their once subversive spectacle of black identity to draw attention to the politics of race and place in New Orleans.

The Zulus enacted their theme by modifying their parade route on Mardi Gras Day. Like all other uptown parades, they had to use the same shortened route to accommodate the city's constrained budget for police presence. However, after their floats rolled through Saint Charles Avenue and Canal Street and reached the Superdome, the riders reassembled on foot and, accompanied by a brass band, led a second-line procession to their clubhouse in the historically black Tremé.[71] This was no ordinary second line—its symbolism was heightened by the parade's trajectory from the Superdome, the site of so much suffering in the immediate aftermath of Katrina, to the neighborhood that is considered home of New Orleans's black musical traditions.

For Mardi Gras Indians, whose multiple "tribes" hailed from the city's most flood-ravaged neighborhoods, the situation was even more dire—many lost their homes and, with them, the supplies necessary to make a new costume. The tradition of Indian "masking" requires each tribe member to craft a new suit every year. The usual materials that go into a suit—colorful feathers, beads, and

Young spectators greet the Zulu parade on Jackson Avenue. New Orleans, February 28, 2006. Photo by Alexey Sergeev.

sequins—are pricey and difficult to find on a short notice. Suits are sewn by hand, and the meticulous process of beading can take months. Floodwaters also robbed the tribes of their usual places to meet and practice their singing. Displaced from their ancestral homes and isolated from their communities, Mardi Gras Indians were perhaps the most endangered of carnival traditions.[72]

Nevertheless as early as the end of October 2005, according to a *Times-Picayune* report, at least six tribes were planning to parade on Mardi Gras.[73] To encourage as many Indians as possible to return for the celebration, blues musician Monk Boudreaux, big chief of the Golden Eagles, and Jazzfest producer Quint Davis raised funds from two jazz foundations and purchased the essential components for building the suits. Using his cell phone to locate and contact the displaced Indians, Boudreaux was able to summon eighty-eight of them to Tipitina's, a nonprofit foundation and nightclub, to pick up their supplies—"more than 170 pounds of large plumes, 4 pounds of two-tone dyed plumes, 3 pounds of quills and 905 links of marabou."[74]

In post-Katrina New Orleans, showing off new costumes on Mardi Gras was, more than ever, a matter of civic duty. As Larry Bannick, chief of Golden Star Hunters, stated, "We may not make a big show, but when the history books write the story of 2006, they [are] going to say the Mardi Gras Indians played their part."[75] Big Chief Boudreaux's son, Joseph Hills, told a *Times-Picayune* reporter:

"This isn't about costuming. Being an Indian is a part of our identity, our culture, our way of life in New Orleans. . . . It is a social thing that will draw people back, give them a reason to have a house. It's such an important tradition to some that it is even more important than a house."[76] This sentiment underscored the Indians' role as anchors of their neighborhoods' communal life—the keepers of local cultural memory that underlies a sense of community and survives through recurring performance.

On a Mardi Gras morning, several Indian tribes took to the streets of their shattered neighborhoods in a show of defiance and hope, bringing with them crowds of eager second-liners, many of whom journeyed home just for the occasion from distant places such as Houston and Atlanta. Although their costumes did not feature explicit references to Katrina, the Indians' deliberately chosen routes took on an added significance for all those present. The Red Hawk Hunters tribe started their march from the foot of the Clairborne Bridge over the Industrial Canal, close to the levee breach that destroyed the Lower Ninth Ward. The Hard Head Hunters marched through their destroyed Seventh Ward neighborhood. Mohawk Hunters, a West Bank tribe, returned to their stomping ground in Algiers.These symbolic acts, staged against the background of physically wrecked communities, not only affirmed the continuity of the tradition against all odds but also made a vivid statement about the place of this tradition on the map of New Orleans. Through their performance in the presence of others whose prospects of return were similarly precarious, the Indians enacted a claim: "We belong here."

A mere six months after Katrina, New Orleanians symbolically reclaimed their city through a celebration of survival and cultural continuity. Their collective performance featured several kinds of remembrance: of lives and homes lost, of policies and politicians that brought the city to its knees, of cultural traditions that were in danger of disappearing along with the vanished communities. Carnival 2006 also acted as a platform for remembering—in the sense of reconstituting out of parts—the cultural whole that is New Orleans. The carnival pageantry was thus an elaborate and often self-conscious commentary on the heterogeneous heritage of New Orleans as well as a defense of this heritage as vital to the future of the city.

Mediating Mardi Gras

Unlike carnival celebrations of preceding years, the residents' performances were addressed first and foremost to the city itself—it was, as one reveler put it, "one big endorsement of the city, a living, sweaty, friendly, buzzed dissertation on the reasons why people still want to live here and fight through difficulties."[77] The carnival's diverse traditions thus served as "a world-confirming strategy of address that performs solidarity and asserts righteousness."[78] At the same time,

New Orleanians were hopeful that the attention given to this particular carnival by national and international media would allow them to "communicate that . . . the need for more help remains acute" while letting the world know that their "traditions and culture are intact."[79] As an ephemeral performance, the carnival's multivoiced promotion of the city's cultural identity relied on media organizations' archival function to craft "prosthetic memories" for the wider audience in order to invite the rest of the nation to experience the ambient sociality of New Orleans. Yet although the repertoire and the archive "usually work in tandem," Taylor reminds us that "the live performance can never be captured or transmitted through the archive."[80] Hence while I am generally convinced by Alison Landsberg's thesis that "prosthetic memories," such as the ones we receive through film and television, can enrich our "archive of experience" and enable empathetic identification with strangers,[81] I note that any effort to forge "prosthetic memories" via distance communication technologies is subject to the conventions of representation of specific journalistic and entertainment genres as well as the politics of media organizations. These conventions, I suggest, influenced the extent to which radio and television audiences could suture themselves into the carnival experience and consequently come to appreciate the urgency of the current situation as well as the complexity of New Orleans culture. In the remaining pages, therefore, I examine how this stylized "dissertation" was translated to national television and radio audiences.

When New Orleans mayor Nagin and business leaders condensed the carnival schedule and redirected all officially registered parades along the same route in the presentable parts of town, they were trying not only to keep the city's expenses down but also to ensure the most photogenic scenery for countless journalists. Although the locals' fear that the media would dwell excessively on "girls gone wild" antics on Bourbon Street did not come true, the national coverage zoomed in on big floats and crowds of cheering onlookers rather than the satirical and bawdy pageantry of walking revelers or the Mardi Gras Indians. Seen through the lens of television networks especially, the first post-Katrina Mardi Gras appeared orderly, safe, and inoffensively fun. Compared with the apocalyptic images that flooded television screens a mere six months before, the portrayal of carnival was comforting and uncontroversial. The presentation of Mardi Gras as a glitzy spectacle promoted the official claim about New Orleans "recovery" and excused viewers to their mundane preoccupations.

Against this general trend, three efforts stood out. National Public Radio's reports, a PBS documentary about New Orleans, and the HBO fictional drama series *Treme* all attempted to convey the city's cultural uniqueness while emphasizing its residents' continuing struggles. The methods they employed were distinct, however: NPR "mainstreamed" New Orleans to appeal to the sensibilities of Middle America, PBS used didactic retrospection to depict the city as a laboratory of American democracy, and *Treme* conveyed the frustrations as well as the rewards of the "after the storm" existence of residents from different walks of life.

NPR covered New Orleans regularly after Katrina, and at the time of the carnival both correspondents from the national office and New Orleans–based commentators reported on the festivity as it unfolded over the weeks leading to Ash Wednesday. NPR set out to capture the "hidden Mardi Gras" to counter the media stereotype of the city as a hedonistic mecca. In doing so NPR reporters saw themselves acting on behalf of embattled New Orleanians. Karen Grigsby Bates, for example, related how all locals she spoke with expressed the same concern: "Please go back home and tell folks the Mardi Gras they see on TV, with the drunks and the flashers, that's not our Mardi Gras."[82] Heeding this plea, reporters vividly described how the various Mardi Gras traditions—marching bands, the Zulu parade, Mardi Gras Indians, and the walking societies—adjusted to post-Katrina realities. Judging by laudatory responses featured on the program in a "From Our Listeners" segment, the coverage met the expectations of those intimately familiar with carnival. As one listener, a native of New Orleans now living in Maine, wrote: "NPR demonstrated a thorough understanding of the nature of this event. Mardi Gras is not about bare breasts, beer, and beads on Bourbon Street, that's what the tourists do. The real story is much deeper."[83]

Although they pointed out the diversity of Mardi Gras, NPR stories depicted the event as a fascinating interlude in the beleaguered lives of New Orleanians rather than a central forum for "talking about Katrina." The real story, for most journalists, lay beneath the mask of celebration. Shifting the focus of coverage from the festive spectacle to daily struggles of New Orleanians, NPR was balancing the jovial image of the city with a more prosaic portrait of normal Americans undeservedly suffering from a combination of bad luck and failed policies. Rather than dwell on extreme suffering in the aftermath of the flood, however, reporters chose to follow the plight of residents of Honeysuckle Lane, a neighborhood in east New Orleans within a twenty-minute drive from the city center. Robert Siegel, who covered this neighborhood for several months, described it as "*a perfectly average place* (my emphasis) with middle income residents such as cops and school teachers living in midsized houses. . . . The punishment Katrina inflicted in Honeysuckle Lane was average by comparison: some roof damage, mostly standing water."[84]

The selection of Honeysuckle Lane as a paradigm of post-Katrina recovery is rhetorically noteworthy as an appeal to an average middle-class listener who is more likely to identify with the trials of an all-American suburb populated by neighbors aiding each other when misfortune strikes.[85] Interviewed at the time of Mardi Gras, those returning to Honeysuckle Lane were not certain of the future of their community—New Orleans was still awaiting FEMA flood maps that would determine which low-lying areas could be rebuilt. Until then they were "homesteading" on their own property. Prompted by Siegel—"You are a kind of a suburban frontier"—one resident affirmed, "Absolutely. Like pioneers, starting over again."[86] Tapping into the archetypal mythology of the frontier,[87] Siegel and his subjects transformed the predicament of many displaced New Orleanians into a saga of self-reliance and perseverance that, unlike the motley and potentially bewildering phantasmagoria of carnival, spoke in a familiar, all-American idiom.

Documentary filmmakers also hastened to pay tribute to New Orleans in the wake of Katrina's destruction. Commissioned by PBS's *American Experience* series, a documentary directed by Stephen Ives aspired to "capture the essence of the city that no longer existed."[88] Having begun filming only three months after the storm, Ives had difficulty tracking down archival materials and people to interview. Yet he found that "even in its shattered state," the city showed "a great sense of buoyancy and resilience." The film's main argument is that it is the city's culture, especially participatory cultural events that bring people together, that both lends it its uniqueness and marks it as a distinctly American metropolis.

"Documentary," Jonathan Kahana observes, "is an essentially transitional medium; it carries fragments of social reality from one place or one group or one time to another, and in transporting them, translates them from a local dialect into a lingua franca."[89] The film *New Orleans,* too, pieces together archival photographs and moving images to produce an account of three centuries of New Orleans history. Guided by the voiceover narration and punctuated by commentary by local artists, musicians, and intellectuals, the film presents the city as a site of "a radical experiment in American democracy," a reflection "of the best and the worst of what we are."

The film's voiceover narrative and onscreen commentary emphasized that culture is what has kept the city together despite the history of racial violence, segregation, and class warfare. The tradition of participatory street parades shows the democratic potential of festive life, of "total unity and absolute diversity existing without contradiction." Mardi Gras, in particular, represents a site of diversity and unity: people signal their social status by joining particular parading organizations; at the same time, "everyone is mingling in the street." The film's frequent mentioning of episodes from Mardi Gras history—from the entrance of Comus onto the scene to Louis Armstrong's reign as King Zulu to the post-Katrina footage of Krewe du Vieux and the Rex ball—highlights this tradition's centrality as a civic ritual. Far from being a sideshow, Mardi Gras, in this documentary's depiction, is an integral part of the American democratic experiment.

Still the film's ability to elicit audience identification with New Orleans "experience" suffered from the typical didactic style that relies on narration to guide the viewer's interpretation of visuals. Reviewing the film in the *New York Times* (whose readership seemed most likely to tune in to the PBS broadcast of the film), Neil Genzlinger remarked that the history of racism, corruption, and poverty shown by the footage was "completely at odds with the talking heads' glowing comments." This "feel-bad history," the critic opined, was "fascinating to look at," whereas most of the laudatory statements "could apply to many other cities as well."[90] The documentary's effort to translate the "local dialect" of street celebrations into a liberal-democratic "lingua franca" resulted in abstract platitudes that could hardly inspire empathetic stranger identification.

Here one is reminded of Michael Warner's point about the tension between the "poetic world making" function of performed types of "stranger sociability" and the "rational-critical" norms typical of the public sphere.[91] Although New Orleans carnival is not strictly "counter-public" in Warner's sense (although Mardi Gras Indians can be considered "subaltern" publics), the world it temporarily imagines is an inversion and often a critique of mainstream social order as well as a projection of a more egalitarian and reciprocal vision of stranger sociability. Yet, as cultural critic Rebecca Solnit described the ethos of cooperation and bonhomie engendered by the locals' post-Katrina experience and displayed during Mardi Gras, "theirs was an old-fashioned conviviality that could be too bacchanalian to meet the earnest desire for civic revival held by many social critics."[92]

As distinct from news coverage and didactic documentary retrospection, HBO's dramatic series *Treme* furnishes a more intimate "prosthetic memory" of New Orleans after Katrina by simulating the ambient qualities of experience and eschewing narrative frameworks and tropes that would make New Orleans and its cultural traditions easily legible to outsiders. Cocreator David Simon asserted in a number of interviews that he cared about the reaction of only one audience—New Orleanians themselves. However he also expressed hope that his series might "actually pick up people who are tired of being spoon fed by TV and who are willing to experience a new culture in a way that doesn't give them all the answers right away."[93]

Set in part in the oldest African American neighborhood of Tremé, the show tracks the interlocking lives of several New Orleans residents "three months after." In addition to actors playing the main characters—including a trombone player, his ex-wife bar owner, a Mardi Gras Indian chief, a disc jockey, a struggling chef, a lawyer, and a Tulane English professor—the series employs numerous local and internationally famous musicians and features many beloved musical and food venues. Indeed *Treme* is so thick with local references that a *Times-Picayune* reporter created an online column to explain each of the ten episodes of the first season. In this way the show constructs its ideal viewer as a sophisticated kind of tourist—the one who avoids the usual attractions on a bus route and ventures instead into local bars and clubs to learn from the natives.[94]

Cinematically the effect of authenticity is produced through a succession of shots and scenes that amplify visual and aural particulars. As the *New Yorker* television critic Nancy Franklin describes, "your gaze is always brought from the general to specific, or—more specifically—to a dense mesh of details that don't always appear to make sense or add up easily."[95] Such an approach, especially in a television drama, can be unsettling to viewers expecting every scene to fit into a recognizable narrative arc. In *Treme* the audience's usually unproblematic work of fixing the identity of dramatis personae and their relationships and motivation is significantly more difficult.

While the work of watching *Treme* can be taxing to the uninitiated outsider, the show rewards patient viewers by granting them intimate access to the minute elements of lived experience. Not only do we get to dwell on the visual and aural details without knowing exactly how they would add up; we also get a more profound look at each of the characters. For example when viewers follow Mardi Gras Indian chief Albert Lambreaux as he returns to his flooded home in the neighborhood of Gentilly and tries to gather the dispersed members of his tribe, they gradually gain insight into the Mardi Gras Indian ritual and develop an appreciation of the physical and psychological challenges facing many residents. When the Chief and his Indians are singing their chants during a practice session, one hears a beeping background noise—most likely belonging to a Bobcat loader scooping refuse, a ubiquitous aural presence in post-Katrina months. By contrast in the Lower Ninth Ward, where Albert goes searching for his tribe's missing "wild man" (whose corpse is found inside his house), one is struck by the unnatural silence—no birds, no children, no cars. The quiet forms an unnerving background to the landscape of ruined houses and cars, either abandoned or gutted. *Treme* thus invites the audience vicariously to inhabit the post-Katrina scene and to empathize with its residents.

On the other side of town, in the Garden District home of lawyer Toni Bernette and her English professor husband, Creighton, we become privy to a conversation about the making of a Mardi Gras costume. Toni comes home to find her husband and daughter busy fashioning costumes out of white sheets; as it turns out, they are planning to impersonate sperm in a parade following a Krewe du Vieux float. On Mardi Gras Day, the Bernettes go into the streets in matching blue tarp costumes. The last detail is both an evocative local reference and a comment on the Bernette family's civic-mindedness: although their own uptown house was mostly unharmed, they expressed solidarity with less fortunate fellow residents by donning the "tarp couture."

Treme is not about Mardi Gras—it is about New Orleans "after the storm"—but the festivity serves as a narrative intersection for its main protagonists. In the episode "All on a Mardi Gras Day," all characters (except Big Chief Lambreaux, who is in jail after a confrontation with the police) lay aside their daily cares to participate in the ritual. Eschewing commentary, "the episode expertly and seamlessly walks viewers to and from multiple Mardi Gras experiences," writes *Times-Picayune* columnist Dave Walker; "it happens pretty much just like this every year on a weekday during which the rest of the world is at work checking e-mails and sitting in meetings."[96] That year, however, the ritual of social integration was also an enactment of cultural survival.

Filmed four years after Katrina, *Treme* intertwines the account of residents' hardships with a celebration of the redeeming power of living cultural traditions. "The city came back on the weight of culture," said Simon in an interview at the beginning of the show's first season. "There was no political leadership that stood up, there was no socioeconomic reason that New Orleans had to return. This city came back over the last five years one trombonist, one sous chef, one Mardi Gras Indian, one Social Aid and Pleasure Club member at a time."[97] What in the *American Experience* documentary *New Orleans* is advanced as a proposition supported by archival sources and commentaries in *Treme* emerges as an implied conclusion at which the audience is encouraged to arrive independently, by piecing the thesis out of the intersecting storylines and the wealth of visual and aural particulars.

Conclusion

At stake in celebrating Mardi Gras 2006 was the definition of New Orleans as a cultural whole and a civic community. And Mardi Gras was arguably the only participatory forum that allowed residents to enact the complexities and contradictions of the city's self-definition. While the rich and privileged carried on their festive tradition of parades (seen in the streets) and exclusive private balls (covered by local television stations), other Mardi Gras traditions were just as defiantly reenacted all over town, many amid ruins and debris. This multifarious spectacle demonstrated that, despite the massive exodus of the population, New Orleans culture was still composed of many strands, none of them completely dominant over the rest. The post-Katrina carnival thus displayed the potential of participatory public celebrations to promote social and cultural diversity as a civic ideal despite the continuous efforts of political and business elites to commodify this diversity by turning it into a sanitized tourist attraction.

Many New Orleanians, however, were concerned that visitors and media audiences would only get a glimpse of floats on the main parade route and then go home without understanding or caring about the complexity of local culture as lived tradition. In the words of Codrescu, "For outsiders—and that includes the national media—there is no Uptown, Tremé, Ninth Ward, downtown, Bywater, Marigny, the French Quarter (well, maybe the French Quarter)."[98]

To their credit some members of the national media did go beyond the French Quarter in an effort to document the fate of New Orleans residents. Listeners to National Public Radio learned of a variety of carnival traditions and became involved in the unfolding story of the frontier-like existence of a middle-class neighborhood in New Orleans east. Viewers of PBS—at least those who tuned in to watch *American Experience* on the eve of Mardi Gras 2007—were invited to imagine New Orleans as a test of whether the American experiment in democracy can succeed. And, going against many conventions of television drama, *Treme* re-created the irreducible complexity of New Orleans.

As a performed popular memory, however, this carnival was an ephemeral, multisited event that could not be preserved intact through archiving. Its transmission—or, rather, translation—through various forms of mediation therefore affected how its pageantry could engage audiences. What may have been a cathartic and world-affirming experience for many local revelers and returning residents became either a fleeting fragment of a cheerful spectacle to an average television viewer or a colorful yet politically inconsequential respite to a listener to National Public Radio. Ironically it is the fictional portrayal of New Orleans in *Treme* that comes closest to displaying the power of lived cultural traditions that make up the ambient citizenship of this politically, culturally, and racially heterogeneous metropolis.

4

Eyes Wide Open

Reflecting on Patriotism and the Cost of War

How does one commemorate an ongoing war, especially if this war is being waged under false pretenses and its military and civilian toll is kept out of public discussion?[1] This was precisely the challenge faced by groups and persons opposed to the United States–led invasion and occupation of Iraq (2003–11). Frustrated by the apparent indifference of the government and mainstream media to the mounting casualty count, many communities, citizen groups, and individuals took matters into their own hands in order to make visible, and sometimes to protest, the human cost of the Iraq War. Their interventions often took a conspicuously nonmonumental form and sprang up in locations far away from the National Mall.[2]

Temporary war memorials that cropped up around the country since the deployment of U.S. troops in Afghanistan and Iraq testify to the closing of distance between events and their commemoration that is a mark of contemporary memorial culture. But unlike other projects designed to preserve and display materially fragile popular memories, such as the September 11 Digital Archive, these memorials are not driven by a fear of obsolescence. Although they enable private acts of memory by creating places for families and loved ones to mourn the fallen, temporary war memorials also draw the attention of distracted citizenry to realities of contemporary wars waged in the name of—and financed by the taxes of—"the American people." In this way they can fulfill the role of a makeshift civic forum for people who hold dissimilar political values and subscribe to contrasting notions of patriotism.

This chapter addresses one such commemoration, the touring exhibit *Eyes Wide Open,* in order to explore the dynamic, interactive possibilities of participatory grassroots memorializing. Sponsored by American Friends Service Committee (a Quaker organization), *Eyes Wide Open* was conceived as a visual reminder of "the human cost of the Iraq War" and a place for public mourning. Its major design feature is the juxtaposition of a field of combat boots, each pair standing in for an American soldier who died in Iraq, and a collection of civilian shoes to symbolize dead Iraqis. In addition to the boot and shoe display, the exhibit also includes a wall of remembrance depicting "dreams and nightmares" of the Iraqi people. The exhibit made its first appearance in Chicago's Federal Plaza in January 2004, when the number of U.S. military casualties reached five hundred. By spring 2007 it had been divided into state-specific exhibits due to its growing size and popularity. Since the withdrawal of U.S. combat troops from Iraq at the end of 2011, *Eyes Wide Open* has continued to display the cost of wars in Iraq and Afghanistan.[3]

Eyes Wide Open is by no means a conventional war memorial. American war memorials, argues Erica Doss, "cue Americans to concepts of citizenship, patriotism, and unity as they simultaneously whet national appetites for further martial adventures."[4] They do so by foregrounding the notion of sacrifice by citizen soldiers and by erasing from public consciousness any reference to the realities of warfare. By contrast *Eyes Wide Open* insists on commemorating casualties on both sides of the conflict, rather than honoring only the American lives lost. In the course of its tour, *Eyes Wide Open* has performed what Carole Blair calls "confrontation" by unsettling expectations about the proper way to honor the dead.[5] If "visitors typically go to memory sites expecting to be inspired by, grateful for, and more deeply connected to the accomplished virtues of their imagined community,"[6] this memorial asks its audiences to reconsider familiar notions of patriotism. Moreover, unlike traditional monuments made of bronze or granite, this memorial relies on a simple visual vocabulary and spatial arrangement to attract visitors and make their contributions part of the exhibit. The memorial is also decidedly ephemeral, as it is not fixed in one location but instead evolves through time and space. Each new location furnishes a set of different rhetorical opportunities and constraints depending on its cultural and political peculiarities and the input from volunteers and visitors alike.

Because of its multidimensional character and relatively open authorship, *Eyes Wide Open* resists characterization along traditional lines of analysis. Scholars of public memory have long urged a reconsideration of an approach to memorials as representations of political values written in stone. Arguing that memorials by themselves "remain inert and amnesiac," James Young presses critics to go beyond the formal-aesthetic dimensions of monuments, memorials, and commemorative displays: "Public memory and its meanings depend not just on the forms and figures in the monument itself but on the viewer's response to the monument, how it is used politically and religiously in the community, who sees it under what circumstances, how its figures enter other media and are recast in new surroundings."[7]

As I have noted earlier, those who study public memory from a rhetorical perspective have similarly stressed the need to shift the interpretive focus from the intention of memorial artifacts to their function—from questions about their potential symbolic power to questions about their impact on actual audiences. Blair and Michel write, for example, "rhetoric typically does not address the material presence or practices of audiences"; however, they warn, "if we fail to deal with audiences as real, material beings and their experiences as significant, we almost certainly overlook differences that *make* a difference in how discourses are used, consumed, and redeployed."[8]

My purpose therefore is not to celebrate the aesthetic originality of *Eyes Wide Open* as a novel grassroots war memorial. Rather what interests me, given this book's concern with commemorations as sites of civic engagement, is how and with what effect the memorial's symbolism has enabled its multiple audiences to take on an active role in the commemorative process. *Eyes Wide Open* helps the viewer to inhabit a "perspective by incongruity"—a spectator position that involves seemingly contradictory attitudes of grateful acknowledgement and political awareness. The memorial's symbolism provokes reflection on the tension between patriotism and dissent, private grief and public outrage, and memory and political action. This argument develops in three stages. First I examine the symbolic resources the exhibit deploys to create a space of mourning and contemplation and to encourage audience participation. In the second part of the chapter, I turn to the spatiotemporal aspect of the memorial to show how it evolved through time and how each new destination on its tour provided a distinct context for memorial enactments by volunteers and visitors. Finally I attend to the issue of mediation, as the spatial and interactive possibilities of the memorial undergo a transformation when it becomes an object of representation in other media.

Visual Perspective by Incongruity

Instead of inventing new symbols to elicit public awareness of the growing cost of war, *Eyes Wide Open* appropriated display strategies that had been already in use. The memorial invokes two distinct, even incompatible, traditions of mourning the dead: the tradition of national military cemeteries and the grassroots memorializing epitomized by the NAMES Project AIDS Memorial Quilt. The juxtaposition of these traditions within the space of the same memorial yields what Kenneth Burke termed "a perspective by incongruity," a "vantage point from which to see the inaccuracies of a situation."[9] The display of U.S. military boots and civilian shoes asks the audience simultaneously to honor the soldiers' sacrifice and to mourn them as victims of the unjust war alongside Iraqi civilians. In so doing the memorial promotes reflection on the proper way to remember the war dead, mediates between private grief and public advocacy, and affirms the connection between memory and political action.

At first sight the orderly formation of military boots that greets visitors at the *Eyes Wide Open* display conjures the regularity and solemnity of American military cemeteries such as the Arlington National Cemetery and the cemetery at Gettysburg, which were designed not only as sites of repose for the war dead but also as civic lessons for the living. As such they were meant to convey patriotism, egalitarianism, and transcendence of faction in favor of a unifying national ideal. The shape and layout of the gravestones at Gettysburg, for example, signaled the equality of sacrifices for the Union cause regardless of rank. In the words of Abraham Lincoln's celebrated address at the consecration of Gettysburg, these war dead "gave their last measure of devotion" in defense of "the proposition that all men are created equal."[10]

National military cemeteries owe much of their power to induce feelings of pride and awe to environmental aspects—the environment separates visitors from the immediate concerns of the day and summons them to contemplate eternity. Modeled after Victorian rural cemeteries, both Gettysburg and Arlington cemeteries are set in picturesque and tranquil surroundings amid sloping lawns and shady groves.[11] Many contemporaries noted the transcendent quality of the landscape in these cemeteries and its healing effect on the human psyche. A short story by Constance Woolson published in the *Christian Union* in 1879 offers a glimpse of such a reaction on visiting Arlington. The ritual of mourning is performed, paradigmatically, by a female visitor, whose sorrow for the loss of young lives is mitigated and transcended by patriotic pride: "I often came here at sunset; the quiet beauty of the place seemed to shed a soothing influence over the close of my day. The uniformity and regularity of the close, low ranks of the dead made their number more apparent. Sixteen thousand. Think of only one thousand men marching in there together, how many they would seem! The sixteen thousand are all here; now lying close together under the grass; still and motionless. God has their souls! . . . I went slowly back . . . , my mind full of thoughts of the dead, sad, yet sweet; for I, too, had lost loved ones on the field of battle, and mourned for them, yet felt proud of them, also, through every fiber of my being."[12]

Similarly a National Park Service walking tour guide at Gettysburg instructs the viewer to "observe the simple elegance the National Cemetery planners had hoped for. . . . As you finish your walk to the Visitor Center and pass beneath the broad shade trees and along the neatly trimmed gravestones, take time to reflect upon the inscriptions around you. They remind us of the devotion to country and the payment in human life Americans have given, and may be called on to give, to insure the freedoms we enjoy today."[13] The layout and setting of American military cemeteries thus nurture the attitude of grateful acceptance of military sacrifices as a price for the nation's immortality and as models of civic excellence.

Because *Eyes Wide Open* pays homage of sorts to the U.S. tradition of honoring dead soldiers, Doss believes that despite its desire to speak truth about the war in Iraq, the exhibit is "conflicted by the problematic obligations of gratitude" and therefore cannot help but function as an "agent of national thanksgiving."[14] However grateful contemplation of patriotic sacrifice at the *Eyes Wide Open* exhibit is mitigated—if not denied—by the presence of civilian shoes. Seen together en masse, military and civilian footwear connote mortal calamity rather than the nobility of warfare. By displaying the loss of both military and civilian lives as a collective tragedy, *Eyes Wide Open* quotes the tradition of ephemeral grassroots memorializing most famously represented by the NAMES quilt. The quilt was created by thousands of people in response to the AIDS epidemic. Comprising individually crafted three-by-six-foot panels, each memorializing a particular person who died of AIDS, the quilt not only made the disease impossible to ignore but also turned "what was perceived to be a 'gay disease' into a shared national tragedy."[15]

Eyes Wide Open borrows from the NAMES quilt several inventive strategies; chief among them are the use of "found" materials and the incorporation of visitors' offerings into the texture of the exhibit. The quilt is distinct from most public memorials in its "phenomenology" and "authorship."[16] Instead of a durable medium, it was made of fragile materials; instead of a uniform catalog of names, it described each person individually through inscriptions as well as various images and objects sewn into the panels. This variability owed to the diversity of authorship—panels were made by romantic partners, friends, family members, colleagues, and even complete strangers. The fact that anyone could contribute to the production of the quilt made the project into more than a collection of multiple testimonies about lives lost to the epidemic. The quilt works as an expression of grief and individual mourning as well as "a sounding board about issues about AIDS: some panel makers use it to speak to specific audiences, both those who already understand and those who need to be taught."[17] The discourse of consolation implied by the quilt's tactile quality and its cultural association with homey virtues of family craft traditions thus exist in a state of tension with political advocacy and protest.

Eyes Wide Open also echoes the quilt's activist political stance. Many contributors indeed regarded the quilt as a kind of war memorial, except it memorialized the war that was still being fought. The death toll of the AIDS epidemic was often compared to that of the Vietnam War, and the U.S. government, rather than the virus, was portrayed as the biggest enemy. As Sturken comments, "the AIDS Quilt intends to end the 'war' it memorializes. As such the debate it produces is very different from that raised by the Vietnam Veterans Memorial: it is a debate not only about how to remember the dead but about how to effectively end the dying."[18] By taking on an explicitly political role in relation to the epidemic, the quilt goes beyond the rhetoric of war memorials, even antiheroic ones like the Vietnam Veterans Memorial.

Although the Vietnam Veterans Memorial can be seen as a screen for the projection of disparate memories of the war, its implied antiwar stance is muted because the memorial was joined by unequivocal representations of military sacrifice on the Mall. The quilt, however, is not fixed in one location, its mobility both a sign of the marginal status of the gay community and a reminder that political visibility is contingent on a continuing collective effort. It therefore "accuses more strongly than the Vietnam Veterans Memorial because it is not as easily subsumed into the nationalistic discourse of the Washington Mall."[19] When the quilt did come to Washington, its organizers wished to turn the Mall into a site of protest, to "call attention to the nation's conscience" and "make an accusation, bringing the evidence of the disaster to the doorstep of the people responsible for it."[20]

The two traditions adopted by the *Eyes Wide Open* exhibit, then, illustrate contrasting ways to pay tribute to the war dead. National military cemeteries present an orderly array of generic grave markers to emphasize patriotic sacrifice. They move visitors to mourn the fallen individually in private and to praise them collectively in public. The cemeteries' scenic placement, away from the bustle of everyday life, renders them into sanctuaries of civil religion. By contrast traveling grassroots memorials accent collective loss while bringing private idiosyncratic memories into the public. Their mobility allows them to take over existing public places and thereby to "summon citizens for public advocacy in the presence of others."[21]

By drawing on both traditions, *Eyes Wide Open* issues an invitation to mourn and honor the dead on both sides of the conflict collectively and individually, to ponder the meaning of patriotic sacrifice, and to question the cost of war. The most distinctive design feature of the *Eyes Wide Open* exhibit is the juxtaposition of combat boots standing for dead American soldiers and civilian shoes to symbolize dead Iraqis. A tag listing the soldier's name, rank, age at the time of death, and home state is attached to each boot. Since names of the fallen military personnel are public information, organizers did not request permission to put names on tags. But if someone's family objected, the name was removed at their request. Civilian shoes were added to the display on July 4, 2004, in Philadelphia, when the names of about three thousand dead Iraqis became available.[22]

The uniform rows of military boots—one for each soldier lost to the war in Iraq—recalls the minimalist aesthetic and egalitarian ethos of national military cemeteries. Unlike gravestones, however, the boots do not mark the fallen soldiers' final resting place but instead prompt the visitor to think of the men and women wearing them as if they were standing at attention. This somber and

Eyes Wide Open boots display in Washington, D.C. Photo by American Friends Service Committee.

decorous display signifies respect for the soldiers' ultimate sacrifice. In contrast with iconoclastic antiwar protests of the Vietnam era, it aspires to acknowledge the dedication of men and women in uniform who voluntarily signed up to defend their country. As Mary Zerkel, the AFSC spokesperson, explained, "The decision to arrange the boots this way may not have been a conscious strategy, but this arrangement made the display look respectful of the military, which was important especially early on, when public opinion largely supported the war. We did consider our audience—the 'movable middle'—and wanted people from different ends of the spectrum to participate. We were not hiding from our [antiwar] position, but did not want to beat people over the head with the message."[23] By foregrounding the rows of boots as the display's central feature, *Eyes Wide Open* upholds the decorum and solemnity of the tradition of mourning the war dead.

At the same time, empty boots are an unmistakable reminder of loss—not only the current body count but also impending deaths. Similar to the panels of the NAMES quilt, new boots will continue to be added until U.S. troops return home. The naming of the dead will go on. According to Mary Ellen McNish, then general secretary of the American Friends Service Committee, *Eyes Wide Open* prompts a question: "How many more boots will be standing at silent attention before the war ends, before Iraqis and American soldiers are out of harm's way?"[24]

The exhibit highlights the sense of futility of this loss by featuring the collection of civilian shoes that represent dead Iraqis—men, women, and children. Because these dead were too numerous compared to the U.S. military death toll, their fate was symbolized by a pile of random shoes donated by volunteers and visitors.[25] Their varying size and color present a stark contrast to the orderliness and uniformity of meticulously tagged boots. In some locations shoes were arranged in concentric circles around one pair of untagged boots to underscore the point that two hundred Iraqi citizens had died for every one American military casualty. Beyond their numerical magnitude, the civilian shoes possess a strong emotional appeal because they conjure up the iconographic dossier of crimes against humanity—one immediately thinks of heaped shoes as a symbol of Nazi death camps. During the Iraq War, the display of civilian shoes vividly challenged the Bush administration's rhetoric of "Operation Iraqi Freedom," and it continues to give the lie to the sanitized discourse of "collateral damage" as the United States carries on its warfare against terrorist networks in Afghanistan.

In 2006, for the exhibit's Washington, D.C., appearance, the organizers set up "Dreams and Nightmares: An Exhibit on Life and Death in Iraq" to educate the audience about the cost of war to the Iraqis. The exhibit consists of thirty-two eight-foot panels covered with images and text on both sides. The majority of this makeshift wall's surface is inscribed with the names of Iraqi civilians killed during the war. Interspersed with the names are stories of several people, young and old, from the list of casualties. Photographs of grieving Iraqis—a young girl in tears, men and women weeping over dead bodies of their relatives, a sobbing

Eyes Wide Open civilian shoes and "Dreams and Nightmares" exhibit. Photo by American Friends Service Committee.

father holding a dead child—reveal the anguish and suffering that could not be captured by numbers alone. Finally some panels allow the audience to imagine the consequences of the United States–led occupation of Iraq as though the war were waged on U.S. territory.[26]

The exhibit has been described by the news media as "at once monumental and mundane."[27] Seen together the boots and shoes overwhelm. On the other hand, a welcoming layout and intimate character of the boots and shoes foster interaction and contributions from visitors. These contributions—in the form of photographs, mementos, letters, and other tokens of tribute, affection, and grief—personalize and break the uniformity of the rows of boots while preserving the overall message of collective loss. Combat boots are among the objects most frequently left at the Vietnam Veterans Memorial in Washington, D.C.[28] Here they are miniature memorials in themselves, acting as magnets for visitors' offerings.

The artifacts left by family, friends, and strangers often illustrate the tension between the expression of conventional patriotism and the mourning of lives lost. Along with flowers and American flags, visitors frequently attach family and school photographs, letters, poems, and other intimate mementos. These gestures amplify and personalize the meaning of "the cost of war"—young lives

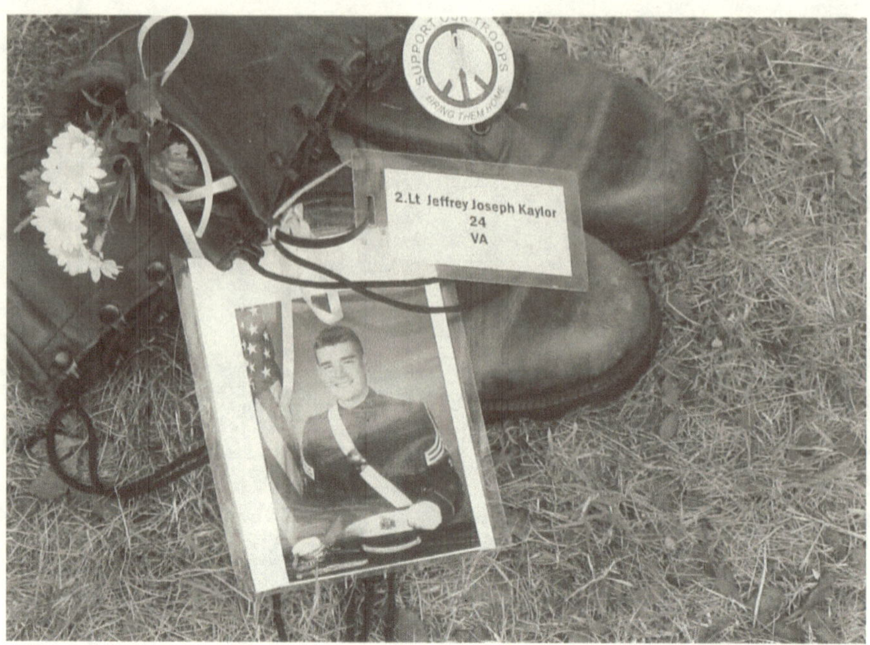

Visitor contributions to *Eyes Wide Open*. Photo by American Friends Service Committee.

interrupted, families grief stricken, dreams shattered. Some contributions explicitly advocate against the war: such is the message telegraphed by buttons that merge the yellow ribbon with the peace symbol and a logo "Support our troops—bring them home." Incidentally these buttons are a prime example of perspective by incongruity themselves, as they juxtapose the two ideologically antagonistic signifiers—the yellow ribbon from the first Gulf War and the peace sign of the antiwar protests of the Vietnam era.

As distinct from similar offerings left at the Vietnam Veterans Memorial—which are collected and archived for posterity by the Park Service—those added to the *Eyes Wide Open* exhibit are shipped along with the boots and shoes to the next destination. This changes the status of these objects from private mementos to public testimony. Some items originally taken from a public source, such as a clipped newspaper article, were transformed into a private message to the dead and then, after their inclusion in the exhibit, assumed a new public meaning. For example, a newspaper article was attached to the boots standing for S.Sgt. Aaron Reese, who drowned in the Tigris River. The article quoted an army officer as saying his Ohio National Guard unit received life vests three days after Reese's drowning.[29] In the context of the display, this article became at once a message of regret and sorrow addressed to the deceased and a public accusation of the authorities responsible for the sergeant's unnecessary death.

By drawing on the visual lexicon and spatial arrangement of both military cemeteries and mobile grassroots memorials, *Eyes Wide Open* sets up a space within which visitors are encouraged to engage in a variety of memorial gestures. It is not a blank space, to be sure, for the "perspective by incongruity" frustrates one's desire to see the memorial only as a tribute to fallen soldiers or as an accusation directed at warmongers responsible for both military and civilian casualties. Rather it summons visitors to confront their biases and blind spots, thus enabling "maximum consciousness."[30] And by traveling to multiple destinations, the exhibit amplifies its appeal to a variety of audiences. It is to this conjunction of space and time as a significant display strategy that we now turn.

Taking (Over) Place

All commemorative rhetoric is situational insofar as public discourse responds to a sociopolitical and cultural context. Permanent memorials, similarly, while commemorating past events, simultaneously reflect the historical conditions under which they were created. But what about those memorials that are not anchored in a particular site and are designed to adapt to a continuously evolving situation? As the preceding discussion of *Eyes Wide Open*'s design shows, the simplicity of the exhibit's conception translated into the relative ease of installation and travel. This, in turn, allowed organizers and volunteers to adapt to changing political circumstances and to capitalize on the significance of various places and occasions to engage audiences.

The initial impetus for *Eyes Wide Open* was the lack of public acknowledgement of the human cost of the Iraq War. As one Quaker volunteer pointed out in 2005, there was "no disturbing press coverage of deceased military personnel returning home in flag-draped caskets," and "thousands of Iraqi deaths [were] reduced to vague statistics through the lens of the mass media."[31] When *Eyes Wide Open* was first shown in January 2004 in Chicago's Federal Plaza, the number of American casualties was 504. As the body count continued to rise despite President Bush's assurance of "mission accomplished," the number of combat boots multiplied. By May 2007 the exhibit was too large to tour nationally, so the organizers adopted a state-by-state approach, displaying the boots to signify casualties from a single state. Although some feared that showing fewer boots would dilute the power of the full national exhibit, the strategy succeeded in bringing home the human cost of the Iraq War. Within one year, between June 2007 and June 2008, state exhibits were shown in forty-eight states, with an estimated attendance of more than 220,000 and an estimated media audience of more than 6.5 million.[32]

Despite the war's waning popularity, however, the Bush administration continued its policies without major opposition in Congress. To raise public awareness of the *economic* costs of war, the AFSC added the *Cost of War* exhibit to the familiar boots and shoes display. *Cost of War* consisted of a series of banners that listed the price tag of one day of the Iraq War—$720 million—and a question: "How would you spend it?"[33] Thus asking the audiences to draw a connection between the current war and other programs that could be funded instead, the pairing of *Cost of War* with *Eyes Wide Open* motivated visitors to move beyond mourning to advocacy.

The modification of the exhibit's contents to convey the growing costs of war—both human and economic—is not the only persuasive strategy afforded by its mobility. What made *Eyes Wide Open* a timely intervention into the national conversation on the war in Iraq was its appearance in places set aside for other purposes, some of them seemingly uncongenial to the exhibit's goals. Instead of a special sacred space postulated by Pierre Nora's notion of *lieu de memoire,* or site of memory, ephemeral memorials are not attached to a specific site.[34] Instead they may temporarily occupy a variety of locations, some already imbued with sacredness, others more profane and prosaic. Historian Steve J. Stern offers a more flexible construct—a "memory knot"—to account for interventionist memory practices: "Memory knots on the social body . . . force charged issues of memory and forgetfulness into a public domain. They make claims or cause problems that heighten attention and consciousness, thereby unsettling reflexive everyday habits and euphemisms that foster numbing."[35]

In order to "heighten attention and consciousness," ephemeral interventions depend on felicitous conjunction of time and place that is likely to yield maximum audience exposure. *Eyes Wide Open* exhibits are often timed to political events and other anniversaries that draw public attention. For example during the 2008 election cycle, the exhibit was shown in the vicinity of both the Republican and Democratic National Conventions. In Minneapolis, where the RNC was held, a Minnesota volunteer group organized three *Eyes Wide Open* events with different degrees of success. The one near the Xcel Center, the RNC convention site, attracted very few visitors: "few conventioneers wandered out of the Xcel Center into it, most local folks avoided the areas populated by the thousands of riot police." In contrast, at the exhibit mounted in conjunction with the Veterans for Peace rally at the Minnesota State Capitol Mall, "hundreds of people took time to walk through the boots" and volunteers "spoke with a lot of media people, many from outside the United States."[36]

Organizers of *Eyes Wide Open* in Denver, Colorado, the location of the Democratic National Convention, timed the exhibit to coincide with the Tent State Music Festival to End the War and used a lottery for free tickets to a Rage against the Machine concert as a device to draw visitors. As a result, Colorado coordinator Sarah Gill reports, "15,000 Rage fans walked past our booth to register for tickets. I'm pretty certain of my assessment that many of these folks had never heard of AFSC before, and while they may have shared some of our convictions, we gave them a way to make those convictions known to others."[37]

In the course of its tour, *Eyes Wide Open* capitalized on the symbolic significance of various locations. Tethering the exhibit to sites already imbued with symbolic history allowed its message to resonate differently in different places. For example on the day of George W. Bush's second presidential inauguration in 2005, *Eyes Wide Open* was displayed at the National Cathedral in Washington, D.C. In Memphis *Eyes Wide Open* was shown next to the Lorraine Motel, the site of Martin Luther King Jr.'s assassination. Strawberry Fields in New York City's Central Park, named after the Beatles song as a memorial to John Lennon, also became host to the exhibit.

Not only iconic locales hosted the display. More often than not, the goal of organizers, in the words of AFSC spokesperson Mary Zerkel, was "to attract an accidental tourist," someone who was not planning to attend the exhibit. According to Zerkel, there have been some "offbeat decisions" about locations that turned out very successful, such as a Walmart parking lot in Pennsylvania, where shoppers in search of cheap goods stumbled upon the display. In Kansas City volunteers used stretchers to make a mobile exhibit and carried it through a busy art fair.[38]

Organizers expected some locations to be friendlier to *Eyes Wide Open* than others. There was little doubt, for example, that Boston and San Francisco, both sites of massive demonstrations against the war in Iraq, would welcome the memorial. In 2007 the Massachusetts state exhibit formed a backdrop to an antiwar rally attended by nearly ten thousand people.[39] On the other end of the spectrum, the exhibit faced opposition by prominent members of local communities who lobbied their officials not to allow the display. In Largo, Florida, some residents objected to the showing of shoes representing Iraqi deaths as a "political" act inappropriate to the spirit of Memorial Day and urged the city to deny the organizers a permit. After negotiations Largo officials agreed to display both boots and shoes as long as the sponsors promised not to make speeches, pass out literature, or wave signs.[40]

Especially in the early years of the war, when public opinion was still sharply divided on the subject of the U.S. invasion, organizers anticipated local opposition to the exhibit. An AFSC online guide for college campus volunteers, for example, instructed them to acknowledge those who disagreed with the exhibit's antiwar message: "Although Eyes Wide Open is a memorial to fallen service people, it does have an anti-war sentiment at its heart, which some people find objectionable. Handle counter demonstrations with respect, and let them know that you are willing to listen to their point of view. If possible, invite them to have a calm, reasonable conversation with you about their views. Do not turn Eyes Wide Open into a rally against any group. Remember that each pair of boots represents a real person who is no longer living. We must give them the utmost respect and not use their death for our own purposes."[41] Asking volunteer "curators" to show sensitivity to local context and to practice openness to criticism and opposition, the exhibit's organizers welcomed its audience's active role as participants in a conversation about patriotic sacrifice. In this manner *Eyes Wide Open* promoted citizenship as a way of being together, as a rhetorical "action performed collaboratively by both speakers and listeners."[42]

This approach paid off. A volunteer from Helena, Montana, described how a fellow volunteer "spent half an hour engaging a well-known local right-wing commentator in conversation about the war at the exhibit, and in the end they found they agreed on everything—the war was a mess, we never should have started it in the first place, etc.—except that he believes in following orders from the commander-in-chief, and she believes in helping the commander-in-chief make the right orders."[43] At an exhibit in Hofstra University before the final presidential debate in 2008, a volunteer from New York State recalled how "a father showed up to remove his son's boots and name tag from the display. He was angered by the fact that AFSC would use his son's death in this way. . . . He argued with the AFSC coordinator about how we must kill the terrorists, and his son did not die in vain, and we had some nerve doing this, and then he handed her a DVD of the latest right-wing garbage propaganda 'Obsession' detailing how 'all of Islam' wants us dead because of our 'freedoms.' The rest of us stood aside and let him rant, feeling his pain, anger, and frustration."[44]

The same volunteer also remembered a number of encounters with initially hostile viewers that ended in a more positive way, including the one in Staten Island, "a conservative borough dominated by the Republicans." As she tells the story: "One time we were in a park, and there were people jogging around. One fellow (who turned out to be a navy captain) came over and started screaming at us, telling us that we were hippies and communists, even though we were flying the American flag. He left and then came back in an hour, much calmer, and said, 'Teach me what you know.' He stayed and talked to the vets who were there with us. Apparently, he lost someone in Iraq and didn't know how to deal with that."[45]

In some locations, on the other hand, "the anticipated resentment and anger never materialized." As a coordinator from Nevada, a swing state during the 2008 election, related, "Displaying the [exhibit] gives me a different context for dialogue to engage people on a more heartfelt level than political races are able to touch. Emphasizing that we're non-partisan keeps people's attention, and holding both major parties accountable resonates with most folks."[46] These examples suggest that the "confrontation" prompted by the exhibit provoked further—often transformative—interactions among those present in the space of display, whether they came there on purpose or happened upon it accidentally. By showing their willingness to listen and empathize, coordinators and volunteers provided a context for a productive civic conversation.

The temporary nature of the memorial is also part of its appeal. Because it is not offered for contemplation in perpetuity, its existence depends on the labor of volunteers and the participation of audiences. Since most *Eyes Wide Open* displays are laid out outdoors, they have to be taken down for the night. The act of setting up and dismantling the exhibit is part of the performance of memory; volunteers and visitors become curators and guardians of memory. Occasionally visitors were recruited as "accidental volunteers," as happened in Denver during the time of the 2008 Democratic National Convention. The exhibit's coordinator wrote in the AFSC newsletter, "Mornings and evenings, we invited everyone at the exhibit or nearby to help us put up or take down the exhibit. If they agreed, I'd give them these instructions: As you pick up a pair of shoes or boots and place them in a bag, say the name of the person—out loud, or to yourself. . . . Many of these 'accidental volunteers' thanked me for offering them such a moving experience."[47]

The reading of names was envisioned by the exhibit's organizers as an integral part of the memorial. When volunteers and exhibit guests read the names, they also mention the person's age and the date on which he or she was killed. "Reading chronologically by the date of death can be very emotional," a volunteer admitted. "Sometimes, ten–twelve soldiers were killed on the same day—so when you read names and say the same date a dozen times, everyone sort of gasps."[48] Some volunteers took the practice a step further and added drama to the ritual of reading names. During the exhibit's sojourn on the Hofstra University campus, for example, viewers were confronted by the "March of the Dead," a procession of students dressed in black with white-faced masks symbolizing the dead from Iraq and Afghanistan.[49] The solemnity of paying tribute to American war dead therefore did not preclude unorthodox gestures that drew attention to casualties on the other side. In this way the "perspective by incongruity" communicated by the juxtaposition of military boots and civilian shoes was augmented by embodied performances of participants.

Volunteers also showed much ingenuity and spontaneity in adapting their display tactics to local circumstances. On August 7, 2007, New York State activists deployed the exhibit on Staten Island's Midland Beach, during the National Night Out against Crime. An annual event sponsored by three police precincts, it serves as a recruiting and public relations venue for the area's law enforcement. As one of the organizers remarked, *Eyes Wide Open* expanded the theme of the evening to include "war crime." Ironically the booths sponsored by vendors at the National Night Out against Crime attracted young visitors by allowing them to hold weapons—grenades and firearms. When these visitors—quite a few of them youths contemplating signing up for military service—wandered through the *Eyes Wide Open* display, they were made aware of the war's toll and encountered veterans who could explain to them the cost of war from a soldier's perspective.[50] In this case, then, the exhibit's pedagogical agenda received an improbable boost thanks to its proximity to a display whose purpose could not be more different.

A highly portable memorial, *Eyes Wide Open* exists as a series of unique enactments in space and time and depends on volunteers and visitors as well as specific locations for whatever persuasive effect it ultimately generates. Besides "bringing home" the human and economic cost of war, the exhibit also reclaims public spaces and emboldens strangers to enter a dialogue over the meaning of the memorial, the value of military sacrifice, and responsibilities of democratic citizenship.

Mediating the Ephemeral

Because it is ephemeral by design, *Eyes Wide Open* does not persist beyond the temporary installations. Unlike the panels of the NAMES quilt, which are unique and visually arresting aside from their function as a traveling memorial, *Eyes Wide Open*'s physical components are utterly prosaic. After the exhibit is taken down, it literally becomes a heap of plastic containers stuffed with boots and shoes. As I have argued so far, it is the performances of memory prompted by the display that make all the difference. At each location on its tour, the memorial takes on a distinct character, as volunteers arrange the rows of boots and shoes and visitors come to mourn, witness, and argue. I am not suggesting that the embodied experiences of the exhibit are unmediated—on the contrary they are positioned vis-à-vis strategic spatiotemporal arrangements as well as spontaneous, contingent performances of others whom visitors encounter in and around the memorial of display. However these "spaces of attention," as Zagacki and Gallagher would call them,[51] do not retain their multimodal and spontaneously interactive character once their contents are re-presented by a different medium. Therefore while different forms of visual and discursive representation may aspire to capture the experience of the exhibit, they constitute a distinct performative modality, subject to a different set of narrative possibilities and technological constraints, not to mention institutional and political biases of media organizations.

Perhaps due to its emphasis on quiet contemplation over dramatic protest, *Eyes Wide Open* scarcely appeared on national television. Designed to attract foot traffic and to persuade visitors to work through a perspective by incongruity created by the juxtaposition of military boots and civilian footwear, the exhibit did not offer itself as a camera-ready "image event."[52] For example when the exhibit was set up near the Xcel Convention Center, the site of the 2008 Republican National Convention, "most media people sought out the clashes between the police and protestors. Quiet memorials were not in vogue."[53]

On the other hand, corporate media's lack of coverage may be attributed to the radical novelty of the concept of representing the dead on both sides of the Iraq conflict as casualties of war. Elaine Brower, a volunteer from Staten Island, commented, "National media don't touch the antiwar stuff." The exhibit did receive favorable coverage from local and regional television stations, says Brower, but often their "positive spin rendered the memorial's chief message as that of 'honoring the sacrifice for our freedoms.' They ignored the fact that we had an Iraqi flag, a peace flag, and a globe flag next to the American flag there."[54]

To document the reception of the exhibit throughout the country, the website of the American Friends Service Committee kept a log of its national tour through a selection of media stories, photographs, and narratives supplied by local coordinators and volunteers.[55] Not surprisingly newspaper reporting, compared to television's episodic representation, was far more attentive to detail and context. Reporters related the stories of local coordinators and sponsors, examined artifacts left at the exhibit, and interviewed visitors. Combined with accounts of tour managers, local volunteers, and coordinators, the archived coverage helps capture to some extent the ephemeral presence and impact of the memorial in its multiple destinations. However, maintaining such an archive electronically requires resources and labor. As of July 2009, several of the links to media coverage on the site did not function, and the list of locations had not been updated for at least a year.[56]

Outside of mainstream media, however, the exhibit was featured in numerous online publications and blogs, many of which combined still images of *Eyes Wide Open* with reporting and commentary. The profusion of coverage on the Internet confirms the observation that today "everyone is a media outlet."[57] Unconstrained by considerations of neutrality espoused by corporate media, these independent reporters are free to editorialize on the perceived significance of the exhibit.

Eyes Wide Open originated as a Quaker project, and especially during its first year on the national tour, Quaker volunteers were instrumental to it success. Although the AFSC did not use religiously colored language in describing the project's goals, many sympathetic participants saw the exhibit through a religious lens. Inspired by the exhibit to meditate on Jesus's admonition to "count the cost," one Quaker blogger imagined how God might meditate on the display's message in "the Maker's Monologue": "I see that you have spent $155 billion of your children's and grandchildren's money making war in Iraq. You realize you could have invested exactly this amount of money doing any of the following?—fully funded world anti-hunger efforts for 6 years; fully funded world-wide AIDS programs for 15 years; ensured that every child in the world is given basic immunization for 51 years. Any of these alternatives would be promoting life, making it literally more abundant as I intend, instead of inflicting death and grievous injury while *talking* about promoting life."[58] This entry interprets the "cost of war" not only in terms of lives lost but also as a waste of resources and opportunities to sustain life. It also endorses a more global view of citizens' responsibilities, expanding one's field of caring beyond the nation state.

To many of its supporters, the memorial's value was in rallying a broad coalition of antiwar groups in an effort to end the war in Iraq. An independent online publication based in Staten Island, *Next Left Notes,* which describes itself as "fiercely New Left and anti-authoritarian," covered a number of *Eyes Wide Open* events over several years. During its numerous appearances, the exhibit brought together members of local chapters of Veterans for Peace, Military Families Speak Out, and Movement for Democratic Society, among others. The "Arlington New York State" exhibit—combining *Eyes Wide Open*'s boots and shoes with crosses similar to those erected by Veterans for Peace in Southern California—was a particularly poignant display of solidarity, as activists were joined by members of the clergy and local politicians. According to one of the organizers, the group of participants "could be the most diverse coalition Staten Island has ever seen—and is reflective of the country's waning enthusiasm for war, particularly in light of the economic disaster that is the U.S. economy."[59]

The exhibit also garnered recognition for its unconventional approach to commemorating the dead from an international online project called "The Polynational War Memorial," dedicated to conceptualizing and designing "a war memorial for all wars since World War II, which will include the names of more than 10 million killed soldiers and civilians."[60] A correspondent from Sweden noted the radical character of *Eyes Wide Open*'s effort to "memorialize all killed, regardless of their nationality, the side of the conflict they were participating on, and whether they were military personnel, civilians, aid workers or insurgents."[61] The author pointed out that even Maya Lin, the designer of the Vietnam Veterans Memorial, when asked in a recent interview about the appropriateness of including names of the Vietnamese killed in the war alongside the names of U.S. soldiers on the wall of the VVM, did not think Americans were ready for such a gesture either during the construction of the memorial or now.

Although hostile responses to the memorial online were few, their tenor seemed to underscore precisely the point made by Lin. A blogger who visited *Eyes Wide Open* in San Francisco in March 2005 argued against the display commemorating Iraqis on the grounds that it conflated "Iraqis" and "civilians." In this visitor's opinion, the United States "has gone to extremes to minimize civilian casualties," so "it seems fairly obvious that a substantial portion—I'd estimate 75% at least—of the casualties were (in order, from the start of the war) soldiers of Saddam Hussein's army, Republican guard troops, Ba'athist 'insurgents,' Sunni militia members, foreign jihadists, and all manner of thugs, fanatics, and killers." Incensed by the alleged display of "moral equivalence between the terrorists and those who fight terrorism," the blogger invoked the Manichean "us versus them" commonplace of the Bush administration rhetoric: "Which side are you on, boys, which side are you on?"[62]

The wider impact of the exhibit is evident in the creative output it has generated in the form of still photography as well as amateur and professional films. Thanks to YouTube, it is now possible to share footage of the exhibit with the widest possible audience. The majority of YouTube videos featuring *Eyes Wide Open* simply record its main features and actions of volunteers and participants, from setting up the boots to giving speeches at press conferences. Two films available on YouTube, however, are notable as artful interpretations of the memorial—independent producer Patricia Boiko's short "The Corporal's Boots" and blues musician Robert Cray's music video for "Twenty," the title song of his 2005 album.

"The Corporal's Boots" is a seven-and-a-half-minute documentary narrated by a middle-aged woman, exhibit viewer Jeannie Graves. Her point of view and emotional response to *Eyes Wide Open* resemble the Victorian visitor's response to the Arlington National Cemetery quoted earlier in this chapter, with one important exception: she is not comforted by the notion that the young soldiers gave their lives for a worthy cause. The first words uttered by the narrator testify to the memorial's perceived ambiguity: "It's an interesting question whether the exhibit is antiwar or prowar. Some people have taken it as an antiwar statement; some people have taken it as a tribute, a memorial to our fallen heroes." Rather than resolve this issue, she takes the audience on her journey through the boots and shoes before relating her encounter with one pair of boots—those representing Cpl. Jonathan Santos, who died in Iraq at the age of twenty-two. The narrator notices Santos's mother trying to attach a pendant to her son's boots. Her voice trembling, she describes how the mother "untied and retied the laces and tried to fix the boots so they were standing up straight. . . . As I watched her, I thought: how many times does a mother tie her child's shoes?" A military mother herself (her son had served in Kosovo), the narrator readily identifies with Mrs. Santos: "My worst fears are what this woman was actually living through."[63]

The film enacts cathartic witnessing and foregrounds empathy and consolation as the exhibit's chief rhetorical effects. Private grief is publicly acknowledged via the narrator's testimony and the bereft mother's expression of gratitude for honoring her son. Although the film raises the question about the exhibit's meaning, it does not urge a single interpretation of it. This "strategic ambiguity" allows opposing interpretations of the display to coexist and converge in praise of the film.[64] Indeed all of the comments posted on YouTube in response to the video lauded its emotional power, even though for some the film was about "our fallen heroes" and "sacrifice for freedom" while for others it was a poignant reminder of "the cost of war" and a "must see for everyone including our politicians."

In contrast with the documentary's ambiguity, Robert Cray's "Twenty" passionately testifies against the war in Iraq. It is a blues ballad that tells the story of a young American soldier who questions his military mission in Iraq and is killed before his tour of duty is over.[65] Cray wrote this "most explicitly political"[66] of his songs at the end of 2004, when *Eyes Wide Open* was completing the first year of its national tour. AFSC assisted Cray in setting up the boot display in the rolling hills of a farm in New Hampshire.[67] The video uses the boots as a framing device for the song's narrative, which at first appears to be a homecoming tale of a soldier returning from Iraq to a picturesque northeastern town. Cray's refrain, "When you're used up, where do you go, soldier?" signals that this story is without a happy ending. As he is riding on a bus and gazing out the window at an idyllic autumn landscape, the young man is haunted by flashbacks of Iraq—soldiers in desert uniforms, explosions, dead Iraqi civilians. The soundtrack relates the soldier's thoughts: "Standing out here in the desert/Trying to protect an oil line/I'd really like to do my job but/This ain't the country that I had in mind/They call it a war on terror/I see a lot of civilians dying/Mothers, sons, fathers and daughters/Not to mention some friends of mine."

While the lyrics are silent on the connection between the war in Iraq and the trauma of Vietnam, the video makes it explicit: when the soldier steps off the bus, he offers a cigarette to a wheelchair-bound man holding a sign that says "Vietnam Vet." The parallel between the young soldier who has been "used up" and the disabled veteran of Vietnam hints at the uncertain future for those who do return home—even those whose bodies seem intact may, in fact, be psychologically damaged. As the video's final scenes reveal, however, the soldier is no longer among the living, and his homecoming is imagined by the artist. After his encounter with a Vietnam veteran, the young man continues on to a field outside of town, where the boots have been set up in neat rows. The soldier walks among the boots and then, coming across a pair bearing a tag that says "Name not yet reported," he pulls the boots on. In the next scene, we see him clad in a desert uniform and standing at attention among the sea of boots and then vanishing as Cray sings his lament: "Late in 2004/Comes a knock at the door/It's no surprise/Mother dry your eyes."

The song stresses the soldier's integrity and dedication ("Mother dry your eyes/that's what I've signed up for") and presents his opposition to the conflict as a realization that he was "trying to protect an oil line" and thus "fighting the rich man's war." Casting the soldier as the war's primary victim along with Iraqi civilians, the artist exonerates the warrior while condemning the war. The story's authenticity is enhanced by the fact that the soldier in the video is played by an actual Iraq War veteran—reservist Aidan Delgado, who became a conscientious objector while serving at Abu Ghraib.[68] Unlike Boiko's film, in which military mothers perform the act of cathartic remembrance, Cray's ballad does not offer the comfort of closure: although the soldier's guilt and shame no longer haunt him, the audience is made witness to his traumatic memory and therefore must come to terms with it.

Various forms of mediation of *Eyes Wide Open* demonstrate both the limitations of mainstream media and the vitality of new and emerging media. In contrast with mainstream media's reluctance to cover unconventional war memorials, responses to the exhibit on the Internet exemplify polemical possibilities of online forums. Yet while they are not facing the institutional and ideological constraints of big media, they also tend to address their audiences as a collection of like-minded persons.[69] Unlike the actual spaces of encounter among strangers furnished by many locations of *Eyes Wide Open*, these forums lack the environmental possibilities of spectatorship in common. Even such evocative films as "The Corporal's Boots" and "Twenty" are unable to narrativize fully the display's representation of Iraqi casualties: in Boiko's documentary civilian shoes remain in the background of the story as a depressing spectacle; in Cray's video the shoes are not featured at all, and instead Iraqi deaths haunt the soldier's conscience. Still these forms of mediation amplify the emotional impact of the memorial by relating deeply felt responses of other witnesses.

Conclusion

The *Eyes Wide Open* exhibit is a plea for its own obsolescence. In contrast with most war memorials, it was erected while the war was still going on and was intended to hasten the war's end. As a reminder of the human cost of war, the memorial invites its visitors not only to remember and mourn the casualties on both sides of the Iraq conflict, but also to question whether any war, including the one waged in Iraq, could be considered just. While the latter is clearly the belief shared by the Quakers and other antiwar groups who actively supported *Eyes Wide Open* throughout the country, the exhibit does not argue this directly—instead it allows audiences to derive their own conclusions from the spectacle presented by the juxtaposition of military boots and civilian shoes.

But this is only part of the memorial's appeal, as the display also forms a backdrop to a panoply of memorial gestures—from expressions of private grief to conventional symbols of patriotism to explicit antiwar statements. Because the memorial's visible surface was augmented by various contributions from visitors, it can be regarded as a product of collective authorship. In addition to memorial artifacts, interaction among those present at the exhibit is integral to its success as a space of mourning and advocacy. By bringing together committed volunteers, concerned visitors, and accidental tourists, the exhibit mediates among various, often seemingly incompatible points of view and visions of civic virtue. Each display thus becomes a forum for mourning, witnessing, and argument.

The ephemeral spectacle provided by *Eyes Wide Open* transformed accidental tourists into citizens who were self-consciously present to each other at the time when the commemorated events were still unfolding. The exhibit's rhetorical power stemmed not only from the unconventional and visually arresting presentation of the human cost of war but also from the performances of memory in the space of the display. In this way the exhibit offered not closure but awareness, asking its visitors to open their eyes to the realities of war waged in their name and thereby to convert their act of remembrance into a public testimony in the presence of fellow citizens.

Of the four instances of participatory commemorations discussed in this book, *Eyes Wide Open* offers the strongest example of civic engagement. Like all the other cases reviewed here, it is inclusive, accessible, and open to diverse opinions and values. Yet it also stages its displays to heighten attention to controversial issues and to further interaction among strangers—something that was lacking in decidedly apolitical approaches of the "Celebrate the Century" program and the September 11 Digital Archive. While *Eyes Wide Open* upholds the ritualistic solemnity of commemorating the war dead and provides a space for private mourning, it deploys the traditional symbolism in novel ways, thereby fostering a space where both respect for the war dead and criticism of war are accepted. In addition to its welcoming stance, the exhibit has a transformative effect on all who participate in it as it does not simply validate one's political values but exhorts people to examine their values in conversation with others.

5

Toward a Participatory Memory Culture

This book began with an observation that ordinary people now expect to be able to "put their stamp on history." But what difference does "putting one's stamp on history" make? Scholars of public memory have been pondering this question, in one form or another, at least since the 1980s, the decade that gave us such nationally prominent unconventional memorials as the Vietnam Veterans Memorial and the NAMES Project AIDS Quilt. To many these memorials signaled both the disenchantment with traditional government-sponsored narratives of the national past and the growing acknowledgment that common citizens deserved recognition as agents of history.

This trend, however, raises a concern over the possibility of national forms of remembrance that can embrace a plurality of citizen voices and identities while projecting some unifying vision. Whereas the VVM and the AIDS quilt can be held up as largely successful examples of such efforts, some scholars worry that the contemporary mnemonic landscape has been overrun by memorials that are tied to identity politics of multiple groups. Calling this phenomenon "memorial mania," Erica Doss sees it as a reflection of "a vastly expanded U.S. demographic" and an index of a troublesome shift toward "rights consciousness."[1] On this view today's memory culture and the discourse of citizenship it feeds are saturated with fractious, feverish expressions of the many by the many that look more like the Hobbesian "war of all against all" than *e pluribus unum.*

If Doss considers today's memory culture a manic and dysfunctional free-for-all, others observe an equally alarming trend toward the privatization of public memorializing. In their survey of recent U.S. memorials, Blair and Michel note how the privileging of "survivors" in constructing memorials to victims of terrorism, for example, has the effect of displacing the public from sites of memory. The emphasis on "family" and on the therapeutic purpose of memorialization, evidenced by the special areas restricted to family members at the Oklahoma City Memorial, prompts the question whether such sites "really are public memorials at all, or whether they are private memorials that merely tolerate public spectators."[2]

These descriptions of contemporary memory culture echo much of the critical commentary about the dangers of fragmentation and polarization in public culture at large and the perceived need for common public experiences that would embolden us "to talk to strangers." The stakes of such engagement are high. Acknowledging fragmentation as a downside of a "participatory historical culture," historian Roy Rosenzweig underlines the importance of memory practices for the collective project of democratic renewal: "Is it possible to build movements for social change without imagining a set of past and present connections to groups of people who aren't kin or ancestors? Is it possible to work for change without a vision of other alternatives that the past can provide? Is it possible to work for change without an understanding of the structures of power that support the status quo?"[3] Rosenzweig's first question in particular emphasizes the need for establishing a trustful connection with others who, by virtue of their different ethnicity, race, class, sexual orientation, or religious affiliation, may not appear to be our "natural" allies.

Can memory practices—especially the ones that valorize "putting one's stamp on history"—be more than mere tools of self-affirmation at the expense of others? This book investigated a handful of participatory acts of retrospection, all of them involving actors with unequal cultural capital and diverse agendas. It evaluated how and to what extent ordinary citizens' participation helps to define "we the people" and contributes to the likelihood of transformative encounters among citizens. Informed by a conception of citizenship as a relationship among strangers, I focused on the manner in which popular commemorations invite and engage their participants in collective production of models of citizenship and judged the potential of these engagements to promote a sense of belonging that mediates between private remembrance and stories of nationhood, between individual interests and public good. One of my guiding questions, to use Benjamin Barber's terms, has been whether spaces of shared remembrance thus constructed can simultaneously create "a place for me" and "a place for us," where individual empowerment and self-assertion can coexist with reaching out to strangers and experiencing alternative identities.

As I stressed in the book's introduction, however, I do not hold that there is a pristine space outside of existing cultural, political, and economic realities that offers opportunities for direct, unmediated expressions of historical experience and performance of citizenship. Even when people aspire to make sense of history on their own terms, they do so within cultural frameworks and with the help of materials that are often not their own. Where other scholars may draw a line between "active firsthand engagement" and "mediation by others who had mysterious and untrustworthy agendas"[4] or between "vernacular" and "official" interests,[5] I see a continuum of practices that combines firsthand engagement and mediation to varying degrees and with different civic consequences. Therefore I am less interested in the question "Is this experience authentic and unmediated?" than in "What modes of civic engagement does this participatory experience promote?" Recognizing the artifice (or artfulness) of all commemorative activity and its relationship with discourses and practices that seem to compromise its purity does not invalidate its value for civic engagement; on the contrary—it allows us to examine, case by case, how people are called upon to participate in constructions of citizen roles and imagined communities.

The four case studies assembled in this book illuminate the process and the means by which contemporary audiences are summoned to participate in historic retrospection and the consequences of this participation for the prospect of democratic renewal. Together these examples illustrate the key rhetorical aspects of popular memories: they testify to the importance of engagement strategies for attracting audiences and participants, highlight the crucial role of popular culture as a source of identification, and confirm the superiority of the interactive, experiential mode in encounters with distant and recent past. Yet these commemorations offer dissimilar lessons in civic engagement based on what model of citizenship they promote and how they manage to foster common spaces for interactions among strangers. In the remaining pages, I review these lessons and reflect on popular memories' potential for civic engagement.

"Celebrate the Century" Program: Converting Citizens into Consumers

The United States Postal Service's "Celebrate the Century" program promised to empower its prospective participants by giving them a sense of control over the contents of the commemorative collection and, by implication, over the nation's historical record. In using the political idiom of voting—it asked participants to cast "ballots" in favor of particular stamp subjects—the program advertised its civic value. At the same time, the process of stamp selection resembled a commercial brand-building campaign. The public, including schoolchildren who were exposed to the program through the corporate-sponsored "Celebrate the Century Kit," was given agency over product design, similar to consumers whose feedback companies solicit to improve products and increase brand loyalty. Whereas voting usually entails deliberative consequences, the narrow range of subjects of celebration—and the interchangeable character of images presented as choices—made "Celebrate the Century" into a superficial exercise in democracy.

Today's audiences are less likely to revere representations of godlike leaders and heroes of the past and more likely to identify with images and stories furnished by popular culture. Compare, for example, the way "the free world" was portrayed in Frank Capra's World War II propaganda film series *Why We Fight* with the "Celebrate the Century" stamp program: the former visualized the American veneration of freedom through a montage of likenesses of heroes of the American Revolution and the Liberty Bell while the latter invited late twentieth-century Americans to connect to the past via the iconography of popular entertainment and consumer products.

Images selected to tell the story of the national experience in the "Celebrate the Century" program are a good illustration of the effort to replace a monolithic narrative of origins and identity with a kaleidoscopic selection of signifiers representing an array of things American. Each of these iconic images can serve as an entry point into the collective story of the century by offering one a more personalized sense of connection to the national past. The century's icons also popularize a more egalitarian ethos: they celebrate not only presidents but also immigrants, women, and counterculture of the 1960s. However the multiplicity of commercial products populating the gallery of U.S. achievements suggests that consumerism is the common denominator of American identity.

In addition to the public's participation in determining the century's icons, the way these icons were presented for public consumption also contributed to the program's civic rhetoric. The arrangement of stamps on the ten panels representing the ten decades of the twentieth century, I argued, produced a narrative of technological and social progress that minimized whatever political differences that may have been read into individual stamps making up the collection. The fact that the stamps were issued on souvenir-like sheets accented their status as depoliticized historical relics.

Besides the narrative arrangement of images, the "Celebrate the Century" program used a number of locations, chosen for their special cultural importance, to vivify the rhetoric of stamps selected to depict the American experience. Many places of memory are set aside to evoke a kind of piety that validates their status as special cultural destinations. In turn visitors are encouraged to take on preferred public identities constructed by memory places. Stamp unveiling ceremonies drew on the existing symbolic resonances of places from the Ellis Island Museum to the Martin Luther King Jr. Historic Site in Atlanta. As much as these locations aided the "experience" of time traveling for those present, they also arguably sealed that experience from potential cross-examination. Each location evoked a particular set of values and historical meanings, but these values and meanings remained isolated, spatially at least, from the lessons of other locations that hosted unveiling ceremonies. In this way display strategies worked to contain public identities in separate settings and implicitly discouraged participants from speaking across differences.

The model of citizenship this commemoration promoted was a rather hollow one, because it presented the century's icons as symbols stripped of political meaning and required the participant-spectator ceremonially to approve the lessons of the past without questioning their political consequences in the present. Ironically, although participants in "Celebrate the Century" were initially hailed as citizens, they were converted into consumers.

The September 11 Digital Archive: A Model of Inclusiveness, a Failure of Dialogue

Organizers of the September 11 Digital Archive expanded their contributor base by making *any* experience of the events, however remotely connected to the physical sites of the tragedy, worthy of being recorded for posterity. If "Celebrate the Century" touted the diversity of its commemorative subjects and public participation in the program as signs of democratic inclusiveness, the archive's open-ended submission policy generated a vast and multifarious collection of verbal and visual artifacts. Not only survivors but virtually anyone who witnessed the events via television coverage in any corner of the globe could participate in the archive's mission. The archive thereby provided a forum where multiple voices could be heard and implicitly affirmed common spectatorship that transcends national boundaries as a paradigm of citizen engagement.

In the spirit of enlisting ordinary people as popular historians, the archive provided a space for a wide variety of accounts in the form of stories, photographs, artwork, and even interactive videogames. Submissions included not only firsthand witness accounts and documentary photography of the events, but also a plethora of diverse reactions to them—from scores of nostalgic family photographs taken against the background of the Manhattan cityscape dominated by the vanquished World Trade Center towers to videogames in which one could fantasize about blowing up Osama bin Laden. In welcoming these submissions, the archive sought to preserve for posterity the rapidly receding historical moment after the attacks, when public participation in history translated into an outpouring of creativity in the streets and squares. At the same time, many of the submissions illustrate how interpretations of experience are often "mediated by existing structures of language and power"[6]—in this case by the tropes of amateur photography and popular entertainment genres. This is especially evident in the way contributors relate their fascination with the spectacle of the burning towers—the sight many describe as a scene from a movie. Scenarios of the destruction of cities by alien invaders are a mainstay of Hollywood science fiction films in which humanity comes together to repel the aggressor under the leadership of fearless leaders. Disturbingly this science fiction formula was also played out in government and media discourses after September 11, especially in President Bush's belligerent calls for national unity and retaliation against the terrorist

"Other." So despite the archive's expressed intention to "create a positive legacy of these horrible events" by involving as many different perspectives as possible, it unintentionally aided in the perpetuation of the rhetoric of victimization and revenge, of the national community united against a common—if elusively defined—enemy.

In evaluating exhibition strategies deployed by the September 11 Digital Archive, I distinguished between its diverse contents and the manner in which visitors are guided to experience them. The archive's display strategy oscillates between undiscriminating inclusiveness and managed diversity. On the one hand, all individual submissions are grouped according to their medium or format rather than topic, so the user can search the archive's contents at will to suit his or her individual preference. On the other hand, the archive on occasion exercises its curatorial discretion to mark certain submissions or to spotlight underrepresented voices among the sea of other entries.

These "special exhibits," especially when they focus on experiences of marginalized ethnic groups, suggest to the visitor that the archive is designed as, among other things, a forum for people of different backgrounds and political views. This exhibition strategy compels the user to imagine the aftermath of September 11 from a perspective not readily supplied by mainstream media coverage. At the same time, other special exhibits accent inclusiveness grounded in the common experience of watching the wounded New York skyline—a multiply mediated and endlessly reproduced spectacle that unified the citizenry in a melancholic trance.[7] Whereas the archive employs some display mechanisms to guide visitors to confront the views of those unlike themselves, there is little opportunity for engaging those views in the virtual space of the exhibit.

The archive's form promotes the value of democratic inclusiveness by inviting ordinary people from all walks of life and with different degrees of proximity to commemorated events to share in the production of public memory. It nevertheless does not furnish a forum for engaging and contesting these collected traces. In this way it offers a depoliticized surface to its users and supports an atomized practice of remembrance that discourages debate and infantilizes citizens.

Carnival 2006: Inspiring Solidarity with New Orleans

The New Orleans carnival, a tourist magnet par excellence, in the wake of "the storm" became an improvised platform for staging the residents' interpretation of the recent catastrophe. The festivity served multiple purposes: it was a citizens' tribunal for accusing the authorities responsible for mishandling the disaster; it was an affirmation of collective resilience; and it was a celebration of the city's endangered performance traditions. The carnival called upon its participants and spectators as carefree revelers, fellow survivors, and sympathetic witnesses all at once. The celebration therefore encouraged those present not only to appreciate the artistry and creativity of costumes and floats—the "authentic" and "diverse" elements extolled by tourism boosters to distinguish New Orleans as a unique cultural destination—but also to join the residents in condemning political corruption, bureaucratic incompetence, and police brutality while praising the values of resilience, camaraderie, and commitment to community.

Performances of carnival revelers in New Orleans also prove that popular culture can be a source of creative expression that serves the disempowered and helps individuals and local communities to assert their agency. Although the hedonism and commercial exploitation of the carnival tradition were perceived by some as incongruous with the gravity of the recent tragedy, New Orleanians reclaimed their tradition in the act of performance and were able to talk about Katrina and the difficult recovery under the guise of frivolity. They put the irreverent symbolism of carnival to use in order to confront their situation and to demand social justice.

Among the book's examples, New Orleans carnival is by far the most experience-rich spectacle. It involves not only sight and hearing but also touch, smell, and taste. This sensory richness has made carnival into an exotic object of consumption that draws tourists to New Orleans to engage in hedonistic pleasures. Spectatorship for many of them entails eating and drinking to excess, watching parades, and competing for parade "throws" with other revelers. Taking a trip to New Orleans for the 2006 carnival, however, also meant coming to terms with the devastation and its potentially dire consequences for the city's demographics and cultural identity. Many exiled residents viewed their participation in Mardi Gras as a civic duty and traveled to New Orleans to affirm symbolically their place on its map at a time when no public authorities could guarantee their right to return. During the carnival numerous spectators held up signs that said "Thank you for parading," while others hoisted placards with names of their flooded streets. Even for tourists, participating in carnival was akin to joining a sprawling reunion party where grief, sarcasm, and defiance mingled in virtually every gesture. The experience that in other historical circumstances may have been solely focused on consumption and recreation in this place and time acquired added significance as a ritual of solidarity with the city left in ruins by forces of nature and government negligence.

While witnessing the carnival in person may have inspired admiration of the city's collective resilience, some forms of mediation—"prosthetic memories," as Landsberg calls them—were successful in encouraging camaraderie with New Orleans. For example the HBO dramatic series *Treme* re-creates the aftermath of Katrina by following the interlocking lives of several New Orleanians. Unlike televised coverage of post-Katrina's flooding and human misery, which cast New Orleans as the abject other, *Treme* makes us see the city from the vantage point of its residents, all of them struggling to reclaim their lives amid chaos and apparent bureaucratic indifference to their basic needs. The series extols the cultural assets of New Orleans—music, food, and festive traditions—by showing us how they are tied to concrete people and neighborhoods. The culture it depicts is both a means of survival and a reason for living in New Orleans in the first place, and this portrayal encourages one to empathize with the residents' fierce loyalty to their local identities. In the age when intentional geographic mobility (as distinct from "mandatory evacuation") is a sign of personal economic success, *Treme* makes us care about people attached to their neighborhoods and local history.

The carnival celebration summoned both visitors and displaced residents to bear firsthand witness to the devastation and to observe the role of culture in keeping communities alive. And a popular television series immersed its viewers in the imaginatively reconstructed experiences of New Orleanians after the storm. Participatory festive traditions and popular entertainment can therefore be leveraged to heighten civic awareness and inspire solidarity with fellow citizens across geographic and social distance and to convert tourists and spectators into empathetic witnesses.

Eyes Wide Open: *Creating Spaces of Attention*

Whereas New Orleans residents capitalized on the appeal of Mardi Gras as a popular tourist attraction, the antiwar memorial *Eyes Wide Open* traveled to its multiple destinations and attracted "accidental tourists" by staging its temporary displays in areas with substantial pedestrian traffic. Its simplicity and solemnity were designed to arrest one's motion along some mundane trajectory (think of shoppers in a Walmart plaza), to capture the attention of tourists who have come to see a different attraction (for example monuments and memorials on the National Mall in Washington, D.C.), or to interrupt the weekend leisure of beachgoers in Southern California or Staten Island. Although the display did allow for expressions of conventional patriotic sentiments in praise of the fallen U.S. soldiers, its unconventional acknowledgment of casualties on both sides of the Iraq conflict prodded visitors to rethink their understanding of patriotic sacrifice.

The stark visual form of the *Eyes Wide Open* inspired a multitude of creative efforts that used its symbolism to tell stories of soldiers whose lives were cut short by "a rich man's war," as the lyrics of Robert Cray's blues ballad "Twenty" put it. Recognizing popular music's power to promote social solidarity, the organizers of the exhibit helped Cray to set up the military boot display as a background for the song's haunting refrain, "When you're used up, where do you go, soldier?" Cray's music video marries the evocative power of a popular song with filmic narrative to create a story that is both vividly particular and universal in its meaning, as it can represent all military men and women whose boots are now standing at silent attention in the space of the *Eyes Wide Open* memorial. This instance of popularization provokes reflection on the value of human life and invites the audience to question conventional justifications of U.S. military action overseas.

As distinct from permanent memorials, the *Eyes Wide Open* traveling exhibit created unique "spaces of attention" wherever it went. The texture of one's experience of the memorial therefore varied from location to location. How one encountered the display of boots and shoes was affected not only by the organizers' strategic choices of location and time, but also by more spontaneous, unpredictable encounters with other visitors and volunteers. One could wander in when new boots were being added to signal the rise in the casualties count, join a pro-peace rally held in conjunction with the exhibit, or witness a counterdemonstration by those who objected to acknowledging Iraqi deaths along with those of American military personnel. The evolving, dynamic quality of the exhibit was to a large extent shaped by those who came together in its space to mourn, to pay tribute, to witness, and—perhaps most important—to be listened to.

The spaces of interaction among strangers temporarily created by the exhibit became provisional public forums where the discussion about the ongoing war in Iraq and its human and economic toll—the discussion banished at the time from mainstream media and politics—could take place. *Eyes Wide Open*'s function as a memorial to lives lost on both sides of the Iraq conflict thus coexisted with its more activist role as a space of discussion and controversy. Distinguished by its tolerance for different points of view, even an expectation of dissent and vociferous opposition, the exhibit welcomed any passerby to reflect and to speak his or her mind to volunteers and engage other visitors. That many "accidental tourists" who stumbled upon *Eyes Wide Open* became "accidental volunteers" is a testimony to its persuasive power.

Popular Memories and the Prospect of Democratic Renewal

It appears that inclusiveness and diversity have become normative aspirations of memory projects that seek to encourage the broadest public participation. Commitment to inclusiveness and diversity can be explicitly proclaimed, as in the case of the "Celebrate the Century" program and the September 11 Digital Archive, or implicitly modeled, as we saw in the examples of the carnival in New Orleans and the *Eyes Wide Open* exhibit. But does this commitment translate into the kinds of representations, performances, and engagements that expand our civic horizons and make us overcome distrust of others who are unlike us?

As the examples of "Celebrate the Century" and the September 11 Digital Archive illustrate, their inclusiveness and diversity, while clearly dependent on popular enthusiasm for history making, hardly produce the kinds of exchanges among participants that go beyond the affirmation of personal experience and identity. Participation here is framed in terms of individual contribution to the collective tableau of memory. "Celebrate the Century" neutralized the political significance of commemorative icons and created separate occasions for separate publics to experience their meaning. It thus created opportunities for privatized remembrance—"a place for me" rather than "a place for us." The September 11 Digital Archive similarly left the act of viewing to the individual visitor of the site while presenting the frozen spectacle of the Twin Towers before the fall as the glue that binds the imagined global community together. Both projects, then, celebrated universal access and the presence of difference as well as valorized the numerical magnitude of participation by "diverse" segments of society. Yet they largely avoided—or missed—the opportunity to animate this diversity by giving the participants a place to interact with one another.

By contrast the first post-Katrina carnival and the *Eyes Wide Open* traveling memorial succeeded in bringing together, in spectacle and conversation, the multitude of interpretations of the recent past and even present. In the case of the carnival, these interpretations took the form of absurdist and satirical depictions of the forces of nature, government agencies, and public authorities. Temporary forums staged by *Eyes Wide Open* exhibits made room for private mourning as well as public advocacy and debate among people from all parts of the political spectrum. In both examples the content of what was displayed or said was as important as the fact of seeing other people partaking in celebration, mourning, or debate. Their inclusiveness and diversity were brought to life by active engagement, making each space of interaction into "a place for us."

One could blame the failure to engage participants in experiencing alternative identities and points of view on mediation and technological constraints and to attribute the spontaneously interactive character of the carnival and temporary antiwar memorials to their grassroots nature and apparent lack of mediation. I, however, do not support this view. "Celebrate the Century" and *Eyes Wide Open* both strategically employed the symbolism of multiple physical locations to display their respective content to visitors. Yet the former asked their audiences merely to applaud the results of the public "vote," and the latter presented visitors with a perspective by incongruity—evoked by the contrast between combat boots and civilian shoes—that interrupted habitual patterns of thinking about the nature of military sacrifice. And as far as technological constraints are concerned, the September 11 Digital Archive could conceivably display a portion of its individual submissions to accent the difference of points of view on the same issue—for example, "What should the US government do in response to 9/11 attacks?" Instead it opted out of the role of moderator and chose to represent "diversity" by introducing some accounts of "minority" experience into the mix of entries.

Like the ultimate democratic value, "freedom," inclusiveness and diversity in themselves amount to little unless they are actualized in the context of civic engagement. Popular memories make for stronger or weaker sites of civic engagement depending on whether they allow for public affirmation of the individual citizen's contribution *and* for experiencing alternative identities and perspectives. Either way they buttress a particular vision of civic life and provide symbolic resources for dealing with present historical exigencies. To recall the civic role of display rhetoric discussed in the introduction, acts of memory can reinforce existing beliefs and ideologies as well as call them into question. Displays of memory, then, are no mere political window dressing—they underlie political decision making in the present.

What can be said of the visions of civic life promoted by the four commemorations examined in this book and their consequences for democratic politics? Motivated by no specific exigency aside from the approaching end of the millennium, the ceremonial discourse of "Celebrate the Century" nevertheless recruited the public to construct a story of social, economic, and technological progress culminating in the present. Although ostensibly celebrating progressive social change over time, the program presented particular milestones of change and the contentious politics that generated them as belonging to the museum of the past. When some citizens took issue with such political obsolescence—as was the case with the Atlanta mayor's objection to embalming Martin Luther King Jr.'s legacy and isolating it from today's issues such as affirmative action—their voices appeared as expressions of special interests rather than calls to examine our collective aspirations. Because of this neutering of political symbols and its celebration of consumerism, "Celebrate the Century" is implicated in propagating the ideology of neoliberalism, whose most palpable accomplishments have been the ascendance of the free-market logic in all areas of public life and the redefinition of citizenship in terms of consumer rights. As a result such issues as civil rights "have been transmogrified . . . into a special interest of minority groups for which most Americans are supposed to have little sympathy."[8]

If the purpose of "Celebrate the Century" was ceremonial, the September 11 Digital Archive was launched in response to an event that was expected to alter the way Americans view themselves and the world. The aftermath of 9/11 brought about a surge of volunteerism and participation in communal life; at the same time, the Bush administration encouraged Americans to continue using their credit cards and to acquiesce to a disastrous domestic and foreign policy in the name of protecting our "freedom." Despite its mission to create a positive legacy of the events, the archive's neutral stance in regard to its contents thus made it complicit in supporting precisely the calamitous philosophy of atomized individualism that it set out to contradict. And its deferral of interpretation to "future historians" suggests that its contents have no present political value.

The aftermath of hurricanes Katrina and Rita in the late summer and fall of 2005 exposed the cracks in the neoliberal policies that have weakened the government's investment of resources into the country's vital infrastructure. As the world watched a great American city drown because of levee failure and tens of thousands of its residents abandon their homes with no promise of return, the U.S. government, led by antigovernment politicians, showed little sympathy or support. Whereas the mainstream media focused on the tragedy as a natural disaster and portrayed the residents of the area as its victims, the first post-Katrina carnival in New Orleans presented an eloquent and irreverent argument for why it was a human-made catastrophe and asserted the residents' commitment to bringing back their city. Carnival performances, I have argued, engaged residents and visitors alike in a more just and egalitarian vision of collective life than anything the country had seen since 9/11. Judging by numerous volunteers who have traveled to New Orleans to assist in rebuilding the city, this vision has been powerful enough to make Americans care about fellow citizens whom President Bush described as "people from that part of the world."

In contrast to the abundant media coverage of September 11 and Hurricane Katrina, the wars in Iraq and Afghanistan, like the protests against them, received hardly any attention from mainstream news organizations. In the absence of public acknowledgement of the cost of American military adventures overseas, numerous antiwar groups and individuals began to count the war dead—some putting crosses in the sand on public beaches, others marking each new death with a small flag in one's front lawn. *Eyes Wide Open,* a project of the American Friends Service Committee, went beyond the sheer counting of names and raising awareness to provoke its audiences into thinking and talking about the nature of patriotic duty and citizen responsibility.

In his brief essay "Creative Democracy: The Task before Us," John Dewey advocates for an experiential view of democracy. For him it is not a static system of rules and citizen roles but a way of life animated by "the faith that the process of experience is more important than any special result attained, so that special results achieved are of ultimate value only as they are used to enrich and order the ongoing process."[9] His vision of this process is at once modest and profound: "The heart and final guarantee of democracy is in free gatherings of neighbors on the street corner to discuss back and forth what is read in uncensored news of the day."[10]

Echoing Dewey, I propose that the value of commemorations is not only in what or whom they commemorate but also how they engender encounters among strangers. Democratic renewal depends in large measure on whether citizens can find a time and a place to examine their shared values as well as their conflicting priorities. If examples in this study are any indication, participatory commemorations can create such sites—even in the midst of a raucous carnival or a public beach. What matters, ultimately, is not who gets to participate but how the participation expands the individual sphere of caring to persuade citizens to embrace the various others—those for whom they have no natural affinity—as fellow citizens.

This prospect is perhaps overly optimistic, given the seemingly deepening chasm between "blue" and "red" states in the last decade and the rancorous calls from the political right to treat those they disagree with as enemies rather than fellow citizens. Yet as Dewey reminds us, democracy requires a leap of faith.

Notes

Introduction

1. On the culture of parades in antebellum Philadelphia, see Davis, *Parades and Power.* On popular parades and festivities in the early American Republic, see Newman, *Parades and the Politics of the Street.* On the early twentieth-century "historical pageantry craze," see Glassberg, *American Historical Pageantry.*

2. Newman, *Parades and the Politics of the Street,* 7.

3. Glassberg, *American Historical Pageantry,* 2.

4. Davis, *Parades and Power,* 166.

5. Anderson, *Imagined Communities;* Bodnar, *Remaking America;* Boime, *Unveiling of the National Icons;* Dubin, *Displays of Power;* Gillis, *Commemorations;* Hobsbawm and Ranger, *Invention of Tradition;* Levinson, *Written in Stone;* Olick, *States of Memory;* Savage, *Standing Soldiers, Kneeling Slaves;* Spillman, *Nation and Commemoration.*

6. Boime, *Unveiling of the National Icons;* Burgoyne, *Film Nation;* Linenthal, *Preserving Memory;* Linenthal and Engelhardt, *History Wars;* Sturken, *Tangled Memories.*

7. On the subordination of "vernacular" expressions to "official" narratives, see esp. Bodnar, *Remaking America.* Bodnar's expressed intent is "to peel back the mask of innocence that surrounds commemorative events" (20). On the "taming" of festive folk traditions by the elites, see Davis, "'Making Night Hideous.'" For a more recent example of the appropriation of "vernacular" voices of U.S. soldiers by the U.S. military's YouTube channel created during the invasion and occupation of Iraq, see Smith and McDonald, "Mundane to the Memorial." On official manipulation of the historical record, see esp. Loewen, *Lies My Teacher Told Me* and *Lies across America.*

8. On the development of this trend in the United States, see Kammen, *Mystic Chords of Memory.*

9. This sense of popularization is a conventional one. For an alternative understanding of popularization as a rhetoric of "reconstitution" addressed to the democratic audience, see Antczak, *Thought and Character.* Antczak contrasts "popularization" with "indulgence" (playing "to the audience's commonplaces for purposes of the speaker's gain") and "vulgarization" (when the speaker "at least tried to change the audience's mind about something, but only about a particular conclusion"). Popularization stands at the top of this hierarchy of appeals insofar as its aim is not an opportunist act of persuasion but an attempt to "reconstitute" the audience's "thought and character," as seen in the efforts of Ralph Waldo Emerson, Mark Twain, and William James (9). For an evocative application of

Antczak's notion of popularization to a historic site, see Halloran, "Writing History on the Landscape."

10. Scholars of public memory often invoke the term *democratization* to capture the manifold transformation in practices of remembrance in the late twentieth century. Kammen describes the "'Roots phenomenon,' a dramatic expansion in the diversity of social groups concerned about their past," in *Mystic Chords of Memory* (620). Noting the "proliferation of anniversaries, memorial services, and ethnic celebrations," Gillis emphasizes the decentralization and pluralization of the national memory culture as key features of the democratized memory culture ("Memory and Identity," 14). In their survey of Americans' attitudes toward history published in 1998, historians Roy Rosenzweig and David P. Thelen stress the value of all stories about the past, "whether 'the past' consists of a 200-year-old narrative, an account from a textbook, a display at a museum, or a tale recounted by a family member over Thanksgiving dinner." See Rosenzweig and Thelen, *Presence of the Past,* 190.

11. Bodnar, *Remaking America,* 13–14.

12. Ibid., 14. It must be noted that the term *vernacular* has been employed by scholars in many disciplines and has become a magnet for different meanings. Bodnar, for example, follows Susan G. Davis, who used the label "vernacular culture" to characterize street parades in antebellum Philadelphia. Davis contrasts vernacular communication with "industrial, commercial, and official modes of communication and media" (*Parades and Power,* 15). Today the boundary between "popular" and "commercial" is often difficult to sustain or even detect: "there is no pure space outside of commodity culture," as Andreas Huyssen argues ("Present Pasts," 29). Rather than focus on the aesthetics and politics of production, scholars in architecture and critical ethnography have moved to the aesthetics of reception. On this view *vernacular* can be applied to the reception or appropriation of existing artifacts. See, for example, essays in Carter and Herman, *Perspectives in Vernacular Architecture, III.* Barbara Kirshenblatt-Gimblett talks of "vernacular practices of connoisseurship" in *Destination Culture,* 259–81. For rhetorical theorists the notion of vernacular still holds the promise of recovering the voices of marginalized groups and "publics" that may have been muted by the technocratic discourse of poll-driven "public opinion." See especially Hauser, *Vernacular Voices,* and Ono and Sloop, "Critique of Vernacular Discourse."

13. Bodnar, *Remaking America,* 14.

14. Foucault, "Film and Popular Memory," 123.

15. For a discussion of this trend in memory scholarship, see Klein, "On the Emergence of Memory."

16. Kammen, *Mystic Chords of Memory,* 681.

17. See Waite, "Identifying Agency."

18. Kammen, *Mystic Chords of Memory,* 682.

19. Critiques of mass culture's influence on memory are numerous, many of them coming out of the Frankfurt School's "culture industry" thesis that equates commercialism with amnesia. For a summary of this literature, see Huyssen, "Present Pasts." For examples of studies that focus on particular forms of popular culture, see Anderson, "History TV and Popular Memory"; Wallace, *Mickey Mouse History.* For a critique of the wholesale dismissal of "popular culture" as a memory resource, see Lipsitz, *Time Passages.*

20. See Patraka, "Spectacular Suffering."

21. Kammen, *Mystic Chords of Memory,* 665.

22. Sturken, *Tourists of History,* 9–10.

23. Kammen, *Mystic Chords of Memory,* 628.

24. On "dark tourism" see Lennon and Foley, *Dark Tourism;* Strange and Kempa, "Shades of Dark Tourism"; Robb, "Violence and Recreation"; and Bowman and Pezzullo, "What's So 'Dark' about 'Dark Tourism'?" On "toxic" tourism see esp. Pezzullo, *Toxic Tourism.*

25. Berlant, "Citizenship," 37.

26. For a useful articulation of "consensual assumptions" that guide scholars of memory, including rhetoricians, see Blair, Dickinson, and Ott, "Introduction." Kendall R. Phillips traces the relationship between rhetoric and memory back to the works of Plato and Aristotle in "Failure of Memory."

27. For a brief introduction to epideictic, see Haskins, "Epideictic Rhetoric." On the epideictic's civic role, see esp. Hauser, "Aristotle on Epideictic," and Condit, "Function of Epideictic." For studies of contemporary display rhetoric, see Prelli, *Rhetorics of Display.* For identification of public commemorative art as epideictic, see, for example, Blair, "Contemporary U.S. Memorial Sites"; Blair and Michel, "Commemorating in the Theme Park Zone"; and Vivian, "Neoliberal Epideictic."

28. Walker, *Rhetoric and Poetics in Antiquity,* 9.

29. For an analysis of the *Menexenus* as a text about cultural memory, see Haskins, "Philosophy, Rhetoric, and Cultural Memory."

30. McGee, "In Search of the People," 243. McGee's student Maurice Charland presented an extension of this theory in "Constitutive Rhetoric."

31. Hariman and Lucaites, *No Caption Needed,* 18.

32. Ibid.

33. Biesecker, "Remembering World War II," 394.

34. Ibid.

35. Balthrop, Blair, and Michel, "Presence of the Present," 191.

36. Vivian, "Neoliberal Epideictic," 15.

37. Ibid., 20.

38. Ibid., 21.

39. Walker, *Rhetoric and Poetics,* 10.

40. Glassberg, *American Historical Pageantry,* 133.

41. Ibid., 135.

42. Cited in ibid., 135.

43. See esp. Asen, "Discourse Theory of Citizenship."

44. Ibid., 202.

45. Carole Blair thus explains materiality of memorial sites: "they construct valenced reaction and depths of visitor experience that cannot be described, much less explained, in terms of their symbolism or by reference to the intentions of their makers" ("Contemporary U.S. Memorial Sites," 50).

46. Halloran, "Text and Experience," 5.

47. Ibid., 13.

48. Blair, Dickinson, and Ott, "Introduction," 27.

49. Hariman and Lucaites, *No Caption Needed*, 33.

50. On publicness as a condition for political organization and democratic self-understanding, see Arendt, *Human Condition;* Paul Woodruff, *First Democracy* and *The Necessity of Theater.*

51. Rosenfield, "Central Park."

52. Allen, *Talking to Strangers.*

53. Barber, *Place for Us*, 76.

54. Ibid., 3.

55. Blair and Michel, "AIDS Memorial Quilt," 14.

56. Ibid.

57. Ibid. For a study of visitor responses to the Quilt, see Lewis and Fraser, "Patches of Grief and Rage."

58. Blair and Michel, "AIDS Memorial Quilt," 32.

59. Morris, "Mourning After," xliii.

60. Hawkins, "Naming Names," 777.

61. Bennett, "Stitch in Time," 134–35.

62. Ibid., 138.

63. Ibid., 135.

64. Ibid., 148.

65. Ibid.

66. Blair and Michel, "AIDS Memorial Quilt," 24.

67. Doss, *Memorial Mania*, 38.

68. Ibid., 48.

69. Levinson, *Written in Stone*, 10.

70. Kenneth Burke uses the phrase "attitudes toward history" to describe not individual attitudes but public vocabularies adopted by rhetors to name historical and political situations as well as to exhort others. See *Attitudes toward History.*

71. Commemorative forms and symbols that underlie enactments of memory are not neutral or infinitely malleable sedimentations of the past. As sociologist Jeffrey Olick puts it, "the materials available to [speakers] in any context—and which they may thereby transform—are historical accretions, the results of long developmental processes as well as of relational contexts rather than formally defined features of an atemporal system" (*Politics of Regret*, 106). Amos Funkenstein (*Perceptions of Jewish History*, 7–9) likens the relationship between individual acts of commemoration and collective memory as their source to the Saussurean distinction between *parole* and *langue.*

72. Musil, "Monuments," 61.

73. For example rhetorical critics Carole Blair and Neil Michel sought to explain why visitors to the Kennedy Space Center showed little interest in the so-called Space Mirror, a seemingly compelling memorial to U.S. astronauts who perished during NASA missions. The authors found that visitors' attitude toward the memorial (their apathy, to be precise) was shaped by a theme-park environment at both the Kennedy Space Center and nearby Walt Disney World, in which tourists are coaxed "to remain immersed within the vista of efficiently fun, safe, technologically enabled happy endings" ("Commemorating in the Theme Park Zone," 55). Visitors appeared to have been distracted from the somber civic message of the astronauts memorial by their immersive, hypnotic experience of a preprogrammed journey through a corporately owned "vacation dreamscape" (69). Their

expectations of a tourist experience in an amusement park were carried over to other landmarks on their itinerary, even those the rhetorical purpose of which was more civic and pedagogical.

74. Lanham, *Economics of Attention*, xi.

75. Clark, "Rhetorical Experience," 119.

76. Confino, "Collective Memory and Cultural History," 1395.

77. Young, *Texture of Memory*, xiii.

78. Ibid., xii.

79. I could not attend the 2006 carnival in New Orleans and thus missed an opportunity to experience the festivity's ambience firsthand. I note, however, that the parade goer's perspective is necessarily tied to a particular location along the parade route and is often framed by the viewfinder of a camera. Performance studies scholars Ruth Laurion Bowman, Melanie Kitchens, and Linda Shkreli, for example, explored the 2006 Spanish Town Mardi Gras Parade in Baton Rouge "by ciphering [their viewing of the parade] through the technical and conceptual apparatus of photography" ("FEMAture Evacuation," 278).

80. I rely on Diana Taylor's definition of scenarios as "meaning-making paradigms that structure social environments, behaviors, and potential outcomes" (*The Archive and the Repertoire*, 28).

81. Joan Scott cautioned cultural critics against valorizing experience: "We need to attend to the historical processes that, through discourse, position subjects and produce their experiences. It is not individuals who have experience, but subjects who are constituted through experience. Experience in this definition then becomes not the origin of our explanation, not the authoritative (because seen or felt) evidence that grounds what is known, but rather that which we seek to explain, that about which knowledge is produced. To think about experience in this way is to historicize it as well as to historicize the identities it produces" ("Evidence of Experience," 779–80).

82. Clark, "Rhetorical Experience," 116.

83. See Landsberg, *Prosthetic Memory*.

84. Rhetorical pedagogy from antiquity to the Renaissance relied on space as a crucial aid to memory. Spatial mnemonics allowed rhetors to fashion and audiences to follow elaborate arguments and narratives by tethering them to either physically present or imaginary locations. See Yates, *Art of Memory*. In contemporary rhetorical scholarship, space is much more than an instrument in an orator's toolbox. Roxanne Mountford, for example, argues that "rhetorical space is the geography of a communicative event," which, "like all landscapes, may include both the cultural and material arrangement, whether intended or fortuitous, of space" ("On Gender and Rhetorical Space," 42). Public memory scholars have paid greater attention to spaces intended to function as memory prompts than to transitory places that are not intentionally set aside for a memorial purpose. According to Clark, "these encounters—these rhetorical experiences that are provided for us more or less ready-made—should be objects of our rhetorical criticism" ("Rhetorical Experience," 116). Blair, Dickinson, and Ott point out that the designation of places of memory marks them "for exceptional cultural importance" and invites a set of responses from those who visit them: the "effort to participate in a memory place's rhetoric almost certainly predisposes its visitors to respond in certain ways, enthymematically prefiguring the rhetoric of the place—at the very least—as worthy of attention, investment, and effort" ("Introduction," 26).

85. In my examination of mediation, I cautiously embrace arguments about mass media as memory agents. For example Landsberg's thesis about "prosthetic memories" posits a radical transformation in practices of remembering brought on by technological innovation. Landsberg contrasts modern mass cultural technologies with traditional modes of memory that aspired to unify people "across differences of class, ethnicity, gender, and region" by "constructing a common national identity that was supposed to supersede these differences" (*Prosthetic Memory,* 9). Prosthetic memories, she argues, "do not erase differences or construct common origins" (9)—on the contrary they "have the capacity to create shared social frameworks for people who inhabit, literally and figuratively, different social spaces, practices, and beliefs" (8). While Landsberg's argument is a valuable critical rejoinder to theories of mass media as forces of commodification and amnesia, it also overgeneralizes the extent to which prosthetic memories help audiences expand their "archive of experience" and thereby facilitate political solidarity across race, class, and gender. Before we make judgments about a particular medium's progressive potential as a technology of memory, I argue, we need to examine how its technological and narrative capacities are used to position spectators with regard to objects of representation as well as these spectators' own culturally conditioned viewing habits. It is therefore appropriate to talk about distinct "affordances" of each medium under consideration and about narrative and display strategies employed in specific instances of mediation. On "affordances" see Kress, *Multimodality,* and Kress and Van Leeuwen, *Multimodal Discourse.*

Chapter 1: "Put Your Stamp on History"

1. An earlier version of this chapter originally appeared as an article; see Ekaterina V. Haskins, "'Put Your Stamp on History:' The USPS Commemorative Program *Celebrate the Century* and Postmodern Collective Memory," *Quarterly Journal of Speech* 89 (2003):1–18; © National Communication Association, reprinted by permission of Taylor and Francis (http://www.tandfonline.com).

2. Bodnar, *Remaking America,* 13–14.

3. United States Postal Service, *Postal Bulletin,* November 6, 1997, 50.

4. United States Postal Service, *Celebrate the Century Express,* http://www.usps.gov/ctc/train/what.htm (accessed July 15, 2001).

5. On the disappearance of the once "sovereign difference" between representations and referents, see Baudrillard, *Simulations.* Baudrillard argues that the Marxist assessment of capitalism as a production of commodities is obsolete because capitalist production now revolves around the manufacture of signs, images, and sign systems rather than commodities. See Baudrillard, *Pour une Critique.*

6. See, for example, Kanfer, "Post Office Stamps Out the 1980s," 11.

7. Lucaites and Hariman, "Visual Rhetoric," 37.

8. Jean-Francois Lyotard gives a classic if limited definition of postmodernity as "incredulity toward metanarratives" in *Postmodern Condition,* xxiv. David Harvey traces a series of cultural transformations associated with postmodernity, especially those linked to the post-Fordist economy of flexible accumulation and technologies that increase the turnover of production and consumption, in *Condition of Postmodernity.*

9. Bellah, "Civil Religion in America."

10. Bellah, *Broken Covenant,* 2.

11. Ibid., 2–21.

12. Ibid., 4.

13. I construct this account with the aid of *The Postal Service Guide to U.S. Postal Stamps.* This philatelist's manual contains photographs of all U.S. postal stamps issued between 1847 and 2000. The first commemorative collection was issued in 1893 in celebration of the four-hundredth anniversary of Christopher Columbus's landing.

14. According to Donald J. Lehnus, *From Angels to Zeppelins,* "government and politics" and "military" are the most frequent subjects featured on postal stamps between 1847 and 1980; two-thirds of all commemorated individuals lived between 1700 and 1899.

15. Gillis, "Memory and Identity," 20.

16. As Albert Boime points out, Rosenthal's recollection of the circumstances in which the photograph was taken underscores the way that a "subjective need of the elevated flag to produce an image of victorious heroism on foreign terrain coincided with the nationalist ideology" (*Unveiling of the National Icons,* 20). For a close reading of the Iwo Jima photograph, see Hariman and Lucaites, *No Caption Needed,* 93–136.

17. United States Postal Service, *The Citizens' Stamp Advisory Committee,* http://www.usps.com (accessed July 15, 2001).

18. On the change in the iconography of the stamps depicting the American Revolution, see Skaggs, "Postage Stamps as Icons."

19. Gillis, "Memory and Identity," 15.

20. Betsky, "Enigma of the Thigh Cho," 22.

21. Ibid.

22. Eco, *Travels in Hyperreality,* 6.

23. Jameson, *Postmodernism,* 19.

24. Ibid., 18.

25. See esp. Debord, *Society of the Spectacle.*

26. Landsberg, *Prosthetic Memory,* 9.

27. See Gelber, "Market Metaphor," 749.

28. Ibid.

29. Gelber describes a number of possible thematic arrangements, as reported by women collectors, including abstract visual design and color. See Gelber, "Market Metaphor," 749–50.

30. Ibid., 752.

31. Betsky, "Enigma of the Thigh Cho," 31. On the audience's role in decoding the meaning of popular texts, see Fiske, "Television." Like Jameson I believe that popular culture contains longings that are subversive of the status quo. See Jameson, "Reification and Utopia in Mass Culture."

32. Gillis, "Memory and Identity," 9.

33. United States Postal Service, "Postal Service Announces Celebrate the Century Program." Release no. 97–095, November 5, 1997.

34. Gillis, "Memory and Identity," 14.

35. Ibid., 17. See also Thelen, "History-Making in America," and Roy Rosenzweig and David Thelen, *Presence of the Past.*

36. Doss, *Memorial Mania,* 37.

37. United States Postal Service, *Postal Bulletin,* November 6, 1997, 53.

38. See Bill McAllister, "Marciano's Postal Punch," *Washington Post,* March 6, 1998; Jeff McLaughlin, "Late Rounds for a Stamp of 'Rocky,'" *Boston Globe,* February 22, 1998.

39. The author visited George's Café in Brockton in January 2002.

40. The Government Relations review of the operations of the CSAC states that although "confidential minutes of each of Committee's meetings are maintained," they "summarize the individual stamp proposals discussed and their current status" but not "strategic policy decisions arrived at by the Committee." The report noted that "Committee members and Postal Service management officials present at the meetings tried to recall past events and decisions without the benefit of any written documentation. Although officials usually agreed, their individual interpretation of past decisions sometimes differed, which sparked debate as to what had previously been decided." Among the "significant issues that were impacted by previous policy decisions" was the issue of "recognition of specific interests, sub-groups, and units." See Deborah K. Willwhite, "Review of the Operations of the Citizens' Stamp Advisory Committee—Management Advisory Report RG-MA-99-005," July 27, 1999.

41. "Letter to Dr. Virginia Noelke, Chairperson, the Citizens' Stamp Advisory Committee," April 8, 1999, http://www.ncd.gov/newsroom/correspondence/usps_4-8-99.html (accessed July 15, 2001). In a telephone interview on September 18, 2001, Dr. Noelke denied knowledge of this petition.

42. United States Postal Service, "Postal Service Partners with the Department of Education's 'America Goes Back to School' Program." Release no. 98–106, September 24, 1998.

43. Ibid.

44. Browne, "Remembering Crispus Attucks," 176.

45. Diane White, "The Sticky Side of Stamp Choices," *Boston Globe,* February 19, 1998.

46. Rainbow Powell, "90s Stamps Take Licking," *Omaha World-Herald,* June 16, 1999.

47. Arthur Hirsch, "Stamp Out Smoking," *Baltimore Sun,* February 20, 1999.

48. Qtd. in David Brown, "Stamped Out," *Washington Post,* March 7, 1999.

49. Virginia Noelke, telephone interview with the author, September 18, 2001.

50. United States Postal Service. *Criteria. Stamp Subject Selection. (Updated 8/01),* http://www.new.usps.com/cgi-bin/uspsbv (accessed August 15, 2001).

51. Al Urbanski, "Don't Mail It In," *Promomagazine,* October 1, 1999, http://promomagazine.com/mag/marketing_dont_mail/ (accessed July 15, 2001).

52. Ibid.

53. Bill McAlister, "The Power of the Ballot," *Washington Post,* November 13, 1998.

54. Condit, "Rhetorical Limits of Polysemy," 111.

55. Barthes, *Responsibility of Forms,* 67.

56. Kirshenblatt-Gimblett, *Destination Culture,* 21.

57. Ibid., 3.

58. Barthes, *Responsibility of Forms,* 28–29.

59. Ibid., 30.

60. Sontag, "Image-World," 174.

61. Berlant, *Queen of America,* 48.

62. Sturken, *Tourists of History,* 9–10.

63. The concept of subject positioning (or interpellation) is explored in Louis Althusser, "Ideology and Ideological State Apparatuses." For a more recent application of this concept in rhetorical criticism, see Brummett and Bowers, "Subject Positions as a Site of Rhetorical Struggle."

64. Dickinson, "Memories for Sale," 18.

65. Burke, *Grammar of Motives*, 3–20.

66. For a provocative critique of the Ellis Island Museum, see Kirshenblatt-Gimblett, *Destination Culture*, 177–87.

67. For a historical perspective on the emergence of market segmentation in the post-WWII United States and its impact on politics and culture, see Cohen, *Consumers' Republic*.

68. Berlant, *Queen of America*, 48.

69. United States Postal Service, "Nancy Sinatra Joins U.S. Postal Service for Unveiling of Peace Symbol Stamp." Release no. 99–086, July 30, 1999.

70. Ono and Buescher, "*De*ciphering Pocahontas," 28.

71. Qtd. in Rhonda Cook, "Affirmative Action Lawsuit: Mayor Gets Political at MLK Stamp Event," *Atlanta Journal and Constitution*, August 29, 1999.

72. Ibid.

73. Victor Volland, "Stamp Unveiling Pales Next to Snazzy Train Exhibit," *St. Louis Post-Dispatch*, May 16, 1999.

74. I have in mind Kenneth Burke's famous definition of form as "an arousing and fulfillment of desires": "a work has form in so far as one part of it leads a reader to anticipate another part, to be gratified by the sequence" (*Counter-Statement*, 124).

75. Kirshenblatt-Gimblett, *Destination Culture*, 259.

76. Vivian, *Public Forgetting*, 81–82.

77. Barber, *Place for Us*, 20.

Chapter 2: The September 11 Digital Archive

1. See, for example, Burgess and Green, *YouTube: Online Video and Participatory Culture;* Burgess, "Hearing Ordinary Voices"; Garde-Hansen, Hoskins, and Reading, *Save as . . . ;* Howard, "Vernacular Web of Participatory Media." Portions of this chapter originally appeared in article form: Ekaterina V. Haskins, "Between Archive and Participation: Public Memory in a Digital Age," *Rhetoric Society Quarterly* 37 (2007): 401–22, reprinted by permission of Taylor and Francis (http://www.tandfonline.com).

2. Nora, "Between Memory and History," 13.

3. Ibid., 12.

4. This formulation resembles the binary of official and vernacular discourse posited by John Bodnar in *Remaking America*, but if Bodnar sees "official memory" and "vernacular memory" as contemporaneous, Nora's environments of memory are, well, history.

5. Numerous scholars have questioned the "logic of the archive" as well as the archive's privileged role as a repository of cultural knowledge. Identifying the logic of the archive as "a logic of the inscription (or deposit) and the storage of information in systematically articulated space, and of ready retrieval on the basis of that articulation," Frow points out that the model of the archive is problematic for at least three reasons: first, "[the] assumption that the past is accessible only because of its physical persistence as a trace; second, its intentionalism (its assumption that meanings taken up are the repetition of meanings laid down); third, its inability to account for forgetting other than as a fault or as decay or as a random failure of access" ("*Tout la memoire du monde*," 225, 227). Similarly questioning the presumptions of "referential plentitude" and objectivity, Biesecker calls the archive

a "scene of invention" and urges scholars to write "critical histories of the situated and strategic uses to which archives have been put" ("Of Historicity, Rhetoric," 130). In *Archive Fever* Derrida points out that "the question of a politics of the archive" is indeed central to any exploration of the subject and argues that "effective democratization can always be measured by this essential criterion: the participation in and the access to the archive, its constitution, and its interpretation" (4).

6. Boon, "Why Museums Make Me Sad," 256.

7. The narrative orientation of archives and museums is evident both in their acquisition policies and display strategies. On the archive's role in constructing a connection between past and present, see Brothman, "Pasts That Archives Keep." In a similar vein, Ball, "Telling Objects," argues that what is being collected is guided by what story the objects on display can tell.

8. Bennett, *Birth of the Museum*, 109.

9. On commemorative practices after the Civil War, see Savage, *Standing Soldiers, Kneeling Slaves.* Foote's study of how Americans have marked sites of tragic and violent events in the last three centuries also suggests that the monumental veneration of heroes and martyrs has been the preferred method of dealing with traumatic memories. See Foote, *Shadowed Ground.*

10. See Duncan, "Art Museums and the Ritual of Citizenship."

11. Taylor, *The Archive and the Repertoire*, 20.

12. Ibid. In a similar response to Nora, Winter argues that "*milieu de mémoire* are alive and well" in places such as Latin America and India, places Nora overlooks due to his "ingrained Eurocentrism" ("Sites of Memory," 315).

13. Taylor, *The Archive and the Repertoire*, 21.

14. Ibid., 19.

15. Ibid., 20.

16. Ibid.

17. Ibid., 22.

18. See Duncan, "Art Museums," 90–92.

19. Ibid., 93.

20. Ibid., 93–94. Museum studies scholar Jennifer Barrett also notes that one of the museum's important functions was "to display the public to itself, so that it was possible to see what it meant to be a model citizen" (*Museums and the Public Sphere*, 57). These arguments are strikingly similar to Michael Warner's influential thesis about publics as products of discourse that addresses them. See Warner, *Publics and Counterpublics.*

21. Kirshenblatt-Gimblett, *Destination Culture*, 138.

22. Ibid,

23. Wodiczko, *Critical Vehicles*, 49.

24. Sonja Foss, "Ambiguity as Persuasion," was one of the first rhetorical critics to address the persuasive power of the Vietnam Veterans Memorial (VVM). Carole Blair, Marsha S. Jeppeson, and Enrico Pucci, "Public Memorializing in Postmodernity," interpret the memorial as a prototype of postmodern memorializing, given its openness to multiple interpretive gestures, its sensitivity to its environment, and its interrogative, critical stance. Peter S. Hawkins sees such popular monuments as the NAMES project AIDS memorial quilt as successors to "the intimate tableaux that mourners continue to create within the

interstices of VVM" ("Naming Names," 756). Marita Sturken views the VVM as "a screen for many projections about the history of the Vietnam War and its aftermath" (*Tangled Memories*, 82). Kristin Ann Hass examines visitors' offerings left at the VVM in *Carried to the Wall.*

25. Sturken, *Tangled Memories*, 79.

26. Doss, *Memorial Mania*, 74.

27. Huyssen, *Twilight Memories*, 252.

28. See Manovich, *Language of New Media*, 27.

29. Warnick, *Critical Literacy in a Digital Era*, 107.

30. This claim must be qualified, of course. As Diana Taylor points out, "A video of a performance is not a performance, though it often comes to replace the performance as a *thing* in itself (the video is part of the archive; what it represents is part of the repertoire)" (*Archive and the Repertoire*, 20).

31. Warnick, "Looking to the Future," 330–31.

32. Landow, "Hypertext as Collage-Writing," 158.

33. Scholars of digital media often describe collective authorship online in terms of the erosion of the boundary between producers and users. Axel Bruns, for example, coined the term *produsage* to describe precisely this category of user-turned-producer. Bruns distinguishes produsage from Alvin Toffler's similar-sounding hybrid term *prosumption*, the latter envisioning "not a shifting of the balance between producers and consumers, but merely the development of even more advanced consumption skills by consumers" (*Blogs, Wikipedia, Second Life, and Beyond*, 11).

34. Foot, Warnick, and Schneider, "Web-Based Memorializing." On the rhetorical construction of web memorials by individual, rather than institutional, actors, see Hess, "In Digital Remembrance." For a provocative—if somewhat eccentric—reflection on the potential of electronic memorializing to deepen democratic self-knowledge, see Ulmer, *Electronic Monuments*.

35. Gurak, *Cyberliteracy*, 44.

36. In *Language of New Media*, Manovich maintains that "to call computer media 'interactive' is meaningless—it simply means stating the most basic fact about computers" (55). He further cautions, "when we use the concept 'interactive media' exclusively in relation to computer-based media, there is the danger that we will interpret 'interaction' literally, equating it with physical interaction between a user and a media object (pressing a button, choosing a link, moving the body), at the expense of psychological interaction. The psychological processes of filling-in, hypothesis formation, recall, and identification, which are required for us to comprehend any text or image at all, are mistakenly identified with an objectively existing structure of interactive links" (57). Upon reviewing recent literature on "interactivity" and synthesizing the various definitions of it, Spiro Kiousis, "Interactivity," suggests that interactivity is both a media and psychological factor that varies across communication technologies, communication contexts, and people's perceptions.

37. Benkler, *Wealth of Networks*, 293. On the culture of collaboration and self-reflexivity among Wikipedia writers and editors, see Reagle, *Good Faith Collaboration*.

38. Dewey, "Creative Democracy," 22.

39. Gillis, "Memory and Identity."

40. Huyssen, *Twilight Memories*, 253.

41. Gillis, "Memory and Identity," 15.

42. At the same time, historians and archivists are concerned that digital data in particular lacks durability. As Daniel Cohen and Roy Rosenzweig point out, "we are rapidly losing the digital present that is being created because no one has worked out a means of preserving it" (*Digital History*, 9–10). On the "fragility of digital assets," see van House and Churchill, "Technologies of Memory."

43. Vivian, *Public Forgetting*, 59. Unlike many public memory scholars, Vivian calls for a reconsideration of forgetting as an unequivocally negative phenomenon. He theorizes "public forgetting" as a "mode of public judgment whereby communities articulate in speech, language, or other symbolic forms the advent of a radically new set of attitudes, beliefs, or customs concerning the meaning of their own past" (171). Still he is careful to distinguish the more salutary modes of public forgetting—like those exemplified by Abraham Lincoln's rhetoric of reconciliation in the Gettysburg Address and his second inaugural speech—from the more pernicious forms that, like the Third Reich's "violently manipulated regime of memory," lead to "recourse to violence, suspension of laws and rights, and other . . . oppressive measures" (176). Vivian argues that "archival abundance" is one of several necessary conditions for productive forms of forgetting: "When accompanied by sufficient (if not abundant) remembrance and documentation, public forgetting stirs a community to remember its past anew" (178).

44. Manovich, *Language of New Media*, 41.

45. See, for example, Miller and Shepherd, "Blogging as Social Action."

46. Blood, "Weblogs."

47. Gillis, "Memory and Identity," 17–18.

48. See, for example, Selnow, *Electronic Whistle-Stops* and Gronbeck, "Citizen Voices in Cyberpolitical Culture." Noting "passivity" (the downside of "interactivity") as one of the major challenges to doing history online, Cohen and Rosenzweig paraphrase literary critic Harold Bloom, who argues that "whereas linear fiction allows us to experience more by granting us access to the lives and thoughts of those different from ourselves, interactivity only permits us to experience more of ourselves" (*Digital History* 12).

49. Pariser, *Filter Bubble*.

50. Gillmor, *We the Media*, x.

51. Berman, "City Rises," 67.

52. Taylor, *The Archive and the Repertoire*, 252.

53. Halloran, "Text and Performance in a Historical Pageant," 5.

54. On the removal of spontaneous shrines from New York City public spaces, see Jennifer Jensen, "Parks Removes Union Sq. Memorial, Fences off Statue," *Villager*, October 10, 2001.

55. "About the Archive," September 11 Digital Archive, http://old.911digitalarchive.org/about/ (accessed August 15, 2013).

56. Livingstone and Beardsley, "Poetics and Politics of Hispanic Art," 105.

57. Ferguson, "Exhibition Rhetorics," 175.

58. Qtd. in Haskins and DeRose, "Memory, Visibility, and Public Space," 384. On the role of museums and galleries in collecting and displaying ephemeral artifacts of 9/11, see Kirshenblatt-Gimblett, "Kodak Moments, Flashbulb Memories."

59. Baxandall, "Exhibiting Intention," 39.

60. "About the Archive."

61. "Contributor Information." September 11 Digital Archive, http://old.911digitalarchive.org/about/faq.html#q1 (accessed August 15, 2013).

62. "Contributor Information," http://old.911digitalarchive.org/about/faq.html#q2 (accessed August 15, 2013).

63. David Simpson argues in *9/11: The Culture of Commemoration* that the victims of September 11, 2001, "have been staged as the victims of a war, a war against America, which in turn has authorized a reactive war on what is called terror. Their deaths are paraded to legitimate more deaths elsewhere—the deaths of others as innocent as themselves" (47).

64. According to Cohen and Rosenzweig, *Digital History,* 185.

65. See Brien and Brown, "September 11 Digital Archive."

66. Lisa Pichoff, Story #11549, September 11 Digital Archive, June 24, 2005, http://911digitalarchive.org/stories/details/11549.

67. Niles Oien, Story #11163, September 11 Digital Archive, November 17, 2004, http://911digitalarchive.org/stories/details/11163.

68. Richard Hiley, Story #10532, September 11 Digital Archive, April 11, 2004, http://911digitalarchive.org/stories/details/10532.

69. Elizabeth Jaeger, Story #8483, September 11 Digital Archive, October 17, 2002, http://911digitalarchive.org/stories/details/8483.

70. David Vogler, Image #2691, September 11 Digital Archive, November 1, 2004, http://911digitalarchive.org/images/details/2691.

71. Jim Occi, Image #1760, September 11 Digital Archive, November 14, 2002, http://911digitalarchive.org/images/details/1760.

72. G. N. Miller, Image #2757, September 11 Digital Archive, June 1, 2005, http://911digitalarchive.org/images/details/2757.

73. Paul Selders, Image #1742, September 11 Digital Archive, November 3, 2002, http://911digitalarchive.org/images/details/1742.

74. Anonymous, Image #2603, September 11 Digital Archive, September 7, 2004, http://911digitalarchive.org/images/details/2603.

75. Vida Dominguez, Image #2673, September 11 Digital Archive, October 12, 2004, http://911digitalarchive.org/images/details/2673.

76. Foote, *Shadowed Ground,* 344.

77. Ibid., 343.

78. Because of this, Doss calls the archive's curatorial approach "critically vacuous: by refusing the work of interpretation it fails to interrogate how and why (and which) experiences and feelings constitute self and national identity" (*Memorial Mania,* 73–74).

79. "Moving Images; Digital Animations," September 11 Digital Archive, http://old.911digitalarchive.org/collections/animations_and_creations (accessed August 15, 2013).

80. "Frequently Asked Questions," September 11 Digital Archive, http://old.911digitalarchive.org/about/faq.html#q11 (accessed August 15, 2013).

81. This warning is part of the annotation for an animation titled "A bin Laden Christmas," an animation that juxtaposes the familiar "'Twas the Night before Christmas" soundtrack with a depiction of an Orientalized character, Osama, who is awaiting Santa's arrival. Instead of Santa, however, he is visited by a cigar-chewing assassin dressed in a Santa suit and lugging a bagful of explosives. Once the assassin is finished with his

job, the soundtrack changes to the tune of Queen's "Another One Bites the Dust" (http://old.911digitalarchive.org/collections/animations_and_creations; accessed August 15, 2013).

82. Steve Golding, "Creator's Statement," September 11 Digital Archive, February 20, 2002. Retrieved from http://old.911digitalarchive.org/moving/goldingstatement.html (accessed August 15, 2013).

83. Mandel, "To Claim the Mundane."

84. See "America Attacked 911," http://attacked911.tripod.com (accessed August 1, 2006).

85. Stephen Brien and Joshua Brown admit that submissions to the archive "tended to be skewed toward particular groups and individuals who were largely white and middle class," so the featured items represent the fruits of "targeted outreach to particular ethnic and national communities" ("September 11 Digital Archives," 105).

86. Ibid., 108.

87. Although a link to it is still displayed on the archive's original home page, the exhibit cannot be viewed. This problem illustrates how technological obsolescence can prevent the permanent preservation of "born digital" materials. According to Sharon Leon, director of public projects at the Roy Rosenzweig Center for History and New Media, "the Google Maps API that enabled the anniversary interactive map has changed and that change resulted in deprecated code" (pers. e-mail to the author, December 2, 2013).

88. Zelizer, "Voice of the Visual in Memory."

89. Tom Scheinfeldt, "Memories: September 11 Digital Archive," History News Network, September 9, 2002, http://hnn.us/articles/959html.

90. Kirshenblatt-Gimblett, "Kodak Moments, Flashbulb Memories," 26.

91. Tom Scheinfeldt, former managing director at the Center for History and New Media at George Mason University, telephone interview with the author, October 20, 2011.

Chapter 3: Carnival after Katrina

1. For example, CNN anchor Anderson Cooper lost his composure on September 1, 2005, while interviewing Louisiana state senator Mary Landrieu when she expressed gratitude to President Bush for his handling of the disaster. A clip of this interview is available at http://www.youtube.com/watch?v=eVPlcY4YA-0&feature=related (accessed October 15, 2010). Even conservative journalists were dismayed at the way stranded New Orleans residents were treated by local authorities. Fox News television anchorman Shepard Smith was outraged by the sheriff-led vigilante blockade of the Crescent City Connection bridge that connected New Orleans to the unflooded side of the river. New Orleans residents and out-of-town visitors stranded in the city by Katrina were turned away at gunpoint. See David Bauder, "Coverage of Katrina Bolsters Standing of Fox's Shepard Smith," *Seattle Times*, September 26, 2005, http://seattletimes.nwsource.com/html/nationworld/2002520970_katshep26.html.

2. See McKernan and Mulcahy, "Hurricane Katrina."

3. Although *Mardi Gras* (Fat Tuesday) is a term that describes the last day before Ash Wednesday (the beginning of Lent) and as such marks the end of the carnival season, the term has often been used interchangeably with *carnival*.

4. Taylor, *The Archive and the Repertoire*, 22.

5. Berlant, *Cruel Optimism*, 230.

6. Ibid., 231.

7. Mitchell, *All on a Mardi Gras Day*, 36.

8. Gill, *Lords of Misrule*, 46–47.

9. The growing distance between performers and spectators evident in late nineteenth-century Mardi Gras parades was part of a national trend—the pageantry that disciplined the crowds by making them into spectators (and sometimes participants) of organized parades and tableaux. See Glassberg, *American Historical Pageantry*, chap. 1.

10. See Gill, *Lords of Misrule*, esp. chaps. 4–6.

11. Taylor, *The Archive and the Repertoire*, 22.

12. Occasionally Mardi Gras floats (especially those of Rex) were exported to other U.S. cities. On the transformation of pageants into a commodity form, see Glassberg, *American Historical Pageantry*, and Mitchell, *All on a Mardi Gras Day*.

13. Stanonis, *Creating the Big Easy*, 187.

14. For example the two "businessmen" krewes formed in the 1930s, Hermes and Mid-City, aspired to democratize the festivity by sponsoring tourist-oriented balls. To advertise the celebration in other U.S. locales, in 1939 Hermes launched the first traveling carnival exhibition. See Stanonis, *Creating the Big Easy*, 183.

15. Superkrewes such as Bacchus, Endymion, and Orpheus often recruited business leaders from Houston, Dallas, and Los Angeles. Gotham quotes one of the Bacchus leaders, who summarized the superkrewe's raison d'être as follows: "Our idea was that Mardi Gras could draw in people with wealth and money that could afford the good restaurants, the hotels and go back and sing praises for New Orleans" (*Authentic New Orleans*, 176). According to Souther, thanks to the efforts of superkrewes, by the 1970s carnival was recast "as a series of discrete, well-planned attractions appearing in quick succession, with the object of wedding Carnival more firmly to the tourism industry" (*New Orleans on Parade*, 148).

16. Gotham, *Authentic New Orleans*, 178.

17. Several walking clubs take to the streets during Mardi Gras, from the oldest, Jefferson City Buzzards (1890), to the most recently formed, the Krewe of Barkus (1993), which includes costumed canines and their owners. Walking clubs are spotlighted in a documentary, *Cutting Loose* (1996), directed by Susan Todd and Andrew Young.

18. On social aid and pleasure clubs and second lines, see Dinerstein, "Second Lining Post Katrina."

19. Sources on the Zulu krewe history include the krewe's website, http://www.kreweofzulu.com/history (accessed October 15, 2010); Gill, *Lords of Misrule*; Mitchell, *All on a Mardi Gras Day*, and a documentary, *All on a Mardi Gras Day*, directed by Royce Osborn (2008).

20. Mitchell, *All on a Mardi Gras Day*, 151.

21. Stanonis, *Creating the Big Easy*, 225.

22. On the controversy over Zulu in the 1960s, see Souther, *New Orleans on Parade*, 135–41.

23. See the club's website: http://www.kreweofzulu.com/history.

24. Souther, *New Orleans on Parade*, 141.

25. On Mardi Gras Indians, see Lipsitz, *Time Passages*, and Harrison-Nelson and Woods, "Upholding Community Traditions."

26. Lipsitz, *Time Passages*, 238.

27. The ritual of Mardi Gras Indians involves both the members of the tribe's hierarchy and the bystanders. On the Mardi Gras Indian singing ritual, see VanSpanckeren, "Mardi Gras Indian Song Cycle."

28. On constitutive rhetoric see Charland, "Constitutive Rhetoric."

29. Chief Montana's funeral was covered locally and nationally. See Katy Reckdahl, "A Colorful Farewell for the Chief of Chiefs," *New York Times,* July 11, 2005, http://www.nytimes.com/2005/07/11/national/11tootie.html.

30. Lipsitz, "Learning from New Orleans."

31. See Mitchell, *All on a Mardi Gras Day*, for a discussion of the influence of the Zulu club and second lines on Louis Armstrong.

32. Qtd. in Kirshenblatt-Gimblett, *Destination Culture*, 166.

33. Berlant, *Cruel Optimism*, 230.

34. For an interactive map of the flooding of New Orleans and adjacent areas, see http://www.nola.com/katrina/graphics/flashflood.swf (accessed October 1, 2010).

35. See esp. Christopher Cooper, "In Katrina's Wake—Old-Line Families Escape Worst of Flood and Plot Future." *Wall Street Journal,* September 8, 2005.

36. On representations of New Orleans and Mardi Gras in literature, popular culture, and commercial advertisement, see Stanonis, *Creating the Big Easy,* and "Through a Purple (Green and Gold) Haze."

37. On the transformation of New Orleans into a tourist destination, see Gotham, *Authentic New Orleans,* and Souther, *New Orleans on Parade.*

38. Thomas Ruys Smith, "Mardi Gras among the Ruins," *New Statesman,* February 20, 2006, 20.

39. Lynne Jensen, "Carnival Finally Provides a Reason to Party," *New Orleans Times-Picayune,* February 18, 2006.

40. McNulty, *Season of Night*, 136.

41. See, for example, Michael Depp, "Mardi Gras Needed for New Orleans' Mental Health," *All Things Considered,* National Public Radio, January 6, 2006. For a resident's story of depression in the wake of Katrina, see Rose, *1 Dead in Attic.*

42. Depp, "Mardi Gras Needed."

43. Mitchell, "Carnival and Katrina," 794.

44. Souther, *New Orleans on Parade*, 151.

45. In her study of tourism and heritage industries, Kirshenblatt-Gimblett observes: "To compete for tourists, a location must become a destination. To compete with each other, destinations must be distinguishable, which is why the tourism industry requires the production of difference" (*Destination Culture*, 152).

46. Qtd. in Brian Thevenot, "Their Mardi Gras . . . Our Mardi Gras," *New Orleans Times-Picayune,* February 19, 2006.

47. Ibid.

48. According to Souther, the influx of "undesirables" into the city during Mardi Gras in the early 1970s prompted the Greater New Orleans Tourist and Convention Commission to abandon its marketing slogan, "The Greatest Free Show on Earth." In its place the commission published a new pamphlet, "The Real Mardi Gras," in which they admonished visitors to "come as a paying guest as you would to any other great city or event" (*New Orleans on Parade,* 151).

49. McNulty, *Season of Night,* 138.

50. Souther, *New Orleans on Parade,* 232.

51. Codrescu, "New Orleans," 1098.

52. In *Authentic New Orleans* Gotham contends that it is misleading to talk about an "'authentic place' corrupted by tourism"; instead he proposes to examine "how tourism can be a mechanism for creating and maintaining place character, including articulating local identities and generating place-specific forms of collective action" (12). He nevertheless admits that the tourism industry tends "to define all ethnic and cultural differences as equal, horizontal, and plural" and thus obscures "the continuing significance of class and race" (208).

53. Abrahams et al., *Blues for New Orleans,* 2.

54. Ibid.

55. Souther, *New Orleans on Parade,* 6.

56. Burke, *Attitudes toward History,* 171; emphasis in the original.

57. McNulty, *Season of Night,* 147.

58. For descriptions of satire directed at FEMA and Brown, see Mitchell, "Carnival and Katrina."

59. A photograph of this float on parade taken by New Orleans author Billy Sothern can be viewed at "Mardi Gras 2006 Highlights: Installation Statues," *Nola Nik* (blog), February 25, 2006, http://nolanik.blogspot.com/2006/02/mardi-gras-2006-highlights.html.

60. In her book on "the extraordinary communities that arise in disaster," cultural critic Rebecca Solnit pointed out how mainstream media coverage of the post-hurricane chaos amplified the "white panic" by circulating rumors of savagery in the flooded metropolis. See esp. the chapter "What Difference Would It Make?" in *Paradise Built in Hell.*

61. Bakhtin, *Rabelais and His World,* 394.

62. Ibid., 378.

63. Ibid., 395.

64. "Krewe du Vieux Says 'C'est Levee.'" *Le Monde de Merde,* February 11, 2006. Issues of *Le Monde de Merde* and photographs of past parades are available on the krewe's website: http://www.kreweduvieux.org (accessed October 1, 2010).

65. "K.A.O.S. Rules FEMA," *Monde de Merde,* February 11, 2006.

66. "T.O.K.I.N.'s Wet Dream," *Monde de Merde,* February 11, 2006.

67. On the ameliorative and regenerative power of laughter, see especially Bakhtin, *Rabelais and His World.*

68. Berlant, *Cruel Optimism,* 227.

69. Joseph Boyden, "Turns out Life Isn't a Carnival," *Maclean's,* March 13, 2006.

70. On the debate among Zulu members over participation in Mardi Gras, see Carol Flake Chapman, "Black Out," *New Republic,* February 27, 2006, 16–17.

71. A video of the Zulu parade and postparade second line is available on YouTube: http://www.youtube.com/watch?v=vwxjM32tpwU (accessed August 1, 2013).

72. Jon Pareles, "Mardi Gras Dawns with Some Traditions in Jeopardy," *New York Times,* February 28, 2006.

73. Bruce Eggler, "Indians to Uphold Carnival Tradition," *New Orleans Times-Picayune,* October 21, 2005.

74. Maria Montoya, “Tribal Revival,” *New Orleans Times-Picayune,* February 27, 2006.

75. Michele Norris, “‘Big Chiefs’ Continue Mardi Gras Indian Tradition,” *All Things Considered,* National Public Radio February 28, 2006.

76. Montoya, “Tribal Revival.”

77. McNulty, *Season of Night*, 47–48.

78. Berlant, *Cruel Optimism,* 238.

79. “Editorial—This Is Why,” *New Orleans Times-Picayune,* February 28, 2006.

80. Taylor, *The Archive and the Repertoire,* 20–21.

81. Landsberg, *Prosthetic Memory.*

82. Karen Grigsby Bates, “The Hidden Mardi Gras,” *Day to Day,* National Public Radio, February 28, 2006, http://www.npr.org/templates/story/story.php?storyId=5237454.

83. “Letters: New Orleans, Red Cross, and Pianist Review.” *All Things Considered,* National Public Radio, March 2, 2006.

84. Robert Siegel, “New Orleans Neighborhood Awaits Key Decisions,” *All Things Considered,* National Public Radio, January 20, 2006.

85. On the NPR “listener base,” see McCauley, “Leveraging the NPR Brand.”

86. Siegel, “New Orleans Neighborhood.”

87. On the rhetoric and politics of “frontier mythology,” see Rushing, “Rhetoric of the American Western Myth.”

88. *New Orleans,* dir. Stephen Ives, *American Experience,* PBS, February 11, 2007.

89. Kahana, *Intelligence Work*, 2.

90. Neil Genzlinger, “City of Feel-Good Music and Feel-Bad History,” *New York Times,* February 12, 2007.

91. Warner, *Publics and Counterpublics.*

92. Solnit, *Paradise Built in Hell*, 268.

93. Alan Sepinwall, “Interview: ‘Treme’ Co-creator David Simon Post-mortems Season One: On Music, Anger and Katrina,” *What's Alan Watching? Inside Television with Alan Sepinwall,* June 20, 2010, http://www.hitfix.com/blogs/whats-alan-watching/posts/interview-treme-co-creator-david-simon-post-mortems-season-one#cKegmUwrTSKooDKF.99.

94. Despite some notable scholarly works that associate tourists with the attitudes of superficiality and detachment (such as MacCannell's *Tourist* and Sturken's *Tourists of History*), there is plenty of evidence to suggest that tourism can be a transformative civic experience. For an astute analysis of post-Katrina tours in New Orleans, see Pezzullo, “Tourists and/as Disasters” and “‘This Is the Only Tour That Sells.’”

95. Nancy Franklin, “After the Flood: The Creator of ‘The Wire’ in New Orleans,” *New Yorker,* April 12, 2010.

96. Dave Walker, “‘Treme’ Explained: ‘All on a Mardi Gras Day,’” NOLA.com, June 6, 2010, http://www.nola.com/tremehbo/index.ssf/2010/06/treme_explained_all_on_a_mardi.html.

97. David Simon and Clarke Peters, interviewed by Steve Inskeep, *Morning Edition,* National Public Radio, April 9, 2010.

98. Codrescu and Rowell, “Andrei Codrescu with Charles Henry Rowell,” 1113.

Chapter 4: Eyes Wide Open

1. Since the Persian Gulf War (1991), the U.S. news media were banned from photographing flag-draped caskets of U.S. soldiers. The Obama administration lifted the ban in

February 2009. Portions of this chapter were previously published in article form: Ekaterina V. Haskins, "Ephemeral Visibility and the Art of Mourning: Eyes Wide Open Traveling Exhibit." In *Rhetoric, Remembrance, and Visual Form: Sighting Memory*, edited by Bradford Vivian and Anne Demo, 89–112. New York: Routledge, 2011. Reprinted by permission of Taylor and Francis Group LLC Books.

2. Three temporary memorials attracted national attention during the years of the war in Iraq: Arlington West, "a cemetery in the sand" erected every weekend by Veterans for Peace and local volunteers on the beaches of Southern California; a memorial on a hillside bordering a major highway in Lafayette, California; and a touring memorial, *Eyes Wide Open*, the subject of this chapter. Erika Doss briefly addresses all three in her *Memorial Mania*. Michael Rancourt discusses Arlington West in his Ph.D. dissertation, "Remembering the Iraq War."

3. As of August 2013, the AFSC web page states: "Eyes Wide Open continues to tell the story of the human cost of war in 46 states with boots representing US deaths in both Iraq and Afghanistan, and shoes representing Iraqi and Afghan civilians" (www.afsc.org/campaign/eyes-wide-open; accessed August 15, 2013).

4. Doss, *Memorial Mania*, 237–8.

5. Blair, "Civil Rights/Civil Sites," 6–9.

6. Ibid., 14.

7. Young, *Texture of Memory*, xii–xiii.

8. Blair and Michel, "Commemorating in the Theme Park Zone," 68.

9. See Burke, *Permanence and Change* and *Attitudes toward History*; Demo, "Guerrilla Girls' Comic Politics of Subversion."

10. On the symbolism of the Gettysburg National Cemetery, see especially Wills, *Lincoln at Gettysburg*.

11. On Gettysburg's connection to the Victorian "culture of death," see ibid., 63–89.

12. Woolson, "Mrs. Edward Pinckney."

13. *National Cemetery Walking Tour*, Gettysburg National Military Park, Pennsylvania, National Park Service, U.S. Department of Interior, n.d.

14. Doss, *Memorial Mania*, 250–51.

15. Hawkins, "Naming Names," 757.

16. Sturken, *Tangled Memories*, 184.

17. Ibid., 189.

18. Ibid., 196.

19. Ibid., 195.

20. Qtd. in ibid., 216.

21. Vivian, "Neoliberal Epideictic," 16.

22. Mary Zerkel, telephone interview with author, July 17, 2008.

23. Ibid.

24. Mary Ellen McNish, "About the Exhibit," http://www.afsc.org/eyes/ (accessed July 15, 2009). "Many times when the exhibit was up," recalls Mary Zerkel, "casualties would be announced on the Department of Defense website and we would have to add boots to the exhibit. During the times of the heaviest casualties, we would have a board with moveable numbers, so that we could change the tally of casualties several times over the course of a few hours and announce the addition of another pair of boots to the crowd" (personal correspondence with the author, February 1, 2010).

25. In late 2006 the AFSC listed the number of Iraqi casualties at 655,000. The following quote on the website explains this estimate: "A study by Johns Hopkins University and Al Mustansiriya University researchers finds that between 420,000 and 790,000 Iraqis have died as a result of war and political violence since the beginning of the US invasion in March 2003. It was published in *The Lancet* medical journal on October 11, 2006" (http://www.afsc.org/eyes/ht/display/ContentDetails/i/5098; accessed July 15, 2009).

26. An interactive page, "Dreams and Nightmares: An Exhibit on Life and Death in Iraq," is available on the AFSC website: http://tools.afsc.org/quicktime/eyes-exhibit/exhibit-inside-qt.htm (accessed July 15, 2009). This component of *Eyes Wide Open* was created in collaboration with Peaceful Tomorrows, an organization founded by family members of those killed as a result of the terrorist attacks on September 11, 2001.

27. Steven Winn, "Memorials Seek to Make Public Grief Personal," *San Francisco Chronicle,* March 31, 2005.

28. For a detailed examination of objects left by visitors at the Vietnam Veterans Memorial, see esp. Hass, *Carried to the Wall.*

29. This contribution to the exhibit is described by Lindsey Millar, "The Shoes of the Soldiers: Iraq Exhibit at Statehouse Overwhelms," *Arkansas Times,* February 2, 2005.

30. Burke, *Attitudes toward History*, 171.

31. Cindy Fowler, "Eyes Wide Open, Every Day: Bringing Home the Human Cost of War," *Friends Committee on Legislation Newsletter,* February 2005, 1–2.

32. "Exhibition Report: The First Year," http://www.afsc.org/eyes/ (accessed July 15, 2009). Most state exhibits were also augmented by boots and shoes representing U.S. military and civilian casualties in Afghanistan. In October 2009, to mark the eighth anniversary of the war in Afghanistan, AFSC staged a display of more than eight hundred boots in Washington, D.C., in front of the White House.

33. Kari Lydersen, "War Costing $720 Million Each Day, Group Says," *Washington Post,* September 22, 2007.

34. Nora, "Between Memory and History."

35. Stern, *Remembering Pinochet's Chile*, 120.

36. Jeannette Raymond, "Cost of War and EWO: A Solemn Memorial among Chaos or [*sic*] RNC," October 2008, http://www.afsc.org/resource/eyes-wide-open-news.

37. Sarah Gill, "Cost of War and EWO Colorado at DNC," October 2008, http://www.afsc.org/resource/eyes-wide-open-news.

38. Zerkel, telephone interview with author.

39. Stephanie M. Peters, "10,000 in Boston Rally against War—Part of Events Held Nationwide," *Boston Globe* October 28, 2007.

40. Demorris A. Lee, "Boots, Shoes to Stand for War's Fallen," *St. Petersburg (Fla.) Times,* May 25, 2008.

41. "Eyes Wide Open Organizing Toolkit," http://www.afsc.org/eyes/ (accessed July 15, 2009).

42. Benson, "Rhetoric as a Way of Being," 320.

43. "Helena, Montana, 19–20, 2006," August 5, 2006, http://peace.chicago.blogspot.com.

44. Elaine Brower, "Prelude to the Debate: AFSC 'Eyes Wide Open' Exhibited on Hofstra Campus," *Next Left Notes,* October 16, 2008, http://antiauthoritarian.net/NLN/?p=494.

45. Elaine Brower, telephone interview with the author, August 4, 2009.

46. Jim Haber, "EWO Work Expands to Nevada," October 2008, http://www.afsc.org/resource/eyes-wide-open-news.

47. Gill, "Cost of War and EWO Colorado at DNC."

48. Brower, telephone interview.

49. Brower, "Prelude to the Debate."

50. Thomas Good, "Eyes Wide Open—at the National Night Out against Crime," *Next Left Notes,* August 9, 2007, http://antiauthoritarian.net/NLN/index.php?s=eyes+wide+open. The story was confirmed by Elaine Brower in a telephone interview, August 4, 2009.

51. Zagacki and Gallagher, "Rhetoric and Materiality," 172.

52. On "image events" see DeLuca, *Image Politics,* and DeLuca and Peeples, "From Public Sphere to Public Screen."

53. Raymond, "Cost of War and EWO."

54. Elaine Brower, telephone interview.

55. "See Where We've Been," http://www.afsc.org/eyes/ht/display/ContentDetails/i/5136 (accessed July 15, 2009).

56. As historians Daniel Cohen and Roy Rosenzweig observe, "surprisingly few digital historians have thought about ensuring that what has been created today in digital formats will survive into the future. Digital materials are notoriously fragile and require special attention to withstand changing technologies and user demands" (*Digital History,* 16).

57. Shirky, *Here Comes Everybody,* 55.

58. "Maker Monologue (Eyes Wide Open and 'Counting the Cost')," *Mike's Weblog about Computing, Politics, and Faith (a Progressive View),* March 12, 2005, http://makimo.net/weblog/heeeres-yhwh.

59. Thomas Good, "Arlington New York State Returns on Memorial Day Weekend," *Next Left Notes,* May 27, 2009, http://antiauthoritarian.net/NLN/index.php?s=arlington+new+york+state.

60. "The Polynational War Memorial," Polynational War Memorial, http://www.war-memorial.net/index.asp (accessed July 15, 2009).

61. Jon Brunberg, "Cross-National Commemoration in the Iraq War," Polynational War Memorial, December 28, 2004, http://www.war-memorial.net/news_details.asp?ID=34.

62. "Eyes Wide Open Anti-War Display," http://zombietime.com/eyes_wide_open (accessed July 15, 2009).

63. "The Corporal's Boots," prod. Patricia Boiko, YouTube video, 7:35. Posted by "dthornto3," October 24, 2006, http://www.youtube.com/watch?v=NolEYfzjoVo (accessed July 27, 2009).

64. On strategic ambiguity, see Ceccarelli, "Polysemy."

65. "Blues: Robert Cray—Twenty," dir. Sue Turner-Cray, YouTube video, 7:52. Posted by Andy Coon, February 9, 2006, http://www.youtube.com/watch?v=hY4JlbC6wQE (accessed July 27, 2009).

66. John Murphy, "Robert Cray—Twenty (Sanctuary)," MusicOMH, 23 May 2005 http://www.musicomh.com/reviews/albums/robert-cray-twenty.

67. For an account of the AFSC involvement in the shooting of the video, see the American Friends Service Committee website, "New Music Video Features 'Eyes Wide Open' Boots," http://www.afsc.org/video/robert-cray-twenty (accessed July 27, 2009).

68. Delgado was honorably discharged in April 2004. He published a biography, *The Sutras of Abu Ghraib,* and was featured along with several other veterans in the

documentary *Soldiers of Conscience,* directed by Catherine Ryan and Gary Weimberg, which was broadcast on the *POV* series on PBS on October 16, 2008 (http://www.pbs.org/pov/soldiersofconscience; accessed July 27, 2009).

69. As this book's chapter 3 discusses, while the Internet promotes a plurality of points of view on any given subject, it can also abet political insularity and fragmentation.

Chapter 5: Toward a Participatory Memory Culture

1. Doss, *Memorial Mania,* 37.

2. Blair and Michel, "AIDS Memorial Quilt," 32.

3. Rosenzweig and Thelen, *Presence of the Past,* 188.

4. Ibid., 195.

5. Bodnar, *Remaking America,* 13–14.

6. Rosenzweig and Thelen, *Presence of the Past,* 188. See also Scott, "Evidence of Experience."

7. Influenced by Freud's conceptualization of melancholia as unsuccessful mourning, several scholars have noted the melancholic quality of the repetitive consumption of traumatic images of 9/11. In this case melancholia is a collective, not individual, affliction. See especially Gunn, "Mourning Speech," and Biesecker, "No Time for Mourning."

8. Barber, *Place for Us,* 41. On neoliberalism, see esp. Harvey, *A Brief History of Neoliberalism.*

9. Dewey, "Creative Democracy," 23.

10. Ibid., 22.

Bibliography

Abrahams, Roger D., Nick Spitzer, John F. Szwed, and Robert Farris Thompson. *Blues for New Orleans: Mardi Gras and America's Creole Soul.* Philadelphia: University of Pennsylvania Press, 2006.

Allen, Danielle S. *Talking to Strangers: Anxieties of Citizenship since Brown v. Board of Education.* Chicago: University of Chicago Press, 2004.

Althusser, Louis. "Ideology and Ideological State Apparatuses (Notes towards an Investigation)." In *Lenin and Philosophy and Other Essays,* edited by Ben Brewster, 127–86. New York: Monthly Review Press, 1971.

Anderson, Benedict R. *Imagined Communities: Reflections on the Origin and Spread of Nationalism.* Rev. and extended ed. London & New York: Verso, 1991.

Anderson, Steve. "History TV and Popular Memory." In *Television Histories: Shaping Collective Memory in the Media Age,* edited by Gary R. Edgerton and Peter C. Rollins, 19–36. Lexington: University Press of Kentucky, 2001.

Antczak, Frederick J. *Thought and Character: The Rhetoric of Democratic Education.* Ames: Iowa State University Press, 1985.

Arendt, Hannah. *The Human Condition.* Chicago: University of Chicago Press, 1958.

Asen, Robert. "A Discourse Theory of Citizenship." *Quarterly Journal of Speech* 90 (2004): 189–211.

Bakhtin, Mikhail M. *Rabelais and His World.* Translated by Hélèn Iswolsky. Bloomington: Indiana University Press, 1984.

Ball, Mieke. "Telling Objects: A Narrative Perspective on Collecting." In *The Cultures of Collecting,* edited by John Elsner and Roger Cardinal, 97–115. Cambridge, Mass.: Harvard University Press, 1994.

Balthrop, V. William, Carole Blair, and Neil Michel. "The Presence of the Present: Hijacking the 'Good War'?" *Western Journal of Communication* 74 (2010): 170–207.

Barber, Benjamin R. *A Place for Us: How to Make Society Civil and Democracy Strong.* New York: Hill & Wang, 1998.

Barrett, Jennifer. *Museums and the Public Sphere.* Chichester, UK: Wiley-Blackwell, 2010.

Barthes, Roland. *The Responsibility of Forms: Critical Essays on Music, Art, and Representation.* New York: Hill & Wang, 1985.

Baudrillard, Jean. *Pour une Critique de L'Economie Politique du Signe.* Paris: Gallimard, 1990.

———. *Simulations.* Translated by Paul Foss, Paul Patton, and Philip Beitchman. New York: Semiotext(e), 1983.

Baxandall, Michael. "Exhibiting Intention." In *Exhibiting Cultures: The Poetics and Politics of Museum Display,* edited by Ivan Karp and Steven D. Lavine, 33–41. Washington, D.C.: Smithsonian Institution Press, 1991.

Bellah, Robert N. "Civil Religion in America." *Daedalus* 96 (1967): 1–21.

———. *The Broken Covenant: American Civil Religion in Time of Trial.* 2nd ed. Chicago: University of Chicago Press, 1992.

Benkler, Yochai. *The Wealth of Networks: How Social Production Transforms Markets and Freedom.* New Haven: Yale University Press, 2006.

Bennett, Jeffrey A. "A Stitch in Time: Public Emotionality and the Repertoire of Citizenship." In *Remembering the AIDS Quilt,* edited by Charles E. Morris III, 133–58. East Lansing: Michigan State University Press, 2010.

Bennett, Tony. *The Birth of the Museum: History, Theory, Politics.* London: Routledge, 1995.

Benson, Thomas W. "Rhetoric as a Way of Being." In *American Rhetoric: Context and Criticism,* edited by Thomas W. Benson, 293–322. Carbondale: Southern Illinois University Press, 1989.

Berlant, Lauren. "Citizenship." In *Keywords for American Cultural Studies,* edited by Bruce Burgett and Glenn Hendler, 37–42. New York: New York University Press, 2007.

———. *Cruel Optimism.* Durham, N.C.: Duke University Press, 2011.

———. *The Queen of America Goes to Washington City: Essays on Sex and Citizenship.* Durham, N.C.: Duke University Press, 1997.

Berman, Marshall. "The City Rises: Rebuilding Meaning after 9/11." *Dissent,* Summer 2003, 67–70.

Betsky, Aaron. "The Enigma of the Thigh Cho: Icons as Magnets of Meaning." In *Icons: Magnets of Meaning,* edited by Aaron Betsky, 20–51. San Francisco: San Francisco Museum of Modern Art, 1997.

Biesecker, Barbara A. "Of Historicity, Rhetoric: The Archive as Scene of Invention." *Rhetoric and Public Affairs* 9 (2006): 124–31.

———. "No Time for Mourning: The Rhetorical Production of the Melancholic Citizen-Subject in the War on Terror." *Philosophy and Rhetoric* 40 (2007): 147–69.

———. "Remembering World War II: The Rhetoric and Politics of National Commemoration at the Turn of the Twenty-First Century." *Quarterly Journal of Speech* 88 (2002): 393–409.

Blair, Carole. "Civil Rights/Civil Sites: '. . . Until Justice Rolls Down Like Waters.'" National Communication Association Carroll C. Arnold Distinguished Lecture 2006 Boston: Allyn and Bacon, 2007.

———. "Contemporary U.S. Memorial Sites as Exemplars of Rhetoric's Materiality." In *Rhetorical Bodies,* edited by Jack Selzer and Sharon Crowley, 16–57. Madison: University of Wisconsin Press, 1999.

Blair, Carole, and Neil Michel. "The AIDS Memorial Quilt and the Contemporary Culture of Public Commemoration." In *Remembering the AIDS Quilt,* edited by Charles E. Morris III, 3–41. East Lansing: Michigan State University Press, 2010.

———. "Commemorating in the Theme Park Zone: Reading the Astronauts Memorial." In *At the Intersection: Cultural Studies and Rhetorical Studies,* edited by Thomas Rosteck, 29–82. New York: Guilford, 1999.

Blair, Carole, Gregg Dickinson, and Brian L. Ott. "Introduction: Rhetoric, Memory, Place." In *Places of Public Memory: The Rhetoric of Museums and Memorials,* ed. Greg Dickinson, Carole Blair, and Brian L. Ott, 1–54. Tuscaloosa: University of Alabama Press, 2010.

Blair, Carole, Marsha S. Jeppeson, and Enrico Pucci. "Public Memorializing in Postmodernity: The Vietnam Veterans Memorial as a Prototype." *Quarterly Journal of Speech* 77 (1991): 263–88.

Bodnar, John E. *Remaking America: Public Memory, Commemoration, and Patriotism in the Twentieth Century.* Princeton, N.J.: Princeton University Press, 1992.

Boime, Albert. *The Unveiling of the National Icons: A Plea for Patriotic Iconoclasm in a Nationalist Era.* Cambridge: Cambridge University Press, 1998.

Boon, James A. "Why Museums Make Me Sad." In *Exhibiting Cultures: The Poetics and Politics of Museum Display,* edited by Ivan Karp and Steven D. Levine, 255–77. Washington, D.C.: Smithsonian Institution Press, 1991.

Bowman, Michael S., and Phaedra Pezzullo. "What's So 'Dark' about 'Dark Tourism'? Death, Tours, and Performance." *Tourist Studies* 9 (2009): 187–202.

Bowman, Ruth Laurion, Melanie Kitchens, and Linda Shkreli. "FEMAture Evacuation: A Parade." *Text and Performance Quarterly* 27 (2007): 277–301.

Brien, Stephen, and Joshua Brown. "The September 11 Digital Archive: Saving the Histories of September 11, 2001." *Radical History Review* 111 (2011):101–9.

Brothman, Brien. "The Pasts That Archives Keep." *Archivaria* 51 (2001): 48–80.

Browne, Stephen H. "Remembering Crispus Attucks: Race, Rhetoric, and the Politics of Commemoration " *Quarterly Journal of Speech* 85 (1999): 169–87.

Brummett, Barry, and Detienne L. Bowers. "Subject Positions as a Site of Rhetorical Struggle: Representing African Americans." In *At the Intersection: Cultural Studies and Rhetorical Studies,* edited by Thomas Rosteck, 117–36. New York: Guilford, 1999.

Bruns, Axel. *Blogs, Wikipedia, Second Life, and Beyond: From Production to Produsage.* New York: Lang, 2008.

Burgess, Jean. "Hearing Ordinary Voices: Cultural Studies, Vernacular Creativity and Digital Storytelling." *Continuum: Journal of Media and Cultural Studies* 20 (2006): 201–14.

Burgess, Jean, and Joshua Green. *YouTube: Online Video and Participatory Culture.* Cambridge, Mass.: Polity, 2010.

Burgoyne, Robert. *Film Nation: Hollywood Looks at U.S. History.* Minneapolis: University of Minnesota Press, 1997.

Burke, Kenneth. *Attitudes toward History.* 3rd ed. Berkeley: University of California Press, 1984.

———. *Counter-statement.* 2nd ed. Berkeley: University of California Press, 1968.

———. *A Grammar of Motives.* 2nd ed. New York: Prentice-Hall, 1952.

———. *Permanence and Change: An Anatomy of Purpose.* 3rd ed. Berkeley: University of California Press, 1984.

Carter, Thomas, and Bernard L. Herman, eds. *Perspectives in Vernacular Architecture, III.* Columbia: University of Missouri Press, 1989.

Ceccarelli, Leah. "Polysemy: Multiple Meanings in Rhetorical Criticism." *Quarterly Journal of Speech* 84 (1998): 395–415.

Charland, Maurice. "Constitutive Rhetoric: The Case of the Peuple Quebecois." *Quarterly Journal of Speech* 73 (1987): 133–50.

Clark, Gregory. "Rhetorical Experience and the National Jazz Museum in Harlem." In *Places of Public Memory: The Rhetoric of Museums and Memorials,* ed. Greg Dickinson, Carole Blair, and Brian L. Ott, 113–35. Tuscaloosa: University of Alabama Press, 2010.

Codrescu, Andrei. "New Orleans: A Lecture." *Callaloo* 29 (2007): 1098–1102.

Codrescu, Andrei, and Charles Henry Rowell. "Andrei Codrescu with Charles Henry Rowell. American Tragedy: New Orleans Under Water." *Callaloo* 29 (2007): 1107–14.

Cohen, Daniel J., and Roy Rosenzweig. *Digital History: A Guide to Gathering, Preserving, and Presenting the Past on the Web.* Philadelphia: University of Pennsylvania Press, 2006.

Cohen, Lizabeth. *A Consumers' Republic: The Politics of Mass Consumption in Postwar America.* New York: Knopf/Random House, 2003.

Condit, Celeste Michelle. "The Function of Epideictic: The Boston Massacre Orations as Exemplar." *Communication Quarterly* 33 (1985): 284–99.

———. "The Rhetorical Limits of Polysemy." *Critical Studies in Mass Communication* 6 (1989): 103–22.

Confino, Alon. "Collective Memory and Cultural History: Problems of Method." *American Historical Review* 102 (1997): 1386–1403.

Davis, Susan G. "'Making Night Hideous': Christmas Revelry and Public Order in Nineteenth-Century Philadelphia." *American Quarterly* 34 (1982): 185–99.

Davis, Susan G. *Parades and Power: Street Theatre in Nineteenth-Century Philadelphia.* Philadelphia: Temple University Press, 1986.

Debord, Guy. *Society of the Spectacle.* Detroit: Black & Red, 1983.

Delgado, Aidan. *The Sutras of Abu Ghraib: Notes from a Conscientious Objector.* Boston: Beacon, 2007.

DeLuca, Kevin Michael. *Image Politics: The New Rhetoric of Environmental Activism.* New York: Guilford, 1999.

DeLuca, Kevin Michael, and Jennifer Peeples. "From Public Sphere to Public Screen: Democracy, Activism, and the 'Violence' of Seattle." *Critical Studies in Media Communication* 19 (2002): 125–51.

Demo, Anne T. "The Guerrilla Girls' Comic Politics of Subversion." *Women's Studies in Communication* 23 (2000): 133–57.

Derrida, Jacques. *Archive Fever: A Freudian Impression.* Trans. Eric Prenowitz. Chicago: University of Chicago Press, 1996.

Dewey, John. "Creative Democracy: The Task Before Us." In *Hatred, Bigotry, and Prejudice: Definitions, Causes and Solutions,* edited by Robert M. Baird and Stuart E. Rosenbaum, 21–24. Amherst, N.Y.: Prometheus Books, 1999.

Dickinson, Greg. "Memories for Sale: Nostalgia and Construction of Identity in Old Pasadena." *Quarterly Journal of Speech* 83 (1997): 1–27.

Dinerstein, Joel. "Second Lining Post Katrina: Learning Community from the Prince of Wales Social Aid and Pleasure Club." *American Quarterly* 61 (2009): 615–37.

Doss, Erika Lee. *Memorial Mania: Public Feeling in America.* Chicago: University of Chicago Press, 2010.

Dubin, Steven C. *Displays of Power: Memory and Amnesia in the American Museum.* New York: New York University Press, 1999.

Duncan, Carol. "Art Museums and the Ritual of Citizenship." In *Exhibiting Cultures: The Poetics and Politics of Museum Display,* edited by Ivan Karp and Steven D. Lavine, 88–103. Washington, D.C.: Smithsonian Institution Press, 1991.

Eco, Umberto. *Travels in Hyperreality.* Translated by William Weaver. New York: Harcourt Brace Jovanovich, 1990.

Ferguson, Bruce W. "Exhibition Rhetorics: Material Speech and Utter Sense." In *Thinking about Exhibitions,* edited by Reesa Greenberg, Bruce W. Ferguson, and Sandy Nairne, 175–90. London: Routledge, 1996.

Fiske, John. "Television: Polysemy and Popularity." *Critical Studies in Mass Communication* 4 (1986): 391–408.

Foot, Kristen, Barbara Warnick, and Steven M. Schneider. "Web-Based Memorializing after September 11: Toward a Conceptual Framework." *Journal of Computer-Mediated Communication* 11 (2005): 72–96.

Foote, Kenneth E. *Shadowed Ground: America's Landscapes of Violence and Tragedy.* Rev. ed. Austin: University of Texas Press, 2003.

Foss, Sonja. "Ambiguity as Persuasion: The Vietnam Veterans Memorial." *Communication Quarterly* 34 (1986): 326–40.

Foucault, Michel. "Film and Popular Memory." In *Foucault Live (Interviews, 1966–84),* edited by Sylvère Lotringer, translated by Lysa Hochroth and John Johnston, 122–32. New York: Semiotext(e), 1996.

Frow, John. "*Tout la memoire du monde:* Repetition and Forgetting." In *Time and Commodity Culture: Essays in Cultural Theory and Postmodernity,* 218–46. Oxford: Oxford University Press, 1997.

Funkenstein, Amos. *Perceptions of Jewish History.* Berkeley: University of California Press, 1993.

Garde-Hansen, Joanne, Andrew Hoskins, and Anna Reading, eds. *Save as . . . Digital Memories.* Basingstoke, U.K. & New York: Palgrave Macmillan, 2009.

Gelber, Steven M. "The Market Metaphor: The Historical Dynamics of Stamp Collecting." *Comparative Studies in Society and History* 34 (1992): 742–69.

Gill, James. *Lords of Misrule: Mardi Gras and the Politics of Race in New Orleans.* Jackson: University Press of Mississippi, 1997.

Gillis, John R., ed. *Commemorations: The Politics of National Identity.* Princeton, N.J.: Princeton University Press, 1994.

———. "Memory and Identity: A History of a Relationship." In *Commemorations: The Politics of National Identity,* edited by John R. Gillis, 3–24. Princeton, N.J.: Princeton University Press, 1994.

Gillmor, Dan. *We the Media: Grassroots Journalism by the People, for the People.* Sebastopol, Cal.: O'Reilly, 2004.

Glassberg, David. *American Historical Pageantry: The Uses of Tradition in the Early Twentieth Century.* Chapel Hill: University of North Carolina Press, 1990.

Gotham, Kevin Fox. *Authentic New Orleans: Tourism, Culture, and Race in the Big Easy.* New York: New York University Press, 2007.

Gronbeck, Bruce E. "Citizen Voices in Cyberpolitical Culture." In *Rhetorical Democracy: Discursive Practices of Civic Engagement,* edited by Gerard A. Hauser and Amy Grim, 17–31. Mahwah, N.J.: Lawrence Erlbaum, 2004.

Gunn, Joshua. "Mourning Speech: Haunting and the Spectral Voices of Nine-Eleven." *Text and Performance Quarterly* 24 (2004): 91–114.

Gurak, Laura J. *Cyberliteracy: Navigating the Internet with Awareness.* New Haven, Conn.: Yale University Press, 2003.

Halloran, S. Michael. "Text and Experience in a Historical Pageant: Toward a Rhetoric of Spectacle." *Rhetoric Society Quarterly* 31, no. 4 (2001): 5–17.

———. "Writing History on the Landscape: The Tour Road at the Saratoga Battlefield as Text." In *Rhetorical Education in America,* edited by Cheryl Glenn, Margaret Lyday, and Wendy B. Sharer, 129–44. Tuscaloosa: University of Alabama Press, 2004.

Hariman, Robert, and John Louis Lucaites. *No Caption Needed: Iconic Photographs, Public Culture, and Liberal Democracy.* Chicago: University of Chicago Press, 2007.

Harrison-Nelson, Cherice, and Clyde Woods. "Upholding Community Traditions." *American Quarterly* 61 (2009): 639–48.

Harvey, David. *A Brief History of Neoliberalism.* New York: Oxford University Press, 2005.

———. *The Condition of Postmodernity: An Enquiry into the Origins of Cultural Change.* Cambridge, Mass.: Blackwell, 1990.

Haskins, Ekaterina V. "Epideictic Rhetoric." In *The International Encyclopedia of Communication,* edited by Wolfgang Donsbach, 4238–40. Oxford: Wiley-Blackwell, 2008.

———. "Philosophy, Rhetoric, and Cultural Memory: Rereading Plato's *Menexenus* and Isocrates' *Panegyricus.*" *Rhetoric Society Quarterly* 35 (2005): 25–45.

Haskins, Ekaterina V., and Justin P. DeRose. "Memory, Visibility, and Public Space: Reflections on Commemoration(s) of 9/11." *Space and Culture* 6 (2003): 377–93.

Hass, Kristin Ann. *Carried to the Wall: American Memory and the Vietnam Veterans Memorial.* Berkeley: University of California Press, 1998.

Hauser, Gerard A. "Aristotle on Epideictic: The Formation of Public Morality." *Rhetoric Society Quarterly* 29 (1999): 5–23.

———. *Vernacular Voices: The Rhetoric of Publics and Public Spheres.* Columbia: University of South Carolina Press, 1999.

Hawkins, Peter S. "Naming Names: The Art of Memory and the NAMES Project AIDS Quilt." *Critical Inquiry* 19 (1993): 752–79.

Hess, Aaron. "Digital Remembrance: Vernacular Memory and the Rhetorical Construction of Web Memorials." *Media, Culture and Society* 29 (2007): 812–30.

Hobsbawm, Eric, and Terence Ranger, eds. *The Invention of Tradition.* New York: Cambridge University Press, 1983.

Howard, R. G. "The Vernacular Web of Participatory Media." *Critical Studies in Media Communication* 25 (2008): 490–513.

Huyssen, Andreas. "Present Pasts: Media, Politics, Amnesia." *Public Culture* 12 (2000): 21–38.

———. *Twilight Memories: Marking Time in a Culture of Amnesia.* New York: Routledge, 1995.

Jameson, Fredric. "Reification and Utopia in Mass Culture." *Social Text* 1 (1979): 130–49.

———. *Postmodernism or, the Cultural Logic of Late Capitalism.* Durham: Duke University Press, 1991.

Jenkins, Henry, Ravi Purushotma, Katherine Clinton, Margaret Weigel, and Alice J. Robison. "Confronting the Challenges of Participatory Culture: Media Education for the Twenty-First Century." Paper presented at the Media Literacy Conference, Boston, 2007.

Kahana, Jonathan. *Intelligence Work: The Politics of American Documentary.* New York: Columbia University Press, 2008.

Kammen, Michael G. *Mystic Chords of Memory: The Transformation of Tradition in American Culture.* New York: Knopf, 1991.

Kanfer, Stefan. "The Post Office Stamps Out the 1980s." *Manhattan Institute City Journal* 10 (2000).

Kiousis, Spiro. "Interactivity: A Concept Explication." *New Media and Society* 3 (2002): 355–83.

Kirshenblatt-Gimblett, Barbara. *Destination Culture: Tourism, Museums, and Heritage.* Berkeley: University of California Press, 1998.

———. "Kodak Moments, Flashbulb Memories. Reflections on 9/11." *Drama Review* 47 (2003): 11–48.

Klein, Kerwin Lee. "On the Emergence of Memory in Historical Discourse." *Representations* 69 (2000) :127–50.

Kress, Gunther R. *Multimodality: A Social Semiotic Approach to Contemporary Communication.* London: Routledge, 2010.

Kress, Gunther R., and Theo Van Leeuwen. *Multimodal Discourse: The Modes and Media of Contemporary Communication.* New York: Oxford University Press, 2001.

Landow, George. "Hypertext as Collage-Writing." In *The Digital Dialect,* edited by Peter Lunenfeld, 150–70. Cambridge, Mass.: MIT Press, 2000.

Landsberg, Alison. *Prosthetic Memory: The Transformation of American Remembrance in the Age of Mass Culture.* New York: Columbia University Press, 2004.

Lanham, Richard A. *The Economics of Attention: Style and Substance in the Age of Information.* Chicago: University of Chicago Press, 2006.

Lehnus, Donald J. *From Angels to Zeppelins: A Guide to Persons, Objects, Topics, and Themes on United States Postage Stamps 1847–1980.* Westport, Conn.: Greenwood Press, 1982.

Lennon, J. John, and Malcolm Foley. *Dark Tourism: The Attraction of Death and Disaster.* London: Thomson, 2004.

Levinson, Sanford. *Written in Stone: Public Monuments in Changing Societies.* Durham, N.C.: Duke University Press, 1998.

Lewis, Jacqueline, and Michael R. Fraser. "Patches of Grief and Rage: Visitor Responses to the NAMES Project AIDS Memorial Quilt." *Qualitative Sociology* 19 (1996): 433–51.

Linenthal, Edward Tabor. *Preserving Memory: The Struggle to Create America's Holocaust Museum.* New York: Viking, 1995.

Linenthal, Edward Tabor, and Tom Engelhardt, eds. *History Wars: The Enola Gay and Other Battles for the American Past.* New York: Metropolitan Books, 1996.

Lipsitz, George. "Learning from New Orleans: The Social Warrant of Hostile Privatism and Competitive Consumer Citizenship." *Cultural Anthropology* 21 (2006): 451–68.

———. *Time Passages: Collective Memory and American Popular Culture.* Minneapolis: University of Minnesota Press, 1990.

Livingstone, Jane, and John Beardsley. "The Poetics and Politics of Hispanic Art: A New Perspective." In *Exhibiting Cultures: The Poetics and Politics of Museum Display,* edited by Ivan Karp and Steven D. Lavine, 104–20. Washington, D.C.: Smithsonian Institution Press, 1991.

Loewen, James W. *Lies across America: What Our Historic Sites Get Wrong.* New York: New Press/Norton, 1999.

———. *Lies My Teacher Told Me: Everything Your American History Textbook Got Wrong.* New York: Simon & Schuster, 1996.

Lucaites, John Louis, and Robert Hariman. "Visual Rhetoric, Photojournalism, and Democratic Public Culture." *Rhetoric Review* 20 (2001): 37–42.

Lyotard, Jean-François. *The Postmodern Condition: A Report on Knowledge.* Translated by Geoff Bennington and Brian Massumi. Minneapolis: University of Minnesota Press, 1984.

MacCannell, Dean. *The Tourist: A New Theory of the Leisure Class.* 2nd ed. Berkeley: University of California Press, 1999.

Mandel, Naomi. "To Claim the Mundane." *Journal of Mundane Behavior* 3 (2002): 327–35.

Manovich, Lev. *The Language of New Media.* Cambridge, Mass.: MIT Press, 2002.

McCauley, Michael P. "Leveraging the NPR Brand: Serving the Public while Boosting the Bottom Line." *Journal of Radio Studies* 9 (2002): 65–91.

McGee, Michael C. "In Search of the People: A Rhetorical Alternative." *Quarterly Journal of Speech* 61 (1975): 235–49.

McKernan, Jerry, and Kevin V. Mulcahy. "Hurricane Katrina: A Cultural Chernobyl." *Journal of Arts Management, Law, and Society* 38 (2008): 217–30.

McNulty, Ian. *A Season of Night: New Orleans Life after Katrina.* Jackson: University Press of Mississippi, 2008.

Miller, Carolyn, and Dawn Shepherd. "Blogging as Social Action: A Genre Analysis of the Weblog." In *Into the Blogosphere: Rhetoric, Community, and Culture of Weblogs,* edited by Laura Gurak, Smiljana Antonijevic, Laurie Johnson, Clancy Ratliff, and Jessica Reyman. http://blog.lib.umn.edu/blogosphere/blogging_as_social_action_a_genre_analysis_of_the_weblog.html.

Mitchell, Reid. *All on a Mardi Gras Day: Episodes in the History of New Orleans Carnival.* Cambridge, Mass.: Harvard University Press, 1995.

———. "Carnival and Katrina." *Journal of American History* 94 (2007): 789–94.

Morris, Charles E., III. "The Mourning After." In *Remembering the AIDS Quilt,* edited by Charles E. Morris III, xxxvii–lxix. East Lansing: Michigan State University Press, 2010.

Mountford, Roxanne. "On Gender and Rhetorical Space." *Rhetoric Society Quarterly* 31 (2001): 41–71.

Musil, Robert. "Monuments." In *Posthumous Papers of a Living Author,* 64–68. Translated by Peter Wortsman. New York: Archipelago Books, 2006.

Newman, Simon P. *Parades and the Politics of the Street: Festive Culture in the Early American Republic.* Philadelphia: University of Pennsylvania Press, 1997.

Nora, Pierre. "Between Memory and History: Les Lieux de Mémoire." *Representations* 26 1989): 7–24.

Olick, Jeffrey K. *The Politics of Regret: On Collective Memory and Historial Responsibility.* New York: Routledge, 2007.

———, ed. *States of Memory: Continuities, Conflicts, and Transformations in National Retrospection.* Durham, N.C.: Duke University Press, 2003.

Ono, Kent A., and Derek Buescher. "Deciphering Pocahontas: Unpacking the Commodification of a Native American Woman." *Critical Studies in Mass Communication* 18 (2001): 23–43.

Ono, Kent A., and John M. Sloop. "The Critique of Vernacular Discourse." *Communication Monographs* 62 (1995): 19–46.

Osborn, Royce. *All on a Mardi Gras Day.* Spyboy Pictures, 2008.

Pariser, Eli. *The Filter Bubble: How the New Personalized Web Is Changing What We Read and How We Think.* New York: Penguin, 2012.

Patraka, Vivian. "Spectacular Suffering: Performing Presence, Absence, and Witness at U.S. Holocaust Museums." In *Memory and Representation: Constructed Truths and Competing Realities,* edited by Dena Elisabeth Eber and Arthur G. Neal, 139–66. Bowling Green, Ohio: Bowling Green State University Popular Press, 2001.

Pezzullo, Phaedra C. "'This Is the Only Tour That Sells': Tourism, Disaster, and National Identity in New Orleans." *Journal of Tourism and Cultural Change* 7 (2009): 99–114.

———. "Tourists and/as Disasters: Rebuilding, Remembering, and Responsibility in New Orleans." *Tourist Studies* 9 (2009): 23–41.

———. *Toxic Tourism: Rhetorics of Pollution, Travel, and Environmental Justice.* Tuscaloosa: University of Alabama Press, 2007.

Phillips, Kendall R. "The Failure of Memory: Reflections on Rhetoric and Public Remembrance." *Western Journal of Communication* 74 (2010): 208–23.

———. Introduction to *Framing Public Memory,* edited by Kendall R. Phillips, 1–14. Tuscaloosa: Alabama University Press, 2004.

The Postal Service Guide to U.S. Postal Stamps. 27th ed. New York: Harper Resource, 2000.

Prelli, Lawrence J., ed. *Rhetorics of Display.* Columbia: University of South Carolina Press, 2006.

Rancourt, Michael. "Remembering the Iraq War: The Rhetoric of Public Memory and the Memory of Publics." Ph.D. diss., Rensselaer Polytechnic Institute, Troy, N.Y., 2013.

Reagle, Joseph M., Jr. *Good Faith Collaboration: The Culture of Wikipedia.* Cambridge, Mass.: MIT Press, 2010.

Robb, Erika M. "Violence and Recreation: Vacationing in the Realm of Dark Tourism." *Anthropology and Humanism* 34 (2009): 51–60.

Rose, Chris. *1 Dead in Attic: After Katrina.* New York: Simon & Schuster Paperbacks, 2007.

Rosenfield, Lawrence W. "Central Park and the Celebration of Civic Virtue." In *American Rhetoric: Context and Criticism,* edited by Thomas W. Benson, 221–66. Carbondale: Southern Illinois University Press, 1989.

Rosenzweig, Roy. "Roy Rosenzweig: Everyone a Historian," 177–89. In *The Presence of the Past: Popular Uses of History in American Life*, by Roy Rosenzweig and David P. Thelen. New York: Columbia University Press, 1998.

Rosenzweig, Roy, and David P. Thelen. *The Presence of the Past: Popular Uses of History in American Life.* New York: Columbia University Press, 1998.

Rushing, Janice Hocker. "The Rhetoric of the American Western Myth." *Communication Monographs* 50 (1983): 14–32.

Ryan, Catherine, and Gary Weimberg. *Soldiers of Conscience.* DVD. New York: Docurama Films, 2007.

Savage, Kirk. *Standing Soldiers, Kneeling Slaves: Race, War, and Monument in Nineteenth-Century America.* Princeton, N.J.: Princeton University Press, 1997.

Scott, Joan W. "The Evidence of Experience." *Critical Inquiry* 17 (1991): 773–97.

Selnow, Gary W. *Electronic Whistle-Stops: The Impact of the Internet on American Politics.* Praeger Series in Political Communication. Westport, Conn.: Praeger, 1998.

Shirky, Clay. *Here Comes Everybody: The Power of Organizing without Organizations.* New York: Penguin, 2008.

Simpson, David. *9/11: The Culture of Commemoration*. Chicago: University of Chicago Press, 2006.

Skaggs, David Curtis. "Postage Stamps as Icons." In *Icons of America*, edited by Ray B. Browne and Marshall Fishwick, 198–208. Bowling Green, Ohio: Popular Press, 1978.

Smith, Christina M., and Kelly M. McDonald. "The Mundane to the Memorial: Circulating and Deliberating the War in Iraq through Vernacular Soldier-Produced Videos." *Critical Studies in Media Communication* 28 (2011): 292–313.

Solnit, Rebecca. *A Paradise Built in Hell: The Extraordinary Communities That Arise in Disasters*. New York: Penguin, 2009.

Sontag, Susan. "The Image-World." In *On Photography*, 153–80. New York: Picador/Farrar, Straus & Giroux, 1977.

Souther, Jonathan Mark. *New Orleans on Parade: Tourism and the Transformation of the Crescent City*. Baton Rouge: Louisiana State University Press, 2006.

Spillman, Lyn. *Nation and Commemoration: Creating National Identities in the United States and Australia*. Cambridge: Cambridge University Press, 1997.

Stanonis, Anthony J. *Creating the Big Easy: New Orleans and the Emergence of Modern Tourism, 1918–1945*. Athens: University of Georgia Press, 2006.

———. "Through a Purple (Green and Gold) Haze: New Orleans Mardi Gras in the American Imagination." *Southern Culture* (2008): 109–31.

Stern, Steve J. *Remembering Pinochet's Chile: On the Eve of London 1998*. Durham, N.C.: Duke University Press, 2006.

Strange, Carolyn, and Michael Kempa. "Shades of Dark Tourism: Alcatraz and Robben Island." *Annals of Tourism Research* 30 (2003): 386–405.

Sturken, Marita. *Tangled Memories: The Vietnam War, the AIDS epidemic, and the Politics of Remembering*: Berkeley: University of California Press, 1997.

———. *Tourists of History: Memory, Kitsch, and Consumerism from Oklahoma City to Ground Zero*. Durham, N.C.: Duke University Press, 2007.

Tapscott, Don, and Anthony D. Williams. *Wikinomics: How Mass Collaboration Changes Everything*. New York: Portfolio, 2008.

Taylor, Diana. *The Archive and the Repertoire: Performing Cultural Memory in the Americas*. Durham, N.C.: Duke University Press, 2003.

Thelen, David. "History-Making in America." *Historian* 53 (1991): 631–48.

Todd, Susan, and Andrew Young. *Cutting Loose*. Videocasette. New York: Richter Productions, 1995.

Ulmer, Gregory L. *Electronic Monuments*. Minneapolis: University of Minnesota Press, 2006.

Van House, Nancy, and Elizabeth F. Churchill. "Technologies of Memory: Key Issues and Critical Perspectives." *Memory Studies* 1 (2008): 295–310.

VanSpanckeren, Kathryn. "The Mardi Gras Indian Song Cycle: A Heroic Tradition." In *Southern Heritage on Display: Public Ritual and Ethnic Diversity within Southern Regionalism*, edited by Celeste Ray and Melissa Schrift, 41–56. Tuscaloosa: University of Alabama Press, 2003.

Vivian, Bradford. "Neoliberal Epideictic: Rhetorical Form and Commemorative Politics on September 11, 2002." *Quarterly Journal of Speech* 92 (2006): 1–26.

———. *Public Forgetting: The Rhetoric and Politics of Beginning Again*. University Park: Pennsylvania State University Press, 2010.

Waite, Jason. "Identifying Agency: The Construction of Rhetorical Agency in Foxfire." Ph.D. diss., Rensselaer Polytechnic Institute, Troy, N.Y., 2007.

Walker, Jeffrey. *Rhetoric and Poetics in Antiquity.* New York: Oxford University Press, 2000.

Wallace, Mike. *Mickey Mouse History and Other Essays on American Memory.* Philadelphia: Temple University Press, 1996.

Warner, Michael. *Publics and Counterpublics.* New York: Zone Books, 2002.

Warnick, Barbara. *Critical Literacy in a Digital Era: Technology, Rhetoric, and the Public Interest.* Mahwah, N.J.: Erlbaum, 2002.

———. "Looking to the Future: Electronic Texts and the Deepening Interface." *Technical Communication Quarterly* 14 (2005): 327–33.

Wills, Garry. *Lincoln at Gettysburg: The Words That Remade America.* New York: Simon & Schuster, 1992.

Winter, Jay. "Sites of Memory." In *Memory: Histories, Theories, Debates,* edited by Susannah Radstone and Bill Schwarz, 312–24. New York: Fordham University Press, 2010.

Wodiczko, Krzysztof. *Critical Vehicles: Writings, Projects, Interviews.* Cambridge, Mass.: MIT Press, 1999.

Woodruff, Paul. *First Democracy: The Challenge of an Ancient Idea.* New York: Oxford University Press, 2005.

———. *The Necessity of Theater: The Art of Watching and Being Watched.* Oxford: Oxford University Press, 2008.

Woolson, Constance. "Mrs. Edward Pinckney." *Christian Union,* August 1879, 105–6.

Yates, Frances A. *The Art of Memory.* London: Pimlico, 1992.

Young, James Edward. *The Texture of Memory: Holocaust Memorials and Meaning.* New Haven, Conn.: Yale University Press, 1993.

Zagacki, Kenneth S., and Victoria J. Gallagher. "Rhetoric and Materiality in the Museum Park at the North Carolina Museum of Art." *Quarterly Journal of Speech* 95 (2009): 171–91.

Zelizer, Barbie. "The Voice of the Visual in Memory." In *Framing Public Memory,* edited by Kendall R. Phillips, 157–86. Tuscaloosa: University of Alabama Press, 2004.

Index

Note: Italic page numbers refer to illustrations

About the author

Ekaterina V. Haskins is an associate professor of rhetoric in the Department of Communication and Media at Rensselaer Polytechnic Institute. She is the author of the award-winning book *Logos and Power in Isocrates and Aristotle* and numerous essays on rhetoric, visual culture, and public memory. Haskins lives in Troy, New York, where she serves on the board of trustees of the Rensselaer County Historical Society.

www.ingramcontent.com/pod-product-compliance
Lightning Source LLC
LaVergne TN
LVHW050153080826
844660LV00002B/199

* 9 7 8 1 6 1 1 1 7 4 9 4 6 *